Turmoil on the Rio Grande

Number Thirty-eight
ELMA DILL RUSSELL SPENCER SERIES
IN THE WEST AND SOUTHWEST

Andrés Tijerina, General Editor

Series Board:
Alwyn Barr
James E. Crisp
Rebecca Sharpless
Eric Van Young

*A list of all books currently available in this series
may be found in the back of this book.*

TURMOIL
ON THE
RIO GRANDE

History of the
Mesilla Valley, 1846–1865

WILLIAM S. KISER

TEXAS A&M UNIVERSITY PRESS
College Station

Library of Congress Cataloging-in-Publication Data

Kiser, William S., 1986–
Turmoil on the Rio Grande : the territorial history of the Mesilla Valley, 1846–
1865 / William S. Kiser. — 1st ed.
p. cm.—(Elma Dill Russell Spencer series in the West and Southwest ; no. 38)
Includes bibliographical references and index.
ISBN-13: 978-1-60344-296-1 (hc-hardcover : alk. paper)
ISBN-13: 978-1-62349-204-5 (alk. paper) ISBN-13: 978-1-60344-685-3 (ebook)
1. Mesilla Valley (N.M.)—History—19th century. 2. Doniphan's Expedition,
1846-1847 3. Mexico. Treaties, etc. United States, 1848 Feb. 2. 4. Gadsden
Purchase. 5. Apache Indians—New Mexico—Fort Fillmore—History—19th
century. 6. New Mexico—History—War with Mexico, 1845–1848. 7. New
Mexico—History—Civil War, 1861–1865. 8. Arizona—History—To 1912. I.
Title. II. Title: Territorial history of the Mesilla Valley, 1846–1865. III. Series:
Elma Dill Russell Spencer series in the West and Southwest ; no. 38.
F802.M4K57 2011
978.9'66—dc22
2011005230

For my parents, Dan and Jerine Kiser,
for always being there.

Contents

List of Illustrations

List of Maps

Acknowledgments

I remember conceiving the idea for this book during my sophomore year as an undergraduate at New Mexico State University. I undertook the task of research, working in Zuhl Library every morning before going to classes and staring into microfilm machines until my eyes watered. I am not sure that I ever expected the project to reach the point of publication; indeed, it began as a project I undertook mostly for fun in my spare time. Obviously, it evolved far beyond that, becoming somewhat of an obsession at various points over the past several years.

Once I had conducted enough research, I took to writing a preliminary draft (little did I know how truly preliminary that draft would end up being). After a draft of the manuscript was completed, I took it to the office of one of my history professors, Mark Milliorn, who at that point knew nothing of my project. I express my most sincere gratitude to Mr. Milliorn, for not only did he take the time to read the manuscript, but he also encouraged me to continue working on it and informed me that it might just be publishable. He directed me to Louis R. Sadler and his colleague, Charles Harris, both professors emeritus at New Mexico State University who have published extensively throughout their careers. Sadler likewise read the manuscript and suggested that I seek publication. Since that time Sadler and Harris have continued to assist me, providing advice and encouraging me to have a lot of patience and stick with it. This project might have never reached fruition had it not been for the continuous encouragement of these three individuals, all of whom have inspired me not only in my writing but in my career aspirations as well. For that I cannot thank them enough. Additional professors at NMSU who served as mentors were Jon Hunner and Jeffrey Brown, both of whom I thank for the opportunity to have worked with them during my undergraduate career.

I am now in my second year as a graduate student at Arizona State University, and during my time here so far I have received a great deal of assistance from several faculty members. I would like to thank Donald Fixico, my faculty advisor and thesis committee chair. He graciously took time to discuss with me the process of publishing with academic presses, and he provided a great deal of advice along the way. Throughout the revision process, Dr. Fixico inspired me with his philosophy that "you don't just want a book in print. You want the best book in print that you are capable of writing."

Christine Szuter, another member of my thesis committee and director of the scholarly publishing program at ASU, has also been an inspiration for me throughout this process. Szuter spent many years at the University of Arizona Press and has graciously shared her expertise with me throughout this process, reviewing portions of my work from the perspective of a veteran in academic publishing. I extend my gratitude to Dr. Szuter, and for her continued support I am very grateful.

Numerous other faculty members at ASU, along with some of my fellow graduate students, have offered support throughout this process. I specifically wish to thank Jannelle Warren-Findley and Peter Iverson, both of whom, through the examples of their careers, have served as mentors. Their advice and words of praise have been much appreciated. I also wish to thank Mark von Hagen and Kent Wright for their support.

Several academic institutions have assisted in the collection of research materials and in making various items of importance available to me. At New Mexico State University, the Rio Grande Historical Collections proved to be an invaluable resource. Of particular assistance at NMSU were Stephen Hussman, head of Archives and Special Collections, and Larry Creider, who graciously obtained copies of microfilm that the library did not already own. At Arizona State University, Edward Oetting at Hayden Library was kind enough to obtain important microfilm sources not already owned by the library. The archivists at the Arizona Historical Foundation have also been helpful throughout the process of my research.

John P. Wilson of Las Cruces, New Mexico, graciously provided two of his personally hand-drawn maps delineating the Confederate Territory of Arizona. The maps serve as an excellent complement to this book, and Mr. Wilson's generosity is greatly appreciated. Joe Werne also assisted with obtaining maps.

I am appreciative of the staff at Texas A&M University Press for their hard work and dedication in publishing this manuscript. In particular, editor-in-chief Mary Lenn Dixon has been an indispensible correspondent, making herself accessible for every question I have had; she has been a pleasure to work with and has made the process of publication an enjoyable experience for me.

I would like to dedicate a brief paragraph to my many friends who have always supported me (and not made fun of me for spending so much time in the library) during the several years I have spent working on this project. There are too many of them to name, but they know who they are.

Finally, I express my sincere gratitude to my family, and especially my parents, who have continually shown their love and support throughout all of my life's endeavors.

Turmoil on the Rio Grande

Introduction

Modern visitors to the Mesilla Valley will encounter an area of bustling farming communities, the heart of which is the city of Las Cruces with a population approaching ninety thousand. The region is defined by its arid desert climate and basin-and-range topography, the presence of the Rio Grande providing the lifeblood of the area's agricultural prosperity. Large retirement communities abound on the eastern and western sides of the valley, and New Mexico State University serves as an academic anchor for the region. The small town of Mesilla, with a population scarcely exceeding three thousand, is today a popular tourist attraction, an excellent place to immerse oneself in New Mexico culture. Yet the Mesilla Valley region of southern New Mexico has not always been this way. The mid-nineteenth century was a tumultuous yet formative time; much of what one sees today was made possible by the events of 1846–65.

The coming of the U.S. Army in 1846 and their subsequent occupation of the province brought about the final chapter in New Mexico's history as a Hispanic entity. The decade of the 1840s had been a troubled time for relations between the United States and the Republic of Mexico, a nation that only recently had obtained its independence from Spain. Diplomatic relations between the United States and Mexico climaxed following the U.S. annexation of Texas in 1845. On May 13, 1846, President James K. Polk encouraged Congress to declare war on Mexico, an action that proved highly controversial.

On June 22, 1846, a force of 1,586 soldiers led by a widely respected army officer, Brig. Gen. Stephen Watts Kearny, took up the line of march for New Mexico. At Bent's Fort, Kearny issued his first of many public proclamations: "The undersigned enters New Mexico with a large military force, for the purpose of seeking union and ameliorating the condition of its inhabitants. This he does under instructions from his government, and with the assurance that he will be amply sustained in the accomplishment of this object. It is enjoined on the citizens of New Mexico to remain quietly at their homes, and pursue their peaceful avocations . . . all who take up arms or encourage resistance against the government of the United States will be regarded as enemies, and will be treated accordingly."[1]

After a march across the Great Plains that occupied some fifty-seven days, Kearny's command arrived in Santa Fe and, following an unpredicted bloodless conquest of the Mexican military forces stationed there, raised the Stars and Stripes over the plaza in the capital city. The vast expanse of territory comprising New Mexico now belonged to the United States. With the arrival of Kearny and his U.S. troops began a remarkable chain of events, as the new U.S. possession began its struggle for recognition in the U.S. government. The ensuing two decades, the subject of this narrative, would be tumultuous times for the infant Territory of New Mexico; the southern region would play a prominent role in many of these events. No sooner had the United States laid claim to New Mexico than the former Mexican citizens residing in the Mesilla Valley, not to mention the various bands of Apache Indians in the vicinity, came to be intimately acquainted with the Americans, their government, and their designs for the future of the area.

There have been many firsthand accounts written by Americans describing the characteristics of the Mexican inhabitants of New Mexico. To these foreigners from the eastern United States, New Mexico possessed a culture entirely different from any in which they had been immersed, and they took no little interest in describing the people residing in this newly acquired U.S. entity.

Many of the available accounts of New Mexico as it existed in the 1850s come from Anglo-American residents and visitors who often found themselves perplexed by the Spanish inhabitants. Although the majority of the Americans venturing to faraway New Mexico during this time period were explorers and ruffians, they nevertheless experienced considerable difficulty coming to terms with the lifestyle of the Spanish (and after 1821, Mexican) inhabitants. Writing to his superiors in Washington, D.C. in 1852, Col. Edwin Vose Sumner described the Mexican inhabitants as "idle and worthless." The government, in Sumner's estimation, would be doing itself a favor by abandoning New Mexico entirely and leaving it to the Mexicans and Indians to fight over among themselves, as they already had for centuries. Many Americans, to varying degrees of accordance, shared this viewpoint. Many of their writings from this time period contain heavily biased and judgmental accounts and must be taken objectively. Nevertheless, these

early writers provide a unique glimpse into mid-nineteenth-century New
Mexican culture.[2]

"At this period, 1857," wrote Lt. William W. Averell in his memoirs,
"popular knowledge of our Territories was quite limited and indefinite. The
reports of U.S. Engineers who had run boundary lines, or of officers of the
army in charge of exploring expeditions, had afforded interesting, but frag-
mentary glimpses of the wonderful topography of these vast regions which
had been under the dominion of the government of the United States only
about nine years."[3] At the time Averell wrote, knowledge of New Mexico had
increased phenomenally since the initial U.S. occupation in 1846. Numerous military and scientific exploring expeditions in the 1850s had divulged
a wealth of data concerning the physical nature of New Mexico. Still, these
reports were never read by the masses of Americans in the eastern United
States, and an utter ignorance of New Mexican culture prevailed among the
greater percentage of the population. The shock and surprise of these people
when arriving in New Mexico is thus explained by the fact that there simply
existed no popular knowledge of the territory. In 1856 U.S. Attorney W. W. H.
Davis wrote, "There is no country protected by our flag and subject to our
laws so little known to the people of the United States as the territory of New
Mexico. . . . The natural features differ widely from the rest of the Union; and
the inhabitants, with the manners and customs of their Moorish and Castil-
ian ancestors, are both new and strange to our people."[4] Not until the mining booms of the 1870s and the arrival of the railroads in the 1880s did New
Mexico's splendor fully manifest itself in the minds of many Americans.

During and directly following General Kearny's occupation of New
Mexico, the U.S. government did not even possess an accurate map of the
territory. Writing to President James K. Polk in 1848, Secretary of State James
Buchanan remarked, "The only separate map of New Mexico, of which I am
aware, [was] . . . published in London in 1812 . . . the department has a copy
of this work and the accompanying atlas, with the exception of the map of
New Mexico . . . this map, it is presumed, is now with the archives of the
United States legation at the city of Mexico."[5] Thus the only accurate and re-
liable map of the territory in 1848 was located somewhere in Mexico. Other
maps existed, all of which contained inaccuracies, so much so in some instances that the traveler might be better off without one.

At this time New Mexico contained only a small Anglo-American population, spread intermittently up and down the Rio Grande valley from Taos in the north to Paso del Norte in the south; yet the influence of these newcomers in territorial affairs would prove to be phenomenal.[6] From business pursuits to military affairs to politics, newly arrived Americans exercised control in New Mexico from the moment they set foot in the territory. In 1856 the U.S. attorney in the territory wrote that fewer than five hundred Anglo-Americans resided in New Mexico (excluding U.S. troops). These Americans, he wrote, "exhibit the energy always manifested by our countrymen wherever met. It may be asked whether the native Mexicans have been benefited by the country coming into the possession of the United States. . . . From my observation, I believe they have been improved in both a social and political point of view . . . [they] are protected in the enjoyment of all their rights, instead of trusting to the caprice of an irresponsible individual as before."[7]

The number of Anglo-Americans residing in the Mesilla Valley was even less. John Russell Bartlett, passing through the valley during the Mexican boundary surveys of 1851, estimated that not more than twenty Anglos lived permanently in the area, all of them acting as merchants and traders.[8] In this early period of the Mesilla Valley's settlement, the population remained almost entirely Mexican. In order to understand the events that took place in the Mesilla Valley region, it is necessary to understand the everyday habits and characteristics of these Mexican inhabitants.

Lieutenant Averell, in a letter home, wrote, "it is a queer people here . . . houses, dogs, dinners, everything is queer & strange. A kind of Indian summer laziness seems to pervade everything and everybody and this influence soon extends to anyone who comes to live here . . . their wants are few—a blanket at night and a little 'chili' tortillas for food . . . chairs are unknown and women sit on the mats and smoke *cigarillos*—but every Mexican is polite and their manners are easy."[9] Another observer, writing in 1857, was equally unimpressed with his perceived laziness of the residents: "With leisure for doing everything, they lounge in squads upon the streets, play monte here, and bask in the sunshine and sleep there, or imbibe aguardiente (a spirit between alcohol and whiskey), swagger and smoke, when not otherwise engaged. These fellows, of course I do not allude to the ladies, give the lie to the proverb, 'there's honor among thieves,' for they are notorious for stealing from each other, or from anyone whenever the occasion offers."[10]

The first item that commanded the attention of the Americans entering

New Mexico was almost invariably the unique architectural features of the territory. This architectural style, while not luxurious or an object of envy to the Americans, nevertheless proved captivating when beheld for the first time. The buildings in every town, seldom more than one story in height, were constructed of sun-hardened mud bricks, or adobes. Rarely did one encounter a structure built of wood or stone. In New Mexico, wrote one observer, "the style of building was borrowed from the East, and is as ancient as the time of Moses, and was essential here in early times because of the hostility of the Indians . . . an *adobe* is about six times the size of an ordinary brick, and they cost, delivered, from eight to ten dollars the thousand. Neither skill nor practice is required in order to make them. In time the walls become quite solid, and houses are in use, built in this manner, which have stood for nearly two hundred years; but they would not last long in the States, amid the great storms that prevail there."[11] This traditional method of building remains prevalent in New Mexico to this day.

Most Americans complained bitterly of these adobe structures. During rainstorms the roofs leaked in torrents, and the dirt floors became a muddy mess. But, all things considered, the adobe houses were well suited for the hot and dry New Mexico environment. Lt. William H. Emory, of the Army Corps of Topographical Engineers, praised the buildings for their practicality: "nothing can exceed the comfort and convenience of the interior. The thick walls make them cool in summer and warm in winter."[12]

Whether they liked them or not, the adobe buildings were something the Americans would become accustomed to. Every military post in 1850s New Mexico was constructed almost exclusively of adobe, owing in part to the scarcity of other building materials throughout the territory. Early U.S. entrepreneurs and traders, from Santa Fe all the way south to the Mesilla Valley, consistently constructed their homes in the same manner as the Mexican inhabitants among whom they lived.

New Mexicans, in one observer's words, represented a melting pot of three separate races: Spanish, Moorish, and Indian. "As would naturally be the case," commented W. W. H. Davis, "a people so various in their origin as the Mexicans, and in whose veins flows the blood of three distinct races, would present a corresponding diversity of character. They possess the cunning and deceit of the Indian, the politeness and the spirit of revenge of the Spaniard, and the imaginative temperament and fiery impulses of the Moor."[13]

The two cultures, Mexican and American, differed in virtually all aspects, and a severe culture shock often ensued when the two groups began working and living alongside each other. There existed countless barriers to progress and understanding between the two races, not the least of which was language. Any Anglo-American coming to the Mesilla Valley in the 1850s would have little choice but to learn Spanish if they wished to become successful as a merchant, trader, or politician.

Among Anglo-American observers, habitual tobacco smoking was among the single most commonly mentioned customs of the territory's Mexican inhabitants during this time. Many perceived it as an annoying habit, one that perhaps more than any other defined the Mexican race in the territory. "One of the first acts of courtesy of the mistress of the house is to invite you to smoke," Davis explained. "She carries about her person a small silver tobacco-box, in which she keeps the noxious weed, and also has at hand a little package of corn-husks, one of which she fills with the fine-cut tobacco, rolls it up into a *cigarrito*, lights it, and hands it to you to smoke. . . . Smoking is habitual with all classes, not excepting the most lovely and refined females in the country. The habit is bad enough in men, but intolerable in women. The *cigarrito* seems to be an abiding presence, being handed round at the dinner-table as a refreshment, and served up in the ballroom; and it is common to see ladies smoking while they are engaged in waltzing and dancing, and some even indulge the luxury while they lie in bed."[14] Davis, along with many others, found this habit to be highly repulsive, as evidenced in their contemporary writings.

Other forms of amusement among the Mexican race captured the attention of outsiders as well. Among the peoples' most popular pastimes was the fandango, or dance, which was enjoyed by all ages and could be encountered in almost any town.[15] "A fandango can no more be described than it can be painted. The life and motion defy us. . . . No introductions were required and one danced with whom he would. When a dance was finished it was *de rigueur* to take the señorita to the refreshment room and regale her with sweetmeats and a glass of wine," wrote an army officer in the 1850s.[16]

There existed two distinct types of dances, depending on the social class and financial status of the individuals hosting the event. W. W. H. Davis explains: "In New Mexico the general names of all assemblies where dancing is the principal amusement is *fandango,* which is not, as many suppose, a particular dance. Those gatherings where the better classes "most do congregate" are called *baile,* or ball, which differs in no other particular from the fandango. All New Mexicans are exceedingly fond of dancing, and, in fact, it seems almost as much a passion with them as with the French. Every class and rank in society participates in the amusement, and very small children are seen whirling in the waltz and tripping in the dance with the same gusto as their more mature companions."[17] In some of the larger towns, such as Albuquerque and Santa Fe, a fandango could be found almost every night of the week, making it difficult for military officers to keep their troops from leaving their posts and partaking in the festivities.

When not busying themselves with dances and other such celebrations, the Mexican population had competitions in which they would engage. One game, called Correr el Gallo, is described thusly:

> Among country people there are various primitive sports, some of which afford much amusement to both the lookers-on and the parties engaged . . . that known as *correr el gallo,* running the cock, thus described by Gregg: 'A common cock or hen is tied by the feet to some swinging limb of a tree, so as to be barely within the reach of a man on horseback; or the fowl is buried alive in a small pit in the ground, leaving only the head above the surface. In either case, the racers, passing at full speed, grapple the head of the fowl, which, being well greased, generally slips out of their fingers. As soon as some one more dexterous than the rest has succeeded in tearing it loose, he puts spurs to his steed, and endeavors to escape with the prize. He is hotly pursued, however, by the whole sporting crew, and the first who overtakes him tries to get possession of the fowl, when a strife ensues, during which the poor chicken is torn into atoms. Should the holder of the trophy be able to outstrip his pursuers, he carries it to the crowd of fair spectators and presents it to his mistress, who takes it to the fandango which usually follows as a testimony of the prowess of her lover.[18]

Still another form of entertainment was cock fighting. An age-old tradition among the Mexicans, throngs of spectators could often be found huddling together on Sunday afternoons eagerly looking on as two roosters fought to the death. "Cock-fighting . . . is a national and favorite amusement with the Mexican people; all classes indulge in it more or less, from the peon in his blanket to the *rico* in his broadcloth, and the priesthood in this *elegant* pastime. The young bloods of the town train their chickens for the ring with as much care and assiduity as gentlemen of the turf bestow upon their favorite horses; and while in [the] course of training, you will see them tied around the houses by a little cord to one leg. . . . Sunday is the favorite day for this pastime, when the best chickens are trotted out and pitted in the ring," explained one observer.[19]

It becomes evident that in most of the events transpiring in the New Mexican villages there existed minimal discrimination between young and old, male and female. It often behooved Anglo-American onlookers to see young boys and girls engaging in afternoon cockfights right alongside the elderly. From a very early age the inhabitants of New Mexico were fully immersed in their culture. While these activities seemed perfectly normal to the Mexican people, outsiders often viewed them scornfully and contemptuously. Due in many respects to events such as these, considered by visitors to be heathen pastimes, the Mexican population quickly gained a negative reputation with the Anglo-Americans in the east.

Despite any practices of questionable character, many Mexicans were devoutly religious and remained prudent followers of their Catholic faith. Sgt. George Hand, an officer in the California Column stationed in Las Cruces and Mesilla during the Civil War, witnessed the people's reverent religious observances. In his diary entry for the day before Good Friday, 1863, the sergeant recorded, "The Catholic portion of the native Spanish are making a great ado about the Crucifixion of Christ. They hold meetings, nights, with one impersonating Jesus, and this evening he is arrested. Pilate's officer and guard take him off to confinement. Large processions go through the streets, nights, with lighted candles, carrying images of Christ & the Virgin Mary . . . they seem very devout."[20] Religious holidays were always observed with fervor by the native Catholic population.

During this early period of New Mexican history, educational institutions were almost nonexistent. This would continue to be the case into the twentieth century, ultimately having a severe hamstringing effect on New Mexico's statehood aspirations. While progress was made toward the establishment of schools following the U.S. occupation in 1846, it was an incredibly slow and tedious process. W. W. H. Davis, writing a decade after Kearny entered the territory, found himself horrified by the prevalent lack of education among the population. "The standard of education in New Mexico is at a very low ebb," he wrote, "and there is a larger number of persons who cannot read and write than in any other Territory in the Union. The census of 1850 shows a population of 61,547 inhabitants, of whom 25,089 are returned as being unable to read or write. I feel confident that this ratio is too low, and that the number may safely be set down at one half the whole population who cannot read their catechisms and write their names. The number attending school is given as 460, which is about one scholar to every one hundred and twenty-five inhabitants."[21]

In the Mesilla Valley, the number of people who could read and write was even fewer. This remained true well into the Civil War era. A humorous testament to this shortcoming is found in an 1860 issue of the *Mesilla Times,* which stated, "The Deputy U.S. Marshal for this District, while engaged in taking the present census, met with some very extraordinary proofs of the fruitfulness of Arizona. One Mexican siñora [*sic*] gave in her own age as twenty and that of 'her oldest' as sixteen. Another gave the age of her two children as nine months and twelve months respectively. Who will now say [this] is not a great country?"[22]

Indeed, the only institutions of learning were private schools in Santa Fe, far removed from the Mesilla Valley. Only the *ricos* could afford to send their children to these schools.[23] The census of 1850 showed a total of eight teachers in New Mexico, all employed at private schools; the same census placed the number of students at 466.[24] Of these, it can be readily inferred that few or none came from the Mesilla area; consequently, the illiteracy rate among the Mexican portion of the valley's population during this period remained high.

With a lack of education came an accompanying low state of morals that prevailed throughout the territory, at least in the eyes of the Americans. "Probably there is no other country in the world, claiming to be civilized, where vice is more prevalent among all classes of the inhabitants," wrote one observer. "They have never received any moral training, in the American sense of the word, and have been allowed to grow up from infancy to manhood without being taught that it is wrong to indulge in vicious habits." Specific mention has frequently been given to the morals of Mexican women, which, in the eyes of the Americans, were considered to be severely lacking: "The standard of female chastity is deplorably low, and the virtuous are far outnumbered by the vicious. Prostitution is carried on to a fearful extent; and it is quite common for parents to sell their own daughters for money to gratify the lust of the purchaser, thus making a profit from their own and children's shame. It is almost a universal practice for men and women to live together as husband and wife, and rear a family of children, without having been married."[25] It should be noted, however, that these observers only came into contact with a small percentage of New Mexican women, and their observations must be taken objectively due to such inadvertent sampling biases.

While this sentiment reflected the opinion of W. W. H. Davis, he did acknowledge that there were exceptions to the rule. "In speaking of vice and immorality in New Mexico," he continued, "I must not be understood as including the whole population in the same category. Amid so much that is corrupt, there are some as pure in mind and morals as can be found in any country, and who are as much alive to all the amenities and proprieties of life."[26] In other words, the Mexican inhabitants were not all that different from every other society in the world; they had their faults and misgivings, but they had their praiseworthy traits as well.

An editorial published in the *Santa Fe New Mexican* aptly read, "the opinion formed by people from the United States in regard to New Mexico is, generally, most erroneous. The men who come here are farmers and mechanics, and expect to see here what they see in the United States . . . and because the *appearance* and *face* of the country presents an aspect less attractive than their fancies had painted for them, they denounce it without stint . . . these conclusions are very rational, but very erroneous."[27] This statement by the territory's predominant 1850s newspaper should be viewed as highly applicable to native New Mexicans in general, and serves to balance the biases portrayed in the observations of newly arrived Anglo-Americans.

After analyzing some of the basic underlying societal differences that existed between the Mexicans and the Americans in 1850s New Mexico, it comes as little surprise that political and personal strife arose so frequently. The historical events analyzed henceforth in this book are, in many cases, a derivative of fundamental underlying variations between the two races then inhabiting the territory.

CHAPTER 1

Doniphan at Brazito

Among the troops who marched across the Santa Fe Trail and assisted in the conquest of New Mexico was an outfit of greenhorn volunteers from the State of Missouri. Mustered into active service on June 6, 1846, this body of troops came to be known as the 1st Regiment of Missouri Volunteers.[1] They marched behind their widely respected young commanding officer, Col. Alexander W. Doniphan, upon whom would soon fall great fame for his leading role in the yearlong ordeal that followed.

Following the initial occupation of Santa Fe by the U.S. troops, numerous incidents of historical significance took place, many of which have warranted their own historical accounts. Kearny enacted a new form of government in the territory, the stipulations of which became known as the Kearny Code.[2] New governmental officials were placed in charge by Kearny, most of the previous Mexican officials having fled on the approach of the U.S. troops, and the laws of the United States thus extended across the land. Their primary objective being accomplished, the commanding officers of Kearny's outfit could turn to other pursuits.

One of these commanding officers was Col. Alexander Doniphan. Born in Kentucky on July 9, 1808, he moved to Missouri where he studied law, a profession in which he continued until being placed at the helm of his prized volunteer regiment in 1846.[3] Of Doniphan, much has been written; by most accounts he was well liked and respected by his men. Several diaries and memoirs, written by members of his regiment, perceive Doniphan favorably and nostalgically. The majority of these accounts agree that the enlisted men were not well disciplined, insinuating that Doniphan generally presided over his men with remarkable coolness and a reserved sense of authority, highly uncommon for an army officer of his time. One of the Missouri volunteers recalled that many of the men referred to their colonel simply as "Bill" or "Doniphan," it apparently being unnecessary in Doniphan's case to adhere to the proper military protocol for addressing a superior officer.[4] Another soldier from the 1st Regiment, Frank S. Edwards, recalled of Doniphan that "his great charm lies in his easy and kind manner. On the march he could not be distinguished from the other soldiers, either by

dress, or from his conversation. . . . The colonel is in the habit of interlard-
ing his language with strong expressions which many eastern men would
call something very like swearing."[5] Thus it is not hard to imagine why the
average frontier soldier would have found Doniphan to be favorable as a
commander.

After a lengthy expedition in northern New Mexico against marauding
Navajo Indians, a pursuit that occupied Doniphan's troops for the entirety
of the month of November, the colonel and his regiment of volunteers returned to Santa Fe. Almost immediately thereafter Doniphan proceeded
southward toward Mexico, where the conflict between that country and the
United States raged. Doniphan led his troops down the Camino Real, across
the Jornada del Muerto, and toward Paso del Norte.[6] On December 23, after emerging from the ninety-mile waterless wasteland that constituted the
infamous Jornada, the Missourians encamped at the small Mexican village
of Doña Ana. Here an advance force, led by Maj. William Gilpin, awaited
their arrival.

Even as Doniphan and his men arrived at Doña Ana, some 280 miles
south of the capital city of Santa Fe, enemy Mexican spies were already in
their midst. Several weeks before, word had reached the northern Mexican provinces of Chihuahua and Sonora that the invading American force
would soon be marching down the Rio Grande. Chihuahua's Governor Ángel Trías, learning of the approach of the Americans, called his men to arms
and issued a statement of support to his troops, which would subsequently
be published in U.S. newspapers. The *New Orleans Daily Picayune,* which
printed the Trías statement in its entirety, mocked it as a "gasconading proclamation of the Governor of Chihuahua, the puissant Señor General Don
Angel Trias."[7]

In his proclamation the Chihuahuan governor warned his troops and
fellow citizens that "the iniquitous invaders of Mexico are approaching the
town of El Paso . . . it is necessary that you should go forward, defenders
of the glories of Mexico, to give a lesson to these pirates." He promised aid
for the citizens of El Paso, telling them that "should the circumstances of
the war demand it, be assured that you will be supported, at whatever cost,
by great reinforcements. For the people of Chihuahua no sacrifice is felt as
costly when demanded by the honor of the Republic." The editors of the
Daily Picayune sarcastically chastised the diatribe, writing that "this fel-

low Trias, however much he pretend to burn, and however eager his zeal to encounter the 'iniquitous invaders' of his sacred soil, is one of the greatest braggarts in all Mexico, a country that produces rare specimens."[8]

As a consequence of the governor's proclamation, Mexican officials dispatched a scouting party that penetrated up the Rio Grande valley as far as Socorro before slipping back into Mexico without Doniphan's column detecting their presence. This contingent of Mexican spies, commanded by Col. Mauricio Ugarte, retreated without directly challenging Doniphan, but they stayed long enough to obtain valuable information relative to the size and firepower of the U.S. invaders.[9] Thus by the time Doniphan and his expeditionary force reached the quiet Mexican settlement of Doña Ana in late December 1846, the Mexicans already knew the size of the army with which they would have to contend. In the meantime, Doniphan and his troops pressed onward down the Camino Real believing that no imminent danger existed.

The column remained at Doña Ana, camping there on the night of December 23, 1846. The village failed to make a favorable impression on the eastern soldiers, one of whom described it as being "a small town, the most poorly constructed of any that I have seen."[10] Here, amid a citizenry foreign to the invaders in every way imaginable, the column of several hundred men encamped "in the [river] bottom, all noisy and drinking."[11] Another observer colorfully described the Missourians' encampment: "From the appearance no one would have imagined this to be a military encampment. . . . There were no regulations in force with regard to cleanliness. . . . The men, unwashed, unshaven, were ragged and dirty, without uniforms and dressed as, and how, they pleased."[12] Obviously the men did not feel apprehensive, nor did their colonel for that matter. At Doña Ana, Doniphan was reunited with his advance column under Major Gilpin. Having already spent a couple of days in the area, Gilpin felt uneasy about the situation, making known his opinion that the march into Paso del Norte would not go unopposed.[13]

Rumors began to circulate that anywhere from 500 to 1,300 Mexican regulars awaited the Missourians a mere forty miles to the south.[14] Accordingly, Doniphan finally ordered out a scouting expedition, under the command of Capt. John Reid, to verify the validity of the reports. Reid's company of spies did in fact encounter a small group of Mexican troops,

Figure 1.1. Col. Alexander William Doniphan. (Courtesy National Archives)

and a skirmish ensued in which two of the Mexicans were killed, a feat supposedly accomplished with only one shot because the slain men rode astride the same horse. However, aside from this small incident, the scouting party returned to Doña Ana with the news that no evidence could be found of a large body of enemy troops being nearby.[15] Because of this incident Major Gilpin, acting as the only cautious man in the entire bunch, quickly dispatched a detachment of sixty troops to serve as a picket. Gilpin ordered that the men proceed to a point twelve miles south of Doña Ana and remain at all times atop the mesas on the west side of the river, which provided a vantage point from which to overlook the entire valley for any sign of approaching danger.[16]

While these events transpired near Doña Ana at the northern end of the Mesilla Valley, the Mexicans did not remain idle at Paso del Norte on the southern end. Changes were quickly taking place among the officers commanding the Mexican army, all of which would play a substantial role in the events to come. On the same day that Doniphan's men arrived at Doña Ana, the commander of the Mexican troops at Paso del Norte was suddenly stricken ill and had no choice but to return to Chihuahua City. In his absence as commander, another officer, Lt. Col. Luis Vidal, received orders from the governor of Chihuahua to proceed with his body of Mexican troops northward up the Rio Grande valley to resist the advancement of the Americans. Vidal, apparently not desiring to lead the troops, quickly transferred command of his army to yet another officer, Lt. Col. Antonio Ponce de León.[17] Thus the Mexican army at Paso del Norte underwent three changes in commanders in a period of only a couple of days, all during a time in which they should have been undertaking more substantial preparations to meet the Missourians in battle.

The orders Vidal gave to his replacement as commander seemed simple: Lt. Col. Ponce de León would engage the enemy "until put to flight, or until the greatest possible advantage over it has been achieved." Vidal went on to hypothesize that the American troops, whom he supposed to be significantly outnumbered by his own sizable Mexican force at Paso del Norte, would be "lanced like rabbits."[18]

Ponce de León's command consisted of "a force of over 500 men, made up of regulars and National Guard; and a howitzer manned by twelve gunners, with the object of attacking the enemy."[19] Later estimates by some of the American volunteers placed the number of Mexicans near 1,100 men (490 cavalry, 100 infantry, 500 militia), an estimate that now seems exaggerated.[20] At any rate the Mexican commander knew the size of his own force and he had rough estimates of the force upon which Doniphan could readily draw. Knowing the numbers to be numerically in his favor, Ponce de León

marched north from Paso del Norte in accordance with his orders from
Lieutenant Colonel Vidal. In one regard, however, the two opposing forces
were equal: both the Mexican and U.S. armies consisted almost entirely of
volunteers with little or no previous training or fighting experience.

On Christmas Eve, Colonel Doniphan continued the march southward.[21]
Not long after leaving the dusty little village of Doña Ana, the column discovered three dead bodies along the trail: two Americans and one Mexican.
The troops presumed that Mexican spies from Paso del Norte had killed the
three men. Amazingly, despite this discovery and the previous day's skirmish, the Missouri volunteers marched onward with little sense of urgency,
strung out in single file along the trail for several miles. Some of them sang
"Yankee Doodle" to pass the time as they trekked through the bottomlands
of the Rio Grande valley.[22] If the Missourians expected an uncontested conquest of Paso del Norte like that which they had enjoyed when taking Santa
Fe, they would be grossly mistaken in their presumptions.

Around mid-afternoon on Christmas Day 1846, Doniphan ordered his
men to set up camp for the evening. Their march down the valley that day
had brought them eighteen miles closer to Paso del Norte, and Doniphan
had chosen a campsite well known to those familiar with the vicinity. It had
been used for decades, even centuries, as a camping place on the Camino
Real. The location, known as Brazito (little arm), was distinct because of a
large, easterly bend in the course of the Rio Grande, heavily shaded by gi-
ant cottonwood trees on all sides. The men comprising Doniphan's advance
guard encamped in the grassy bottomlands on the east bank of the river and
went about their typical camp chores as the stragglers slowly wandered in.
The failure of the officers to maintain stricter discipline along the line of
march would lead to great confusion in the hours to come.

Of that afternoon one soldier recalled that "it was about 2 o'clock P.M.,
and the day was pleasant. Our horses were grazing some distance from
camp at the time."[23] The setting was one of serenity, the mood was laid back,
and the actions of the Americans as they sat about their camp did not even
remotely resemble alarm. Doniphan and his fellow officers sat down in the
shade of a cottonwood and took up a game of cards, with a prized horse as
the object being wagered upon. At about this time Lt. James A. DeCourcey
observed a large cloud of dust rising on the distant southern horizon, and he
urgently reported his discovery to Doniphan. At first the commander took

no precautions, brushing the report aside as unimportant. A false alarm, perhaps. But within minutes the lieutenant returned and confirmed that the cloud of dust was in fact being caused by the approaching Mexican army, the same one Doniphan had heard rumors about two days before. To this Doniphan purportedly stood up and remarked to his fellow card players, "we must stop this game long enough to whip the Mexicans, but remember that I am way ahead in the score and cannot be beaten, and we will play it out as soon as the battle is over."[24] One historian has pointed out that "Doniphan could be criticized for failing to maintain attention to camp security," an observation that is entirely merited.[25] At this point, with a numerically superior enemy force rapidly approaching from the south, the colonel seems to have been a bit overzealous. Ensuing events would ultimately prove otherwise.

Doniphan, finally issuing the call to arms, caught his troops entirely off guard. "Never was a body of men taken more by surprise," wrote Frank Edwards; "when the dust was first observed, there were not one hundred and fifty men in camp, the rest being scattered after wood and water. But all seemed to have found the cause of the rising dust at the same moment, and came in, in double quick time, to get their arms."[26] Indeed, many of the men comprising the rear of Doniphan's column had not even arrived in camp yet. Among the items lagging behind on the trail were the regiment's ammunition wagons. From this standpoint, with the Americans outnumbered, caught by surprise, and lacking any additional ammunition besides what each man's cartridge box already contained, it appeared as though the Mexicans were riding boldly toward a decisive victory.

At this juncture each side pitched their respective lines of battle in the river bottoms in the traditional military style of the times. On the U.S. side, Companies B, C, and E of the 1st Regiment of Missouri Volunteers composed the right flank, commanded by Major Gilpin. Companies A and F brought up the left flank, and Companies D, H, and G filled the center.[27] Ponce de León's army halted atop a slight rise in the terrain to the south of the Americans, at which place they "drew up in good order, with the cavalry on [the] left and a small howitzer in the center—their left flank and body being composed of infantry—and gay enough they looked, their cavalry in bright scarlet coats with bell buttons, and snow-white belts, carrying polished sabers and carbines and long lances, with red and green pennons, while their heads were protected by brass helmets with large black plumes."[28] To another of the Missourians it was "seemingly enough to make one's blood flow chill when he saw the long, bold, and beautiful front of the enemy, forming a striking contrast with our single rank of footmen."[29]

The accounts later given by the Americans suggest that the Mexicans, and especially their widely acclaimed regiment of cavalrymen from Veracruz (the only trained regulars that the Mexican army had on the field that day), presented themselves in full splendor. The Americans, in contrast, boasted a somewhat less impressive appearance. During the Navajo expedition in November, many of Doniphan's men traded various trinkets to the Indians in exchange for clothing articles of Navajo manufacture. Accordingly, when the U.S. soldiers took up the line of battle that fateful December afternoon, many of them were "dressed . . . pretty nearly in the Indian style."[30]

Here a brief standoff ensued in which the two sides faced each other at a distance of about a thousand yards, out of the effective range of musketry. A singular bold officer of the Mexican army, Lt. Manuel Lara, rode out to meet the Americans. As he trotted forward on his horse he carried a black flag bearing a skull and bones motif accompanied with the phrase *Libertad o Muerte* (Liberty or Death).[31] Doniphan responded to this gesture by dispatching a messenger of his own to meet the Mexican lieutenant at the center of the battlefield. The event had all of the components of dramatic entertainment that one might find in a modern-day Hollywood western.

The young Mexican lieutenant delivered his message to Doniphan's courier, Lt. Col. David Mitchell, and his interpreter, Thomas Caldwell. The Mexican commander, Ponce de León, requested a parley with Doniphan. Mitchell curtly refused this request. The interpreter and the Mexican lieutenant bickered back and forth for a few moments in Spanish before the men returned to their respective lines in preparation for the fight ahead. Colonel Doniphan later recalled this particular incident, writing that "with my permission a hundred balls would have pierced the insolent bearer of the pirate flag; but I deemed it most proper for the honor of our country to restrain them."[32]

By taking the time to send out a messenger and request a meeting with Doniphan, the Mexican commander had made the first mistake of the day. Doing so provided the Americans with much-needed time, and as a result many of the stragglers who had not yet arrived at the battlefield when the call to arms was issued were afforded the opportunity to join their ranks before the battle commenced. In this manner the U.S. lines were reinforced for the frontal attack that was soon to come.

However, even with the added manpower, their lines remained uncomfortably thin. More importantly, nowhere in the U.S. lines could there be found any artillery. In an unwitting blunder of foresight, Doniphan and his fellow officers had elected to leave the artillery regiment behind in Santa Fe under the charge of Col. Sterling Price in order to protect the American garrison there in the event of a reprisal by the surrounding Mexican population. Surely Doniphan regretted the decision at this point. "Had we had a single piece of cannon with us [the Mexicans] would have lost more of their men; but having no artillery on our side, we had to act as infantry," complained one of Doniphan's lieutenants after the battle.[33]

An interesting side note arises in regard to Doniphan's artillery. One of his fellow officers, in his report of the events leading up to the battle, remarked that Doniphan had in fact sent an express rider back to Colonel Price at Santa Fe while encamped near Doña Ana on December 23, the same time he began receiving reports that an enemy force was just sixty miles away. Doniphan took the precaution under the inkling that the Mexicans might offer resistance as he neared their stronghold at Paso del Norte, noting in his report that he "sent an order to Major Clarke [sic], of the artillery, at Santa Fe, to join my forces at the earliest moment."[34] These reports contradict the accusations of others claiming that Doniphan failed to take any precautionary measures before the battle. It seems not altogether improbable that Doniphan took the action in relative secrecy without making it known to the bulk of his men.[35]

Patience would ultimately prove to be the greatest deciding factor in what would come to be called the Battle of Brazito. The American lines held steady as Ponce de León's several hundred men commenced their approach. As they marched forward the Mexicans fired two consecutive volleys at the U.S. troops, both of which went unanswered by the patient Missourians. In each instance the Mexicans miscalculated their distance, firing too high and having virtually no effect on their intended targets. Through all of this the ruffians from Missouri held steady and did not fire a single shot. If the men lacked discipline, it certainly did not show here, as they obeyed

Doniphan's command to hold fire with an amazing coolness prevailing throughout the ranks.

The charge of the Mexicans "was a handsome one, but . . . was too coolly met to break [the U.S.] line," recalled one U.S. officer.[36] The Mexican army fired still another volley into their enemy's ranks, this time wounding several of the Missourians. At this point, in Doniphan's estimation, the Mexicans had approached to within a reasonable firing distance, and he ordered his men to let loose upon them the lethal contents of their muskets. By the time the Americans fired their volley, the enemy had approached to within less than one hundred paces of the eagerly awaiting Missourians:

> They advanced within gunshot, and took shelter in the chaparral, discharging three full rounds upon our line before we returned the fire. At this crisis, Colonel Doniphan ordered the men *"to lie down on their faces, and reserve their fire until the Mexicans came within sixty paces."* This was done. The Mexicans supposing they had wrought fearful execution in our ranks, as some were falling down, while others stood up, began now to advance, and exultingly cry out *"bueno, bueno,"* whereupon our whole right wing, suddenly rising up, let fly such a galling volley of yager balls in their ranks, that they wheeled about and fled in the utmost confusion.[37]

Others present at this spectacle reported much the same. "Just as the smoke of [their third] discharge lifted, two powerful volleys were poured in by our men from their rifles, while, at the same moment, the Mexican dragoons charged gallantly down on our left flank."[38] This heavy showering of musket balls at close range took the desired effect among the Mexican troops, immediately throwing their gallant charge into disarray. Although more than one volley would be fired by the Americans that day, it was this first volley that proved the most fatal to the bewildered Mexican soldiers. "The consternation now became general among the ranks of the Mexicans," wrote one soldier, "and they commenced a precipitate retreat along the base of the mountains. Many of them took refuge in the craggy fastnesses."[39]

The most desperate fighting took place on the right flank of the Mexican lines, where the more experienced Mexican regulars comprising the Veracruz dragoons made their stand. According to the report of the Mexican commander, the Veracruz dragoons charged the American ranks in contradiction to orders, the result being that "the whole of the left wing of the cavalry and National Guard also took no part in the combat, but, on the contrary, some of them were already running away."[40] This indicates the breakdown in command and communication that occurred on the Mexican side after the battle began. Mexican sources cite this as a primary contributing factor to their defeat, one individual noting that "the cowardice of the national guard and the lack of discipline on the part of the cavalry decided the victory for the enemy."[41] Rather than attacking in unison, portions of the Mexican army charged from one flank while other portions simultaneously fled from the other flanks. A woeful lack of organization, impudent disobedience of orders, and widespread pandemonium prevailed on the Mexican side of the field.

It was here on the Americans' left flank that Marcellus Ball Edwards was posted during the battle, and his account evidences the level of intensity the fighting reached at that location. "I would not pretend to say which company bore the brunt of battle or the severest fire," he wrote, "as each claims the honor, but our flag, which was borne on the extreme right, was pierced by a greater number of bullets than any other. The large flag of Company C, thribble the size of ours, had not a hole shot in it. But this makes no difference; I don't suppose the Mexicans shot at our banners."[42] Edwards thus suggests that the Missourians, despite composing a single regiment, competed with one another among their respective companies. Each company possessed a sense of staunch pride, and no doubt they strove to excel in the battle to prove the worth of their own respective companies.

With the Mexican army in a state of total disarray and divided into several smaller retreating units across the battlefield, the Americans appeared to have won the day. In the ensuing confusion, several downsized groups of Mexican soldiers desperately charged portions of the U.S. line, but to no avail. One of the targets attacked by the Mexicans was the supply wagons located behind the U.S. front lines. Throughout the battle Edwards commanded a small detachment of some fifteen to twenty men ordered to guard these wagons. As Mexican troops approached, Edwards ordered his men to hide among the brush and tall grass surrounding the wagons. After the Mexicans had marched to within a dozen yards of the wagons, the Americans revealed themselves and fired into the ranks of their unsuspecting enemy, immediately routing the small detachment and causing them to flee in all directions.[43]

As the remnant of this attacking party of Mexican soldiers fled to the nearby hills, "they were pursued by the Americans about one mile; Captain Reid, and Captain Walton, who by this time had mounted a few of his men, followed them still further."[44] Walton gave up the chase after about four miles, leaving the Mexicans to their fates. Several different accounts agree that these Mexicans, after reaching the hills to the east (probably the foothills on the western slopes of the Organ Mountains), were attacked by Apaches "who had been watching the struggle from their concealment, [and] set upon them and killed almost all for the sake of their bright uniforms and arms."[45] This account deserves some consideration, as the Apaches were well known for their astonishment with impressionable clothing articles such as the bright and colorful items worn by the Mexican cavalry at Brazito. This, coupled with a traditional Apache enmity toward the Mexican race, adds weight to the validity of these reports.

In contrast to the Americans, who possessed not a solitary piece of ordnance, the Mexican army had a single small three-pounder they kept at the center of their advancing line, heavily reinforced with infantry troops.[46] After the Mexicans failed in their initial charge, the small three-pound cannon became important for all involved. While the small cannon could not turn the tide of the battle for the hopelessly defeated Mexican army, it might still be fired into the American ranks with deadly results. Realizing this, a group of Americans numbering about thirty men took on the task of capturing the Mexicans' last remaining advantage in the battle. These bold Missourians of Company G, commanded in their feat by Lt. Nicholas B. Wright, charged the fortified position of the Mexican artillery, guarded on both sides by lines of infantry consisting of about seventy-five men each. In their assault the Americans killed several of the men posted to guard the cannon, causing the remainder to flee, and then laboriously hauled their prize back to the American lines.[47]

While perhaps hyperbolized by some of the men directly involved, this emerged as an accomplishment worthy of remark among their comrades. "[The Mexican] infantry having been put to flight, the Howard Company, under the command of Lieutenant Nicholas Wright, taking advantage of the panic, charged upon them, and took their cannon from them," explained 1st

Lieutenant Kribben.[48] "This was a most daring act, almost ridiculous for its fearlessness," reiterated Frank Edwards.[49] Ironically, despite the importance and daring of the action undertaken by the men of Company G, it would prove to be of little importance by the time they returned to the U.S. lines with their captured prize. In the time it took them to drag the cannon back to safety, the remainder of the Mexican army had given up the fight altogether, rapidly retreating back to Paso del Norte.

The entire Battle of Brazito, despite its eccentricities, lasted not more than thirty minutes. The reports given by various officers after the melee differ slightly in their estimations of casualties. It is positively known that not a single U.S. soldier died in the battle, and it is generally accepted that only eight were wounded (although another source says seven), none of them severely. On the Mexican side, the results were much different. Doniphan claimed that forty-three of the enemy lost their lives, the majority of them dying in that first destructive volley fired at close range by the Americans. He estimated 150 additional Mexican troops were wounded, and five were taken prisoner.[50] These numbers of killed and wounded, as initially reported by Doniphan, were almost certainly embellished. The subsequent report of Lieutenant Kribben claims only thirty Mexicans killed and "several" wounded, of which six later died.[51] On the contrary, the report filed by the Mexican commander, Lt. Col. Antonio Ponce de León, likely underestimated the casualties: eleven killed and seventeen wounded, "besides the scattered troops which will be delayed in getting together."[52] Several of the scattered troops to which he referred were without a doubt those of the Veracruz dragoons who had been attacked and killed by the Apaches, which would further increase his estimate of casualties during the engagement. In light of these several conflicting reports, the final tally in terms of Mexican casualties is not precisely known. It seems that at the very least seventeen Mexicans were killed (the eleven initially reported by Ponce de León, and the six others who later succumbed to their wounds); the number of wounded at least equaled, and likely exceeded, the number of killed. Regardless of the actual numbers, there was no question among those involved that the Americans had won the day. "How we came off so well, I cannot make out," said Frank Edwards, "for the bullets rained about [our] troops."[53] Even the Missourians, full of a conquering army's pride, could have never expected to emerge with such a lopsided victory.[54]

The few Mexicans taken prisoner at the battle showed a sense of astonishment by the determination of their foe during the fighting. They obviously expected a less valiant, more timid resistance from the easterners. A Mexican prisoner explained to one of the Missourians that he "could not understand such a people, for, not only did they sustain three volleys without returning one, which, of itself was very puzzling, but, when one row [of troops] was mowed down, up sprang another out of the grass."[55]

Afterward, the men of the 1st Regiment enjoyed the spoils of their victory. From the countless articles that the Mexican soldiers had left strewn about the field during their hasty retreat, the Americans hauled into their camp several kegs of wine "of the best quality," which they passed around until the last drop had been consumed. Bread and cheese, a rare delicacy on the mid-nineteenth-century frontier, provided a well-deserved and lavishly enjoyed Christmas feast for the men. They also took the ammunition left behind by the Mexicans, as well as several cases of surgical tools. "The field was strewed with bodies of men and horses, lances, swords, helmets, trumpets, carbines and other war emblems."[56] That night the Americans spread their tents about the battlefield, and the Mexican and U.S. wounded were sheltered in them. Those of the Mexican army who died were buried in a mass grave on December 26, just before the men picked up camp and headed toward Paso del Norte.

The fact that the Mexican army held a considerable strategic and numerical advantage over the Americans when they first entered the Mesilla Valley on December 23 cannot be disputed. But by the time the two sides confronted each other, numerous catastrophic blunders had been made on the part of the Mexican leaders, both in preparing for the battle and during the battle. In analyzing these mistakes, it becomes clear why the Americans emerged with such a decisive victory.

At least one company of Mexican volunteers was armed only with bows and arrows. This in itself negated that particular company's effectiveness. These men might as well have stood by as observers, as their arrows could not plausibly have had any effect at the distances from which the two armies fired at each other.

Military intelligence and reconnaissance operations also failed for the Mexicans. To be sure, they had sent out spies and were well aware of Doniphan's approach. Even so, most accounts agree that the Mexican commanders underestimated the size of Doniphan's force, thinking it to be only a couple hundred men when in fact it was twice that size. This represents a mistake on the part of the Mexican scouts, who failed to make accurate reports about the size of the enemy. Some scholars maintain that the hasty Mexican retreat could also have been due to a large cloud of rising dust to the north, behind the American lines. Some of the Missourians believed that the Mexicans misinterpreted this as the oncoming of a large body of U.S. reinforcements. Had the Mexican spies been more careful in their reconnaissance operations, they would have known beforehand that Doniphan's men had with them some two thousand sheep. The source of the dust on the horizon was not American reinforcements from Santa Fe; it was merely a herd of harmless sheep, whose effect on the battle surely could not have been too much for the Mexicans to contend with.[57]

Throughout the war with the United States, the Mexican army suffered due to their being less technologically advanced than the Americans. The Battle of Brazito proved to be no exception. Nearly every Mexican soldier who took to the field that day did so dismally equipped with smoothbore, obsolete carbines.[58] The Americans, meanwhile, carried newer firearms, and more of them. The United States enjoyed a stronger economy and wealthier government treasury than did Mexico, and it showed in the equipment of the U.S. troops. This advantage might have been negated due to the fact that the supply and ammunition wagons had not yet caught up with the column at the time the Mexicans approached. But here again the Mexican commandant made a costly mistake in judgment. By sending out a messenger under a flag of truce to meet with the Americans, he allowed sufficient time to pass for the surplus ammunition to reach the Missourians.

One might legitimately contend that the Mexicans had an indisputable advantage in that Doniphan failed to bring the artillery along with him, opting instead to leave it behind in Santa Fe. The final result of the battle shows that this singular oversight by Doniphan did not matter. One can only wonder how many men the Mexican army might have lost had Doniphan in fact had his entire artillery regiment with him, which consisted of not one but several cannon, most of which were much larger than the Mexican three-pounder. Mexican casualties at the battle would have doubled, possibly even tripled, with the presence of Doniphan's artillery.

Finally, the Mexicans simply did not adequately prepare for the enemy force they were to meet on the battlefield. It is obvious that they lacked an organized and articulate chain of command. At least three changes had been made in the commander of the Mexican army, all within a couple days of the fighting at Brazito. It is incredibly difficult for an army to undergo three such changes in leadership in such a short amount of time and still maintain its prior morale and effectiveness in fighting. Additionally, at least one change occurred during the battle itself. The Mexican commandant, Lt. Col. Antonio Ponce de León, gallantly remained at the front lines of his infantry troops during their charge, until he himself was wounded in that fateful first volley fired by the Americans. Unable to continue in his role as commanding officer, Ponce de León had little choice but to relinquish his command to a subordinate officer, Capt. Rafael Carajal. By this time the Mexican army was all but whipped, a fact that is reflected by Carajal's orders when he assumed command: "collect the troops and make as orderly [a] retreat as might be possible."[59] This could partially account for the incredible confusion that plagued the Mexicans after the Americans fired their first shots. The result of all this was simple, and perhaps best summarized by the Mexican commander after the battle: "In short . . . the victory which I had considered certain changed into the complete loss and dispersion of the [army]."[60]

Although the Mexicans had made numerous mistakes, the Missourians still deserve credit for capitalizing on those blunders and for not making similar errors of their own. Throughout the entire incident the Americans never lost their composure. Doniphan's men arrived on the battlefield as a poorly dressed and ragged-looking lot of men, the embodiment of the frontier soldier, with little training and even less fighting experience. But one would have never conceived of such a notion from their actions on December 25, 1846. One enlisted man who fought at Brazito noted, "I thought everything would be serious, but everything was to the contrary. There was more profanity in ranks than I ever heard before. Everyone was trying who could excel in cracking jokes and all was merriment. That night we had quite a spree over the provisions and wine taken from the enemy, and the officers finished their game."[61] So it would seem that despite the excitement of the day the indefatigable Colonel Doniphan never forgot about returning to the card game in which he was so far ahead, and which the Mexican army had so rudely interrupted.

As the Missourians continued toward Paso del Norte, they were joined by an infamous character of western lore, scalp hunter James Kirker. Chihuahuan Governor Ángel Trías owed Kirker some $10,000 for Apache scalps and refused to pay; in consequence, Kirker resolved to join the invading U.S. troops, offering his services as guide. In the ensuing months, Kirker would provide advice and information to Doniphan in many instances and would prove to be an invaluable resource.[62]

On December 27, Colonel Doniphan and his victorious Missouri Volunteers entered Paso del Norte, the northernmost town that still remained a part of Mexico, which bustled with anxiety over the news of their army's defeat. Following the encounter at Brazito, Doniphan had every reason to expect a hearty resistance by the Mexicans from a fortified position at Paso del Norte. Unlike the march before Brazito, caution became the watchword of the U.S. column. One soldier noted, "we fully expected to have another skirmish before entering the city of El Paso, and were, therefore, on the alert."[63] About six miles north of Paso del Norte, a narrow pass afforded a perfect vantage point from which the Mexicans could have opposed Doniphan's advance. "When within two or three miles of this place [the pass], we were continually halting, waiting for the rear to catch up."[64] The men from Missouri, now fully cognizant of the potential danger, approached the Mexican village with attentiveness.

Instead, the conquering troops were never forcefully confronted. A small delegation of Paso del Norte residents met the approaching column under a flag of truce as they entered the town, assuring Doniphan "of the tranquil and friendly disposition of the inhabitants" and surrendering without incident.[65] The citizens living there were naturally curious; for some, this was the first time they had seen white men from the United States. Despite the apprehension they must have felt, many of the people did not display feelings of hostility toward the invaders. The people, recalled Frank Edwards, "came creeping cautiously out of their houses, with baskets of fruit, which they kindly forced the soldiers to accept. By the time I reached the Plaza, I had both holsters and pockets filled."[66]

The Paso del Norte region was at this time a unique cultural crossroads. Writing in 1856, less than a decade after Doniphan's men passed through, W. W. H. Davis noted:

As we rode through the town I was struck with the charming appearance it presented. On every side were vineyards, flower gardens, orchards, and shrubbery, loaded with foliage, flowers, fruit, and little canals carried water along nearly all the streets . . . adding to the pleasantness of the scene . . . when to these natural beauties we add nearly every delicacy and luxury that the heart of man can crave, and a climate that rivals that of Italy, it can easily be conceived that, as a place of residence, it is almost an earthly paradise. [Crossing the Rio Grande into Paso del Norte], I found everything purely Mexican, and even the near proximity of the Americans, without the advantage of their institutions, had failed to start the inhabitants from the Rip Van Winkle sleep in which they have slumbered for centuries.[67]

At Paso del Norte, Doniphan's several hundred troops quickly dispersed, some of them occupying two buildings on the plaza as temporary quarters. Still other companies found shelter at barracks and other various locations throughout the city. Here the Americans would remain for several weeks, awaiting the arrival of the artillery regiment finally being sent from Santa Fe. By now Doniphan understood that he would need the additional firepower as he continued southward into Mexico, where he knew he would once again meet the Mexican army.

The soldiers passed their time at the town in their own respective pursuits. Those men who did not bask in the luxuries of fruits and wine "searched the town for arms, which was attended with great success. They found buried in one place two or three very small pieces of iron cannon and large quantities of ammunition and some musketoons."[68]

While Doniphan did not meet any direct opposition while in Paso del Norte, it should be noted that some individuals there did conspire against the Americans, providing valuable information to Mexican authorities farther south. One such individual, Father Ramón Ortíz,[69] had been present in Paso del Norte for many years. Ortíz supplied information to authorities in Chihuahua City regarding Doniphan's troop strength, along with other details. Doniphan eventually discovered the actions of the priest and had him arrested.[70]

On February 1, 1847, the artillery companies, with Major Clark and Capt.

Richard Weightman in command, reached Colonel Doniphan at Paso del Norte, having made the trip from Santa Fe in fourteen days. The reinforcements consisted of 130 troops, four 6-pound cannon, and two 12-pound cannon. Less than two weeks later, on February 11, the entire command departed Paso del Norte and took the trail to Chihuahua City, where they would once again engage the Mexican army in battle.[71]

By the time Doniphan and his troopers returned home to the eastern states, more than a year after leaving Missouri with Kearny's original column of 1,586 troops, the men were hailed as heroes. The Battle of Brazito had been thoroughly covered by eastern newspapers, especially those in Missouri, who heaped elaborate praises upon their beloved volunteer army.[72] After the nearly flawless victory at Brazito, they fought and defeated the Mexican army again at the Battle of Sacramento, in the process conquering Chihuahua City and essentially neutralizing the threat in northern Mexico. By June 16, 1847, the victorious Missouri volunteers found themselves back in New Orleans, eager to be mustered out after a long and arduous year of service in the Southwest. They had marched six thousand miles, won two decisive and important battles, and performed their duty to the United States to the utmost of their ability.

The exact site of the battlefield in the Mesilla Valley where the clash between Mexican and U.S. forces took place is not exactly known. Several historians and archaeologists have attempted to locate the battlefield in recent years. Some have found minor shreds of evidence, such as fired musket balls, but no strong or conclusive evidence exists. The battle is known to have been fought in the bottomlands of the valley and alongside the river, an area prone to heavy flooding for decades afterward. Any obvious traces would thus have been lost to the elements, either washed away farther down the valley or buried under several feet of sediment. The "little arm" of the river, for which Brazito received its name, is no longer existent to mark the location, the river now running in a relatively straight line through the valley. Additionally, the entire area is now, and has been for over one hundred years, composed almost entirely of farmlands. The continuous plowing of the soil has served to further obliterate any traces of the battle.

It is difficult to accept the minor material shreds of evidence that have been found, especially musket balls, as being positively attributable to the Battle of Brazito. A few years later, in 1851, Fort Fillmore was built near the site and remained a large and important garrison for an entire decade; any artifacts that have been found could likely have been from the soldiers there. Thus the battlefield is a casualty of the passing years, and it will probably be impossible to ever determine the exact site where Doniphan's men made their brave stand against their oncoming foe.

Many of the participants did leave behind clues by which we can ascertain the approximate location. An analysis of estimated distances traveled by Doniphan's column prior to the battle provides a close estimate. However, even these estimates vary by several miles depending on the source.

The Mexicans called the altercation La Batalla de los Temascalitos, which referenced several "sandy little hills" in the vicinity. Well known to locals and travelers for several years after the battle took place, several passersby made note of the site. Susan Magoffin, wife of the famous pioneer and trader Sam Magoffin, passed the location shortly after the battle, writing in her diary that "we nooned it at Brasito [sic], the battlefield long to be remembered by Col. Doniphan and his little band of seven hundred volunteers. I rode over the battle ground (a perfect plain), and brought off as trophies two cartridges, one Mexican and the other Amer[ican]."[73] U.S. attorney W. W. H. Davis, passing the location in the mid-1850s during his circuit of the territory, likewise made specific mention of the battlefield. Davis's account hints at the possible location: "a few miles below the fort [Fillmore] we passed the battlefield of Brazito, where Doniphan fought a severe action with the Mexicans during the war."[74] No matter which source is drawn upon, it can be accurately concluded that the Battle of Brazito was fought at a location in the bottomlands of the Rio Grande valley, on the east side of the river, south of Fort Fillmore and north of the modern-day town of Vado, New Mexico.

What we can be certain of, however, is that Doniphan's success at the Battle of Brazito was of monumental importance for more reasons than one. The victory, critical to his penetration farther into Mexico (eventually to the Gulf of Mexico) and his eventual capture of Chihuahua City, assisted in the victorious emergence of the United States in the war with Mexico from 1846 to 1848. The victory at Brazito laid an even stronger foundation for America's claim to the New Mexico Territory, as the Mexican army, with their retreat from the battlefield that day, essentially abandoned their northernmost province to the Americans. In a sense General Kearny's conquest of New Mexico was finally completed when Colonel Doniphan and his Missouri volunteers drove the last remaining force of Mexican troops out of the territory on that fateful Christmas Day in 1846.

Perhaps most importantly for future regional concerns, Doniphan and his army comprised the first large body of Americans to ever enter the Mesilla Valley. Prior to this, only a few brave American pioneers and traders had passed through the area, and even then at tremendous risk to life and property. The increased American presence, coupled with the U.S. claim to the land, would forever change life for those living along the Rio Grande in southern New Mexico. The people residing there, while still predominantly Spanish in culture and background, were now viewed (though still unofficially) as citizens of the United States of America. This change in sovereignty would have a profound effect on events in the Mesilla Valley throughout the upcoming decade, as the United States attempted to extend throughout the region its laws, its protection, and its hallowed freedoms.

CHAPTER 2

The Treaty of Guadalupe Hidalgo

Colonel Doniphan's victory at Brazito and subsequent march through northern Mexico to the Gulf represents only a small component of the war with Mexico. Nevertheless, as stated, it was an important event for those areas of northern Mexico directly affected by it. The war between the two countries continued for some time after Doniphan and his men triumphantly arrived back at New Orleans in the summer of 1847.

The Mexican War ended with the signing (and subsequent ratification) of the Treaty of Guadalupe Hidalgo by the two warring nations on February 2, 1848.[1] Although many people in the region may not have fully appreciated the ramifications at the time, the treaty would be of tremendous importance to all those living in New Mexico, and especially those in the Mesilla Valley. The treaty included within its provisions the famed Mexican Cession, which included the entirety of New Mexico Territory and the modern Southwest, from Texas to California. This did not, however, immediately make the territory of New Mexico a part of the United States, nor did the residents immediately become citizens.[2] Although the laws of the United States had been extended over the Mexican Cession lands in 1848, the people living in the territory could not call themselves U.S. citizens until September 9, 1850. It was on that date that Henry Clay, the famous congressional negotiator, finally succeeded in pushing through that governing body, the Compromise of 1850, simultaneously conceding to the demands of both pro- and antislavery factions in the eastern United States.

The treaty with Mexico had been signed by Nicholas P. Trist, U.S. minister to Mexico, and now awaited the slow and painful process of ratification.[3] In addition to future citizenship, the treaty required the demarcation of the new international boundary line, the prompt removal of American troops from Mexico, the restoration of customhouses, an immediate end to all hostilities, and the exchange of prisoners of war.[4]

The treaty also included numerous articles and provisions that would prove to be controversial in the years following, and that would lead to increasing diplomatic conflict between the United States and Mexico. Among the more troublesome articles contained in the Treaty of Guadalupe Hidalgo were Articles V, VI, and XI, respectively. All three of these articles would directly affect the Mesilla Valley and the people living there, and would take years to be satisfactorily sorted out.

Article V of the treaty defined the new boundary line between the United States and Mexico, but it did so in a vague and unsatisfactory manner (at least from the U.S. standpoint). According to the provisions of the treaty, each country would appoint able and competent commissioners to survey and mark the new boundary line; once completed, the findings of these scientific surveys were to retroactively become a part of the Treaty of Guadalupe Hidalgo.[5] This concept seemed simple enough, but political strife and self-interest prevailed among the boundary commissions, resulting in countless impediments throughout the process. First and foremost, the men appointed to serve as commissioners could never quite agree on the appropriate placement of the boundary line. In upcoming years the U.S. government would struggle to appoint an able and dedicated boundary commissioner, resulting in lengthy delays and added expenses, not to mention immense confusion. Many of those attempting to solve the problem met with personal frustration or, worse, termination from their positions by the U.S. government. The problem would not be completely resolved until the Gadsden Purchase of December 1853, more than five years after the initial treaty with Mexico had been signed.

As a direct result of Article V, the town of Mesilla came into existence. The creation of Mesilla hinged almost entirely on the issue of boundaries, and of the citizenship preferences of the people living there. Thus the founding of Mesilla can be viewed as a derivative of the Treaty of Guadalupe Hidalgo and the resulting disagreements among Texas, the United States, and Mexico pertaining to the boundary line placements.

Following the Mexican War and the signing of the treaty, the State of Texas claimed all land east of the Rio Grande. Congressional representatives from Texas continued to assert that because of the Texan invasion of New Mexico several years before the treaty with Mexico, all land east of the Rio Grande belonged to their state.[6] The diction of the Treaty of Guadalupe Hidalgo, these politicians further asserted, represented a description of the boundary that they claimed, and therefore they used this treaty in an attempt to legitimize that claim in Congress. Another element used by those in favor of Texas' claim to eastern New Mexico was an act of Congress of

May 13, 1846, in which the United States affirmed the validity of the Texan claim to the Rio Grande as its western boundary. Furthermore, in a message to Congress on December 7, 1847, President James K. Polk made direct reference to the Rio Grande in New Mexico as the Texas boundary, proclaiming, "New Mexico is a frontier province, and has never been of any considerable value to Mexico. From its locality, it is naturally connected with our western settlements. The territorial limits of the State of Texas, too, as defined by her laws, before admission into our Union, embrace all that portion of New Mexico lying east of the Rio Grande."[7]

Matters reached a climax in August 1850 when acting Secretary of War Gen. Winfield Scott dispatched 750 recruits of the 1st Dragoons and 3rd Infantry to New Mexico to complement the military force already in the territory. General Scott instructed Col. John Munroe, commander of the military force in New Mexico, that "these reinforcements are deemed necessary to enable you to protect the people of New Mexico. . . . It is known here, that the Legislature of Texas has been summoned, by the Governor of that State, to meet . . . to adopt measures for extending her political and civil jurisdiction over that part of New Mexico, on this side of the Rio Grande, claimed as a part of Texas." Secretary of War Scott further informed Munroe that it would be highly probable for Texas to raise a body of troops and send them to New Mexico, "if the disputed boundary between Texas and New Mexico, be not earlier established by Congress. Accordingly," Scott continued, "you are hereby instructed, in the case of any military invasion of New Mexico, from Texas, or by armed men from any other State or States, for the purpose of overturning the order of civil government that may exist in New Mexico at the time, or of subjugating New Mexico or Texas, to interpose, as far as practicable, the troops under your command against any such act of violence."[8]

This served only to further aggravate an already complex situation. From this arose a three-way struggle to gain legitimate possession not only of the Mesilla Valley but of the entire eastern portion of New Mexico as well, and Texas made a bold move in threatening the use of military force in asserting their claim.

At the time, Doña Ana was the only Mexican village of any sizable significance in the northern portion of the valley. The people living there, nearly all of Mexican ancestry, retained vivid memories of previous bloody conflicts between Texas and Mexico. They possessed no desire to become Texas citizens.[9]

Although not nearly as old as the more southerly Mexican town of Paso del Norte (founded in 1659), Doña Ana did predate the Mexican-American conflict by several years. Situated on a rise of the eastern bank of the Rio Grande, the town began in 1843 on a Mexican land grant of 35,000 acres that had been obtained from the governor of Chihuahua. Known as the Doña Ana Bend Colony grant, the first successful land grant in the Mesilla Valley, it was issued to Don José María Costales of Paso del Norte, who initially planned to colonize the land grant with about one hundred other pioneering individuals. However, Costales's plans did not materialize, and not until Don Pablo Melendres arrived there in 1843 with a small group of men, who began digging acequias, did the village finally materialize.[10]

There are numerous theories as to where the name *Doña Ana* is derived from. One tale suggests that long before the town existed the daughter of a Spanish military officer, named Ana, was carried off by Apaches in this vicinity and was never heard from again. A letter written in 1693 to the Mexican viceroy referenced a sheep ranch in this area of the Rio Grande valley known as Doña Ana María Niña de Cordoba. The settlers in 1843 might have simply shortened this to Doña Ana. Still another theory pertains to the death of Pedro Robledo, an officer accompanying Don Juan de Oñate's 1598 colonization expedition who died in that area and for whom the present-day Robledo Mountains, a few miles northwest of Doña Ana, are named. The granddaughter of Robledo, supposedly named Ana, is said to have fled south from Santa Fe during the Pueblo Revolt of 1680. When she reached the area now known as Doña Ana, she knew that her grandfather had passed away in the vicinity, and she died there from grief. This latter explanation, likely derived from local lore, seems to be the least believable, but, to be sure, it is not positively known exactly how or why the village came to be known as Doña Ana.[11]

When Doña Ana was originally settled, each family received one hundred acres to farm, with about half that amount being given to men without families. A census taken on January 24, 1844, showed that 261 people called Doña Ana home despite the incessant Apache raids that plagued the town.[12] Doña Ana elected its first alcalde, or mayor, on January 25, 1844, when Don Pablo Melendres rose to the position.[13] Melendres would continue to be an

Figure 2.1. Lt. Delos Bennett Sackett of the 1st Dragoons, surveyor of the Las Cruces town site in 1848. He is shown here in uniform as a Civil War officer. (Courtesy National Archives)

influential figure in the valley for years to come. In the summer of 1848, Melendres would request that Lt. Delos B. Sackett of the 1st U.S. Dragoons, then stationed in Doña Ana to fight Apaches and discourage depredations, proceed several miles downriver and conduct a survey for a new town site, that of Las Cruces.[14]

In the early months of 1848, a far more pressing issue arose in this quiet little farming community in the upper valley. When news of the provisions

of the treaty with Mexico reached the residents of Doña Ana, and they realized the effect it would have, many of them naturally had no desire to change
their ways and become a part of Texas or the United States. Boundary commissioner John Russell Bartlett, present in the Mesilla Valley immediately
following these events and no doubt well acquainted with the matter on a
personal basis, described the situation in his *Personal Narrative:*

> Immediately preceding, and after the war with Mexico, the Mex-
> ican population occupying the eastern bank of the Rio Grande in
> Texas and New Mexico were greatly annoyed by the encroachments
> of the Americans, and by their determined efforts to despoil them
> of their land and property. This was done by the latter either settling
> among them, or in some instances forcibly occupying their dwell-
> ings and cultivated spots. In most cases, however, it was done by
> putting "Texas head-rights" on their property. These "head-rights"
> were grants issued by the State of Texas, generally embracing 640
> acres, or a square mile, though they sometimes covered very large
> tracts. They were issued to persons who had served in wars, like our
> military land-warrants, and also to original settlers.[15]

The troublesome situation arising from the Texan claim to the Mesilla
Valley was thus exacerbated by violations of previous citizens' property
rights through the sale of these Texan head-right claims. The Treaty of Guadalupe Hidalgo contained provisions guaranteeing certain property rights
to individuals already residing on Mexican Cession lands, and the sale of
land claims to outsiders was perceived by the local population as a direct
violation of their own land rights. One such example involved a 640-acre
tract upon which was situated the village of Doña Ana, which was sold in
1850 to Maj. Enoch Steen of the 1st U.S. Dragoons by William Cockburn,
an assistant to Texas commissioner Robert S. Neighbors.[16] Upon learning
of what had transpired, a number of Doña Ana citizens signed a petition
in March 1850, and sent it directly to the military department commander,
Col. John Munroe. The petition explained the circumstances surrounding
the claim: "Texas commissioners that regulated the Political jurisdiction
in this place and vicinity, have sold a land warrant or certificate to Maj.

Steen the military commander of this place . . . with which he has taken one league of land including the houses of the town and the cultivated lands and a grand portion of the adjoining lands." The citizens urged the civil authorities in Santa Fe to take action, stressing that Steen's purchase of the head-right claim "is so directly contrary to the Treaty entered into between the United States of America and the Republic of Mexico. It is contrary to all natural right and contrary to that of the people."[17] Ultimately Steen lost the claim and the land reverted back to the rightful owners, but not before a considerable controversy arose as a result of the local population becoming aware of his actions.

The issuance of these land certificates led many Americans to flock to the Rio Grande valley. In many instances the certificates placed the new-comers on property "which for a century had been in the quiet possession of the old Spanish colonists and their descendents." The Mexicans, in order to avoid inevitable conflicts, "abandoned their homes, and sought refuge on the Mexican side of the river." This was especially true at the village of Doña Ana, which had the added appeal of a permanent garrison of U.S. troops stationed there. The town thus became "an attractive point for speculators, and was in consequence pounced upon by them, and covered by the Texan land-warrants . . . several hundred abandoned their property and homes in despair, and sought an asylum in the Mexican territory, preferring the very uncertain protection they could obtain there to remaining as citizens of the United States."[18]

In response to these troubles the Mexican government devised a plan whereby Mexicans residing in this disputed region could emigrate back to Chihuahua, forming colonies there. This action was in line with the provi-sion of the Treaty of Guadalupe Hidalgo allowing individuals not wishing to become American citizens to move back to Mexico. A federal decree was drawn up on August 19, 1848, providing funding for the establishment of these colonies on the Mexican side of the international border, and Fa-ther Ramón Ortíz, the *cura* at Paso del Norte, received the appointment as Commissioner General of Emigration to oversee the process and issue land grants. Ortíz would be instrumental in the issuance of land grants on the west bank of the Rio Grande, at that time still Mexican territory. The first settlers arrived in what is today Mesilla as early as 1849, although the first influx did not occur until 1850. Ortíz issued several Mexican land grants in and around Mesilla in 1851 and 1852, before the Gadsden Purchase transferred that region to the United States.[19]

By April 1850, partially as a result of the head-right that Major Steen had purchased, and partially because some settlers had already reestablished themselves on the land grants issued by Father Ortíz, the people at Doña Ana had devised a simple solution to their dilemma: they would move across the Rio Grande, the opposite (west) side of which remained a part of Mexico. Doing this meant the people would not be subject to any new laws or regulations imposed by the United States, nor Texas for that matter. Approximately sixty families from Doña Ana, under the guidance of Don Rafael Ruelas (who would become the alcalde of the newly created settlement),[20] moved across the river and founded a new settlement.

The new settlement of Mesilla, and the process by which it came into existence, was described by boundary commissioner John Russell Bartlett in a communication with the secretary of the interior in August 1851. He noted the town to be between eight and ten miles south of Doña Ana and that it contained between eight hundred and one thousand inhabitants. "It consists of mud, or chiefly of stick houses, and has been settled within two years by Mexicans who have abandoned their residences on our side of the river, preferring to be under the Mexican government," he wrote, adding that "one half of these removed from Doña Ana in consequence of the encroachments made on them by the Americans."[21]

With the adoption of the Compromise of 1850, Texas relinquished its original claim to the Rio Grande as its western boundary with New Mexico, and the boundary lines between Texas and New Mexico were placed, for the most part, in their present locations.[22] By the time Congress sorted this out, Mesilla had already become a thriving community on the west bank of the river, which remained a part of Mexico.[23] However, Mesilla's status as a town within the boundaries of Mexico would be short-lived.

Article VI of the Treaty of Guadalupe Hidalgo maintained that Mexico would allow the United States to use the southernmost portions of New Mexico Territory, including the Mesilla Valley, for the construction of a transcontinental railroad to California.[24] It had long been believed by Americans that southern New Mexico and the Gila River valley across modern-day Arizona provided the most plausible route for such a railroad. The matter was important enough in 1848 that the United States insisted on the inclusion of this clause in the treaty. It would prove to be yet another item of dispute between the two countries.

The topic of effective and inexpensive transportation would plague the Southwest for years to come, the roots of which can be traced back to the failure of Article VI. In the late 1840s, supplies arriving on the U.S. side of the Rio Grande at Paso del Norte had to be shipped 850 miles overland at an annual cost of more than $200,000.[25] In the years following the Mexican War, it was the common delusion of many U.S. politicians that the Rio Grande, with its terminus at the Gulf of Mexico, represented a viable option for transporting goods inland to the newly acquired territory of New Mexico. Many believed that the natural obstructions in the river could be removed, making the river navigable as far inland as Santa Fe. At the time, the river could only be navigated inland for a couple hundred miles, but the hope for improvements was prevalent enough that the government appointed numerous army officers and engineers to investigate. Eventually, all involved came to the realization that it could never work. The idea was never again pursued, giving way to the increased importance of a transcontinental railroad across southern New Mexico. The United States began to seriously press the issue in the early 1850s, especially following the discovery of gold in California in 1849. With thousands of fortune-seeking forty-niners striking westward, and the gold being transported back east on ships, the railroad took on an increased importance.

Unfortunately for the United States, the Mexican government did not feel particularly inclined to adhere to this portion of the treaty. When the boundary commissions began working in the early 1850s, this issue arose repeatedly. Manifest Destiny had a firm grip on the United States, with the merchants and businessmen in the east competing with one another over the most plausible location for a transcontinental railroad. It is an item of no little irony that although this was such a hot topic at the time, another thirty years would come and pass before a railroad would actually be built across New Mexico. For the time being it served as yet another disputable object in an already tumultuous and deteriorating diplomatic relationship between the United States and Mexico.

In the eyes of Washington politicians and frontier soldiers alike, the eleventh article represented another problematic clause in the Treaty of Guadalupe Hidalgo. This article addressed the issue of Native American tribes living within the cession lands, stipulating that the responsibility for controlling these Indians belonged to the United States: "[These] tribes . . . will hereafter be under the exclusive control of the Government of the United States, and whose incursions within the territory of Mexico would be prejudicial in the extreme; it is solemnly agreed that all such incursions shall be forcibly restrained by the Government of the United States." Furthermore, when Indian raids could not be prevented entirely by U.S. troops, "[the Indians] shall be punished by the said Government, and satisfaction for the same shall be exacted; all in the same way, and with equal diligence and energy, as if the same incursions were meditated or committed within its own territory against its own citizens."[26]

In other words, the U.S. War Department took on full responsibility for controlling the Indian tribes of south Texas and the entirety of southern New Mexico, which included the troublesome Apaches. This proved to be an impossible task, and many politicians in Washington immediately recognized the futility. While the treaty awaited ratification, James Buchanan was serving as President Polk's secretary of state. Buchanan did not foresee any problem in keeping this promise to Mexico, proclaiming, "The government possesses both the ability and will to restrain the Indians within the limits of the United States from making incursions into the Mexican territory, as well as to execute all the other stipulations of the eleventh article."[27] Had he realized the immense War Department expenditures and loss of life that would result, Buchanan might not have so readily agreed to the inclusion of this clause in the treaty. Despite the hopelessness of fulfilling this obligation, the army tried to the utmost of its ability. Innumerable examples of these efforts will be seen in a subsequent chapter.

Territorial Governor and Superintendent of Indian Affairs James S. Calhoun likewise realized the impossibilities surrounding this stipulation of the treaty. Writing to U.S. Commissioner of Indian Affairs Orlando Brown in February 1850, Calhoun prophesized that this article of the treaty would be the root of many problems in the future. "The Apaches, Comanches, and Utahs are a different people," he wrote, "wholly disdaining to follow peaceful pursuits, and relying, chiefly, upon their skill in making successful depredations, to secure to themselves a necessary subsistence. Without reference to our Treaty with Mexico, it is abundantly apparent, it will require the gravest consideration of the most sagacious Statesmen to devise a system that will secure peace and quiet in this territory."[28]

During discussions prior to ratification, Article XI was adamantly opposed by two U.S. senators: Sam Houston of Texas and Stephen A. Douglas of Illinois. Both men believed that this article bestowed upon the United States unenviable responsibilities that would be impossible to fulfill. Despite the reasonable objections of these two men, Congress passed the treaty without amendment. The final tally of votes showed that the treaty barely passed with the required majority: thirty-eight votes in favor, fourteen against. A change of only four votes would have been enough to defeat ratification.[29] The support of Secretary of State Buchanan, along with the fact that many Washington politicians simply did not understand the difficulty and complexity of controlling New Mexico's Indians, was enough to override the objections of Houston and Douglas.

Less than a year later, primarily as a result of increasing Indian raids in the Mexican border region, President Zachary Taylor suggested that the War Department increase the number of troops available for duty in New Mexico. By 1852 the United States possessed a standing army of some 11,000 men; of those, almost 8,000 were in New Mexico and Texas, trying in vain to enforce Article XI. As might be inferred, the government incurred a considerable annual expenditure as a result of operations in this remote region. Along with an increase in the number of troops came an even more drastic increase in War Department spending. In 1845, before the Mexican War and Treaty of Guadalupe Hidalgo, military-related transportation in the southwest cost $130,053. By 1851 that number had increased to $2,994,408. Clearly, adherence to the eleventh article was costly, and other citizens of the United States not residing in New Mexico and Texas were denied military protection because the majority of the army had been transferred to the Southwest.[30]

In 1853, with Article XI having been in effect for over five years Juan N. Almonte, Mexican Envoy Extraordinary and Minister Plenipotentiary, wrote a detailed thirty-two-page letter to Secretary of State William L. Marcy relative to the failure of the United States to enforce the treaty. Almonte conceded that his government "could not but feel gratified to perceive that the Executive of the United States has acknowledged . . . the obligation in question," but also noted that he "would fail in the performance of his duty [as Mexico's minister] if he were to cease to urge the government of the United States to carry out the stipulations of the treaty." Almonte went on to outline the repeated failures of the United States in preventing Apache depredations in Mexico. He told Marcy that Article XI "seems to have been reduced to a cipher," and lamented the fact that "the greatest portion of the frontier of Mexico has been entirely laid waste . . . by a series of incursions that have neither been prevented nor checked although coming precisely within the pale of the category to which the stipulations of the 11th article ought to be applied." Mexico could no longer "turn a deaf ear to the complaints of her citizens," and Almonte undertook the task of urging upon the United States the importance of fulfilling its obligation to enforce the Treaty of Guadalupe Hidalgo and to obtain indemnities from the U.S. government for Mexican claimants who had been victimized by Indian depredations.[31]

Aside from the protestations of envoy Almonte, however, the Republic of Mexico did little to help the precarious situation along the border. The Mexican government disarmed all of its citizens living in the northern provinces of Chihuahua and Sonora almost immediately following the signing of the treaty in 1848. This left the frontier population defenseless against Apache raids. Now, with the Apaches attacking these northern Mexican settlements unopposed, an increasing number of raids naturally ensued. Compounding the problem, Mexico did not station any of its troops along the border with the United States, maintaining that the responsibility fell squarely upon the shoulders of the U.S. War Department. Not until 1851 did a few companies of Mexican troops arrive in Sonora and Chihuahua, but even then the number amounted to not more that about four hundred men, hardly enough to discourage the dauntless Apaches from depredating.[32]

On the American side, change would be slow in coming. Washington politics began to take a sharp turn toward the slavery issue beginning with the 1848 election of Zachary Taylor, the Whig Party candidate. Although sectional differences demanded the nation's full attention, problems stemming from the war with Mexico remained. Numerous foreign ministers to Mexico were appointed, none of whom proved either able or willing to perform the tasks at hand; one of them, ex-Kentucky Governor R. P. Letcher, publicly stated his personal enmity toward Mexico while simultaneously attempting to serve as the foreign minister there. In the ensuing presidential term of war hero Zachary Taylor, from 1848 to 1850 (cut short by his premature death), three different persons filled the position of secretary of state. Of these only one, Daniel Webster, legitimately addressed the issue.

In 1851 Webster asked the U.S. minister to Mexico to pursue all means necessary to secure a release from Article XI. Although some minor negotiations began, the minister did not have enough funds to satisfactorily accomplish the task. The United States, unable to abrogate the article, remained responsible for preventing Indian raiding in the northern Mexican settlements.[33] With each passing foreign minister and secretary of state, relations between the United States and Mexico deteriorated even more. From these continuously escalating disputes arose three major items of interest pertaining to southern New Mexico and the Mesilla Valley, all of which required immediate attention: the boundary commission and transcontinental railroad, the Gadsden Purchase, and the never-ending Apache wars.

CHAPTER 3

The International Boundary Surveys

For centuries New Mexico had been under the autocratic rule of the Spanish Crown and then for a brief quarter century spanning the years 1821 to 1846 under the rule of the Republic of Mexico. During that time there had been little need for exact political boundaries to be ascertained. Because no other countries laid claim to the land, prominent and well-known geographical features were commonly used to mark approximate boundary lines. In many instances, mountain ranges and rivers sufficed for this purpose. This meant that boundaries were not really permanently fixed. If a river marking an international boundary changed its course (like the Rio Grande did in the 1860s), then so, too, did that boundary change. For the U.S. government, this unobtrusive concept of a boundary line simply did not suffice. A more distinct, scientific method was needed to draw the official line separating New Mexico from Mexico.

When the Treaty of Guadalupe Hidalgo was signed in February 1848, with a provision included therein for the demarcation of the exact boundary line between the United States and Mexico, the United States intended to pursue every means necessary to ensure that this stipulation would in fact be carried out to the highest degree of accuracy. To the greatest extent possible, the boundary would be laid out in the most beneficial manner according to the desires of the United States.

The first issue facing Congress was the proper placement of the boundary between New Mexico and Texas. The State of Texas, as previously noted, initially claimed the Rio Grande as its western and southern boundary, thus drastically reducing the size of New Mexico. This claim would also have given Texas the eastern half of the Mesilla Valley, including Doña Ana; the other half, in which Mesilla was located, would have remained a part of Mexico until the disputes could be sorted out. The Compromise of 1850, signed into law on September 9 of that year, ultimately proved to be the final word on the subject. It used specific language to describe the permanent location of the Texas–New Mexico boundary on the Rio Grande. The compromise stated that the Texas boundary should begin at a point on the Rio Grande twenty miles north of Paso del Norte. This essentially meant

that all towns on the Rio Grande north of El Paso would remain a part of
New Mexico. Henry Clay, a primary sponsor of the legislation, received full
support in this action from President Millard Fillmore, who replaced Zachary Taylor in office following his death on July 9, 1850. "All must now be
regarded as New Mexico which was possessed and occupied as New Mexico
by citizens of Mexico as of the date of the treaty, until a definite line of
boundary shall be established by competent authority," Fillmore instructed
Congress in a message delivered on August 6, 1850.[1]

To this day the line provided for in the Compromise of 1850 remains
the east–west boundary line separating Texas and New Mexico. Texas, of
course, vigorously refuted this, claiming that the southern boundary line
should begin much farther north, thus ceding to Texas the Mesilla Valley.
Every attempt of Texas to gain this boundary line failed, and matters ended
there.

With the Texas–New Mexico boundary trouble being thus resolved,
the eastern side of the Mesilla Valley was clearly to remain a part of the
Territory of New Mexico. This still left the west bank of the river, and the
town of Mesilla, in the possession of Mexico. Thus began several years of
monumental government expenditures and fruitless struggles by boundary commissions and foreign diplomats from both the United States and
Mexico in an attempt to reach an agreement on the boundary separating
the two nations.

Article V of the Treaty of Guadalupe Hidalgo provided a vague description of the proposed international boundary, but during the process of ratification it had been continually revised and its meaning further distorted by
both countries. Numerous locations of significance within the boundaries
of this region would be disputed, the more important among them being
the port at San Diego, California, and the town of Paso del Norte. An additional incentive could be found in the opportunity for the United States
to build a transcontinental railroad extending from Paso del Norte to San
Diego, providing a direct connection with the California coast and facilitat-
ing travel and trade between the two.

An error in a previously drawn map would prove to be the single greatest determining factor in the majority of the international boundary conflicts. When writing the treaty, negotiators from both the United States and
Mexico unwittingly agreed to reference an 1847 map published by John Dis-

turnell.[2] This would have worked fine, except that the map contained significant errors.[3] Woefully inaccurate, the map showed the Rio Grande in the location of the Pecos River and the town of El Paso near the present-day location of Carlsbad, New Mexico—about one hundred miles east and thirty-five miles north of El Paso's actual location.[4]

This placed the United States in a serious dilemma. If drawn according to this map, the boundary would allow Mexico to retain possession of a considerable amount of territory that it had already ceded to the United States according to the treaty of 1848. Clearly, this left plenty of room for debate on both sides, and neither country wished to concede to the other without a thorough investigation into the matter. The United States had a viable claim insofar as Disturnell's map contained blatant errors and should have never been used as a determining factor in the marking of the boundary. At the same time, Mexico had a reasonable defense as well: the treaty, which had already been ratified by the United States and signed by the governing bodies of both countries, clearly stated that the Disturnell map should be used by the boundary commissioners.[5] The outcome would hinge on the willingness of one nation to concede their claim, which, naturally, would not come to pass; therefore, in order to bring closure to the situation, some type of compromise would have to occur.

The temporary boundary line established by the treaty in 1848, until the respective commissions could complete and submit their reports, utilized traditional methods of citing mostly geographical features as guidelines. One such geographical feature was the Gila River, flowing from its source in the Mogollon Mountains of western New Mexico and thence across the entirety of modern-day southern Arizona. It was the land south of this valley that the United States most desired in order to build the transcontinental railroad. But here again, according to provisions of the Treaty of Guadalupe Hidalgo, this region remained a part of Mexico. This, along with the errors contained in the Disturnell map, comprised the two primary arguing points of the United States.

One saving grace was that the treaty also called for the formation of boundary commissions by both countries, supposed to work harmoniously and cooperatively with each other to mark the boundary. As stipulated by the treaty, work by the boundary commissions would begin on May 30, 1849.[6] The commissions appointed by both the United States and Mexico

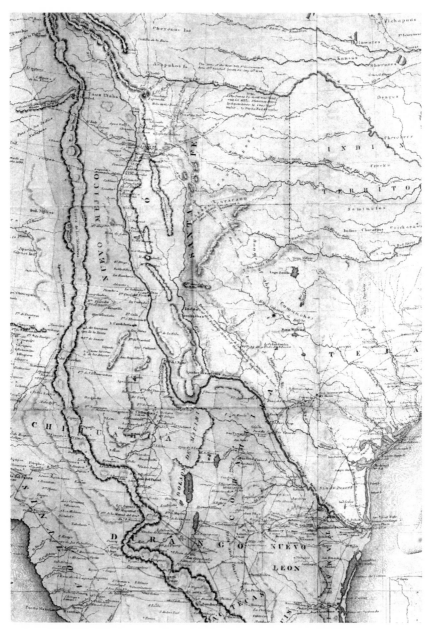

Map 3.1. The Disturnell Map of 1847, used during treaty negotiations with Mexico in 1848. The erroneous placement of the Rio Grande on this map was a direct cause of the ensuing boundary disputes. (Courtesy Dolph Briscoe Center for American History, the University of Texas at Austin, James P. Bryan map collection)

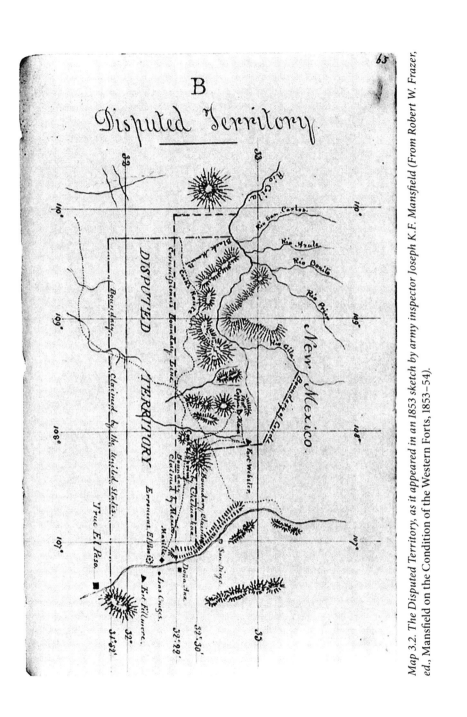

Map 3.2. The Disputed Territory, as it appeared in an 1853 sketch by army inspector Joseph K.F. Mansfield (From Robert W. Frazer, ed., Mansfield on the Condition of the Western Forts, 1853–54).

consisted of a wide array of different persons, both military and civilian; some were experienced and knowledgeable and others were not. With so much diversity, differences of opinion were inevitable, and in a matter of such incredible importance on a national level, minor methodological discrepancies would lead to personal feuds and political turmoil. Needless to say, this undermined the work being done by the two commissions.

The United States commission suffered from internal strife and political struggles throughout the duration of the surveys. In a time of increasing pre–Civil War sectional tension, American boundary commissioners were subjected to intense scrutiny by the nation's northern and southern newspapers, and everything these men did was viewed by elements of the media and government on a magnified level. On January 14, 1849, President Polk appointed John B. Weller to head the American boundary commission. Appointed to serve along with Weller was Andrew B. Gray as chief surveyor and Maj. William Helmsley Emory as chief astronomer. Lt. Amiel Weeks Whipple and Lt. Edmund Hardcastle would serve as Weller's personal assistants.[7] Two of these men, Emory and Whipple, would play a role in surveying the boundary for years to come, long after Weller and Gray had been dismissed from their positions. This first U.S. boundary commission consisted of thirty-nine men, including the above-named individuals, along with two companies of military troops who served as an escort. Weller's surveying party began at San Diego in May 1849 and trekked slowly eastward, with the Mesilla Valley and Paso del Norte designated as the eventual termination point of the surveys.

The Mexican boundary commission did not commence work until the first week in July, when it arrived at San Diego to join Weller's commission. The Mexican contingent was led by Gen. Pedro García Conde[8] with José Salazar Ylarregui[9] serving as his primary assistant. García Conde boasted an impressive background in engineering and geography and was an excellent choice for the position of commissioner. A contemporary of his would later recall that he was "well known as an engineer and a man of science . . . and was constantly occupied with his maps and charts."[10] His earlier cartographic work in the State of Chihuahua further enhanced his credentials.

The Mexican boundary commission came into being pursuant to legislation promulgated by the Mexican minister of foreign relations, Mariano Otero, and passed on November 2, 1848.[11] The commission, once entirely outfitted, consisted of approximately 150 men, including García Conde's son, Agustín, as a second engineer.[12]

In this, the first of many surveys to come, neither commission proceeded very far. Underlying tensions within the U.S. commission, both personal and political, rose to epic proportions. The men simply could not agree with one another about how to do the work. Perhaps the greatest instigating factor in this was the fact that the U.S. commissioner, John B. Weller, openly associated with the Democratic Party, whereas the Whig Party had just recently taken control of both the presidency and Congress. In a time when the two parties found themselves at odds with each other over such volatile issues as slavery and the outcome of the Mexican War, it comes as no surprise that Weller was quickly removed from his position as boundary commissioner and replaced with somebody who more appropriately fit into the Whig Party's agenda. On June 20, 1849, a mere three weeks after he had begun working on the boundary at San Diego, and before the Mexican boundary commission had even started, famed western frontiersman and explorer John C. Frémont was appointed to replace Weller as commissioner.[13] Frémont accepted the appointment, although he never had any intention of working on the boundary. He resigned the position before even beginning, opting instead to seek election as the first U.S. senator from the new State of California, a position far more prestigious than plotting the Mexican boundary.[14]

Weller was not informed of his removal until December 18, 1849, nearly six months after it had taken effect, which only further complicated matters. When he finally learned of his removal, Weller became indignant, even more so because he had continued for six months in a position from which he had already been terminated. The United States thus wasted half a year, and still nothing had been accomplished toward a solution to the boundary disputes. With no newspapers existing in the Mesilla Valley at this time, the people there could not have known the particulars of these events, but surely some of the information reached them by word of mouth. Few of those living in and around Mesilla, uneducated as the majority of them were, must have realized the potential ramifications of the events transpiring between the United States and Mexico at this point. As it were, the Rio Grande continued to delineate the international boundary for the time being, with many of the people perhaps wondering what their eventual fate

would be. Historian Robert V. Hine best summarizes the unfortunate situation up to this point: "In early 1850, two years after the Treaty [of Guadalupe
Hidalgo], the first commissioner was dead, the second was discredited, and
the third had resigned before taking up the work."[15]

Finally, on May 4, 1850, with another five months of idleness having
passed, President Zachary Taylor appointed John Russell Bartlett to serve
as boundary commissioner.[16] Bartlett's appointment to the position, not
unlike many others of the time, owed in large part to the spoils system.[17]
Bartlett was an interesting man in many respects, and, while his boundary
surveys and reports achieved little in the way of productive and lasting results, and in fact necessitated the Gadsden Purchase two years later, he was
by no means a poor choice for the position. Bartlett had moved to New York
City in 1836, and beginning in 1840 he occupied himself as a bookseller,
with his shop located in the Astor House. He continued in this profession,
along with his partner Charles Welford, until the early months of 1850, at
which time he boarded a ship and headed to the great Southwest.[18] Bartlett,
without hesitation, accepted the opportunity for adventure in the untamed
American West, a stark contrast to his monotonous daily routine in his New
York bookshop.

By the time President Taylor appointed him, Bartlett already possessed
some familiarity with Native Americans and the western frontier through
his previous studies, and he was fascinated by the prospect of experiencing
first hand what he had previously only read about. "Although my life and
pursuits had always been of a sedentary character I always had a great desire
for travel," he wrote, "and particularly for exploring unknown regions. I
had, also, ever felt a deep interest in the Indians and was glad of an opportunity to be thrown among the wild tribes of the interior."[19] One New York
newspaper, reporting on Bartlett's appointment, commented that he possessed "habits of industry and great energy of character; he is also a man of
the highest integrity, and thoroughly versed in the natural sciences."[20]

From the beginning Bartlett exhibited a number of tragic flaws that
were derived from his upbringing as a member of the privileged eastern
elite class. His romantic views of Native Americans were a consequence of
literary portrayals common in that time period, Bartlett being closely associated with the likes of James Fenimore Cooper and other authors.[21] Bartlett
was thus predisposed to a somewhat inaccurate perception of Indian life

Figure 3.1. Boundary Commissioner John Russell Bartlett, shown here in the mid-1850s. (Courtesy Rhode Island Historical Society. RHi x3 539, Graphics-Portrait File)

on the western frontier, which would result in much confusion on his part while dealing with the native tribes with whom he came in contact in the Southwest. Another product of Bartlett's upbringing was his lack of familiarity with military protocol and the appropriate professional relationship between military and civil officials. Personal disputes frequently arose as a result of Bartlett's failure to recognize the authority associated with the rank of a military officer, and vice versa.[22]

Bartlett accepted the appointment on June 19, 1850, becoming the fourth boundary commissioner, but only the second to actually serve in that capacity. At the very least, Bartlett would perform the job in a markedly enthusiastic manner, although the end result would be less than satisfactory. Much like the previous commission of John B. Weller, Bartlett's contingent consisted of a wide variety of people: topographical engineers, civilian surveyors, field scientists, mechanics, and soldiers. His brother, George Bartlett, received an appointment as commissary for the expedition. Bartlett's chief topographical engineer, and the person with whom he would be working with most closely, was Bvt. Lt. Col. John B. McClellan. Bartlett would later write that "the most disagreeable duties I ever had to perform were the appointments of officers and assistants for the Commission . . . too many were urged on me by their Congressional friends merely to get them away from Washington."[23] Nevertheless, on August 3, 1850, the appointment process having been completed, Bartlett's invigorated group set out from New York City bound for the gulf coast of Texas. Bartlett himself did not accompany this initial voyage, opting instead to stay behind temporarily, but he finally boarded a ship destined for the Texas coast on the thirteenth of August.[24]

Bartlett endured many of the same privations that Weller had undergone a year before at San Diego. Before even reaching El Paso, the point from which he would begin the survey, a personal feud developed between Bartlett and McClellan, his pretentious chief topographical engineer. McClellan wrote the secretary of the interior, charging Bartlett with, among other things, "unpardonable mismanagement of the public interest and funds entrusted to him . . . [and] conduct unworthy of commissioner of the United States."[25] Bartlett responded by charging McClellan with "habitual drunkenness and conduct unbecoming an officer," and gave him an ultimatum: resign his position on the boundary commission, or else face criminal charges.[26] McClellan absolutely refused, and, in the words of Bartlett himself, "no other alternative remains but to relieve you, as I hereby do, from the duties of chief astronomer to this commission. You may therefore consider yourself no longer connected with the boundary survey."[27] This was communicated to McClellan in a letter dated the sixteenth of December 1850; upon receipt of the notice, McClellan boarded a wagon for the Texas shore, where he boarded a ship back to Washington, still raging and embittered toward the commissioner over his premature dismissal. This represented but one instance in a slew of similar ones with which Bartlett would have to deal in the future. It did not appear as if this new U.S. commissioner was off to a very promising start.

Whereas his predecessor Weller had met with an untimely termination from the position, Bartlett continued forward and remained mostly unperturbed by the troubles with his colleagues. Along with a small group of twenty-four men, Bartlett and a small escort left San Antonio and arrived at El Paso ahead of the bulk of his employees, who followed a few days behind on the trail. On December 3, 1850, a year and a half after Weller began his first survey at San Diego, Bartlett met with Mexican Commissioner Pedro García Conde for the first of what would be many times. The two enthusiastic individuals, both willing to work and compromise with each other to achieve their common goals, would eventually become embroiled in an intense and long-lasting controversy because of it.

García Conde in particular was a man dedicated to mapping the boundary line accurately, although his actions typically leaned toward achieving the best possible result for his native country in spite of what might have been contained in the provisions of the Treaty of Guadalupe Hidalgo. Unlike the troubled American commission, that of Mexico, known as the "Commission for the Limits of the Mexican Republic" was much more simplistic in nature. Composed of only about a dozen actual engineers (in addition to a small detachment of Mexican troops for protection from hostile Indians), all of whom were well-educated graduates of the Mexican Military College (Colegio Militar), the small group of Mexicans assigned to draw the boundary were much less prone to internal tension and conflict than the large, diverse conglomerate of nearly 150 Americans with whom they dealt in these proceedings.[28] Bartlett admitted the superiority of the Mexican commission in a private correspondence. "I am compelled to confess," Bartlett wrote, "that this small number of 10 engineers [composing the Mexican commission] possess more science than the whole American commission."[29] Indeed, this confession by Bartlett, a learned man who maintained a staunch sense of pride, exemplifies the tremendous shortcomings that continually hamstrung the U.S. commission.

It was during their first few meetings at El Paso in the month of December 1850 that Bartlett and García Conde came to an agreement concerning the initial placement of the boundary line on the Rio Grande. The point, they agreed, should be placed on the west side of the river, south of the town of Doña Ana and about forty-two miles north of Paso del Norte.[30] This compromise placed the international boundary at a point just north of the town of Mesilla. "Nothing Bartlett ever did in his entire life would cause so much trouble and controversy as the determination of that point," observes one scholar.[31] This single act by Bartlett, the establishment of the boundary forty-two miles north of El Paso rather than just a few miles, as the

United States had originally aimed for, initiated months of political strife in the capital as the nation's leaders debated whether this was an acceptable boundary placement.

Located at 32° 22' north latitude, the boundary line would proceed from that point on the Rio Grande straight westward for more than one hundred miles before eventually striking a northbound course to meet the Gila River. The compromise that had been worked out between Bartlett and García Conde over the past several months was simple: Bartlett relinquished claim to almost the entirety of the fertile and populous Mesilla Valley. In return, García Conde ceded the rugged mountainous regions of southwestern New Mexico (the southern portions of the Gila Wilderness), including the Santa Rita del Cobre copper mines, to the U.S. government.

From his prior knowledge, Bartlett knew the Santa Rita and upper Gila River regions to be rich in mineral resources, particularly gold and copper, and therefore believed it would be far more economically beneficial to the United States in the long run than the Mesilla Valley, which he saw as nothing more than an agrarian district with little potential to prosper beyond that distinction. García Conde maintained an entirely opposite viewpoint, believing the Mesilla Valley to be the prize at stake in the negotiations. "The determination of the dividing line between our Republic and that of the United States," García Conde wrote, "is resolved most favorably in the interests of the Nation. The boundary . . . [begins] nearly thirty-seven geographic miles straight north from [Paso del Norte], embracing . . . the population of the La Mesilla which today has more than two thousand inhabitants."[32] Indeed, time would prove García Conde to be the victor in this particular compromise agreement. To each of the two commissioners, this seemed like a fair stopping point in their negotiations, and each man left the table satisfied with their diplomatic accomplishments. Their superiors, however, and in particular Bartlett's, would prove to be far less satisfied with the agreement.

On April 24, 1851, after four months of preparation, Bartlett and García Conde met at the proposed location on the Rio Grande, north of Las Cruces and south of Doña Ana, and placed the first temporary boundary marker. Several leading men from each respective commission accompanied them, along with a small detachment of U.S. dragoons from the post at Doña Ana. The agreement, written in both English and Spanish, was signed for the

Figure 3.2. Mexican Boundary Commissioner Pedro García Conde. (Courtesy Nettie Lee Benson Latin American Collection, University of Texas Libraries, The University of Texas at Austin)

United States by both Commissioner Bartlett and Chief Surveyor Amiel W. Whipple (acting in the absence of Andrew B. Gray). Pedro García Conde and his surveyor, José Salazar Ylarregui, signed for Mexico.[33] A small selection of mementos were chosen from among the men's possessions and placed inside an empty sarsaparilla bottle to be buried at the site as a ritualistic observance of the occasion. Among the items deposited at the location was a small chip from the Washington Monument in Washington, D.C., which at the time of this event was a mere three years old. The exact location in the Mesilla Valley where this ceremony transpired is now unknown, and the stone marker placed there in 1851 by Bartlett and García Conde no longer exists; thus the site of this first mutually accepted point of boundary between the United States and Mexico has been forever lost to history.

This agreement meant that Mesilla would remain a part of Mexico, as would the entire western half of the Mesilla Valley. To Bartlett the compromise seemed reasonable inasmuch as García Conde had refuted the Distur-

nell map, and the east–west boundary line would begin at a point on the Rio
Grande farther south than Mexico had originally desired. Perhaps most importantly in Bartlett's estimation, the compromise "secures to us not only
the valuable district known as the gold and copper mines [the Santa Rita del
Cobre mines], but an extent of territory, south of the Gila, more than one-
third the distance between the Rio Grande and the Gulf of California."[34] To
García Conde, this seemed beneficial because Bartlett relinquished claim to
almost the entire Mesilla Valley, and in so doing had refuted the claim of the
United States to a boundary beginning at or near "the town called Paso."[35]
Pleased with the outcome, Bartlett immediately wrote to Secretary of the
Interior Alexander Stuart to inform him of the proceedings. In his letter
to Stuart of December 28, 1850, Bartlett excitedly related that "the happy
result [of the compromise] . . . is to me a source of very great satisfaction.
On arriving here and finding the map of Disturnell so utterly at variance
with truth, as far as the position of the Rio Grande, of the town of El Paso,
and the limits of New Mexico are concerned, I entertained fears that the
joint commission would find it impossible to agree upon a line of boundary
which should comply with the treaty."[36]

The feelings and sentiments in the Mesilla Valley toward the compro-
mises made between Bartlett and García Conde were manifested in a petition written to territorial Governor James S. Calhoun on August 25, 1851:

> We the undersigned citizens of Mesilla beg leave to call your at-
> tention to the unpleasant condition we are placed in, in consequence
> of the great oversight of Mr. Bartlett the Commissioner on the part
> of the United States in placing the Initial Point, or Starting place of
> the Southern Boundary of New Mexico, beyond the limits of the
> Treaty according to Mr. A. B. Gray's (U.S. Surveyors) Arguments,
> which we have had the good fortune to fall in with in writing, a copy
> of which, we beg the honor of presenting to you.
>
> We were of the opinion ever since the line was established that
> it was wrong, and should have taken this step sooner but until the
> arrival of Mr. Gray we was as it were in a perfect state of obscurity,
> and did not know how to proceed.
>
> The town of La Mesilla was settled some time in the early part
> of 1850, by Americans and New Mexican Territory Citizens, under

the Conviction that it was N. Mexican Territory and was Subject to its Laws. Consequently, the town has flourished and now contains some 1500 or 2000 inhabitants most of whom are Citizens of the United States and New Mexico and claim the rights and protection as such.[37]

Unbeknownst to Bartlett at the time of his compromise, the mutual feeling of success between himself and the Mexican commissioner would be short-lived. What the two men had initially thought to be a fair compromise for the interests of all involved turned out to be nothing more than fuel for the fire. Bartlett was lambasted by his superiors in Washington and by newspapers all across the country. Many people contended, although with little merit, that Bartlett was concealing a personal scheme to rob the South, especially the State of Texas, of a transcontinental railroad route to California. Congressman V. E. Howard of Texas, an advocate for the Gila River railroad route, noted in a speech of July 6, 1852, that Bartlett had erred in his negotiations for a boundary line. "All accounts tend to prove that Mr. Bartlett has surrendered the best route for the railroad," Howard lamented; "he has given up to the Mexican Government public land sufficient to construct the road to the junction of the Colorado and Gila [Rivers]."[38] Indeed, his compromise with García Conde ceded to Mexico the railroad route most desired by southern bureaucrats and businessmen.

Bartlett's agreement with García Conde negated any possibility of building a railroad through southern New Mexico, but whether or not Bartlett took this action purposefully was an entirely separate matter. From the available evidence, it seems that this thought was secondary on Bartlett's mind, his primary purpose of gaining the mineral-rich Gila region having been accomplished. Bartlett steadfastly denounced all accusations of sectional preferences, noting the geographic impracticability of the Gila River route. Several years later the commissioner would be exonerated of such accusations when Secretary of State William L. Marcy wrote, "A better knowledge of the country in the vicinity of the Gila has demonstrated the great difficulty—not to say, impossibility—of constructing a railroad along its banks . . . yet a very eligible route for such a road is found at a further distance . . . on the Mexican side of the line but not on the American side of it. . . . It is believed if the United States would acquire this . . . line, they would then have within their territory a good route for a railroad."[39] The lands referred to by Marcy, those south of the Gila River, would later be acquired by the United States through the Gadsden Purchase.

As was typical of the time period, Northern and Southern tensions manifested themselves in the issue. Bartlett was a known Yankee from Rhode Island, but several of the men on his commission were ardent Southerners. This issue sparked many heated correspondences between Bartlett and various other politicians in Washington, led to feuds between himself and his colleagues working by his side, and would eventually result in the disbandment of the entire commission. Even here, ten years before the fact and in the most remote and desolate section of the western United States, could be seen the roots of sectional turmoil that led to the Civil War.

Among those who wholeheartedly opposed the Bartlett–García Conde agreement was Chief Surveyor Andrew B. Gray, absent on leave at the time of the compromise; in July 1851 he vehemently refused to sign his name to the treaty. In support of his refusal to sign, Gray noted that he, as chief surveyor, had the explicit right to have been present during the negotiations, contending that his right to do so had been either ignored or infringed upon by A. W. Whipple, who signed the treaty in Gray's absence.[40] Gray contended that had he been present he never would have allowed the agreement to pass, and would have insisted on the placement of the boundary line at a point just north of the "town called Paso." Washington bureaucrats ultimately concluded that without Gray's signature the agreement was null and void.

Not surprisingly, Gray's refusal to sign led to yet another personal dispute. Gray accused Bartlett of advancing personal and self-serving purposes in making the agreement, denouncing Bartlett's appointment of Whipple as temporary chief surveyor during the time Gray had been absent on leave. With well-aimed sarcasm, the pithy Gray informed Bartlett that by vesting within himself the power of appointing officials at will he was "constituting himself President, and General [García] Conde the Senate, of the United States."[41] The subject eventually reached the leading politicians in Washington, where a staunchly partisan Congress found itself divided on the issue as well. President Fillmore and Secretary of the Interior Stuart of the Whig Party both supported Bartlett in his agreement with García Conde. The Democrats, ironically led by ex-commissioner John B. Weller, steadfastly opposed the agreement, the end result being a continuance in the already three-year-old ordeal.[42]

Surely the Mexican boundary commission, and Pedro García Conde in particular, must have been unspeakably frustrated with the inability of their U.S. counterparts to work in harmony with one another. In the meantime, Bartlett and García Conde had their hands tied and work on surveying the boundary came to a relative standstill while matters were sorted out in Washington.[43]

In his letters to Washington, Bartlett defended his actions to the best of his ability. He noted that the land in the "Mesilla Strip," as he called the Mesilla Valley, and all land westward from there (the region that would eventually be obtained by the United States through the Gadsden Purchase), was neither valuable nor desirable. The Mesilla Valley, he contended, averaged only about a mile and a half in width, and, although possessing potential agricultural benefits, had a monetary value of only about fifty cents to one dollar per acre. The remainder of the land in question, everything westward from the Mesilla Valley to California, consisted of, in Bartlett's words, "a desert without water, wood, or grass, where not one acre can ever be cultivated, where no military post can be sustained, and which can never be inhabited."[44] This claim was, by and large, supported by fact. It would be years before civilization found much use for the land comprising the southernmost extremities of modern-day New Mexico and Arizona. Indeed, much of the parched desert region remains uninhabited to this day.

Bartlett's final line of defense came in regard to the town of Mesilla, which he knew to be of importance to all parties concerned. This town, he asserted, would ultimately prove to be impertinent to the matter of the boundary dispute; according to Bartlett, in the event that the boundary line was drawn near El Paso and Mesilla did in fact revert back into the possession of the United States, the people there would probably just move again to remain a part of Mexico.[45] In this Bartlett would eventually prove to be mistaken, although by the time the final results of the boundary debacle were known, Bartlett was back in his home state of Rhode Island and would have nothing more to do with the matter.

The tradition of American boundary officials being fired did not cease with Weller or McClellan. On November 4, 1851, Andrew B. Gray, whose absence during the signing of the Bartlett–García Conde agreement caused its eventual nullification by the United States, received notice from Secretary of the Interior Stuart that he had been terminated and that his replacement was on the way. This may have been due in no small part to Gray's refusal to sign the Bartlett–García Conde agreement, for the man who fired him, Secretary Stuart, had outspokenly favored the agreement from the beginning. It is not likely that Bartlett had much influence in Stuart's decision to replace Gray, although that possibility should not be discounted.

Whatever the cause may have been, Gray would no longer figure in the grand scheme, and Lt. William H. Emory arrived not long afterward to fill his vacated position.[46] Emory, an 1831 West Point graduate, joined the Corps of Topographical Engineers in 1838. He would prove to be among the more experienced and hard-working men in the boundary surveys, having already gained substantial knowledge during the Northwestern Boundary Surveys of 1844–46 and with General Kearny's Army of the West in 1846–47. Interestingly, Emory received the appointment to the boundary commission in September 1851, a full three months before Stuart actually removed Gray.[47] Emory's first order from Stuart was simple enough: approve the Bartlett–García Conde agreement in order to prevent any further conflict in the matter, thus enabling the surveys to continue.

When Emory finally arrived in New Mexico and joined Bartlett he discovered that, in his personal estimation, "little or no work" had been completed by the commissioner.[48] Writing of the situation to a family member, the frustration of a succinct Emory was clear. "O this line! Of all the assemblages of folly, ignorance, and hypocrisy I ever saw congregated together under the title of scientific corps, [this one] exceeds. Think of two hundred thousand dollars expended here and nothing to show but this: The determination of one point in latitude, the running of a parallel one degree, and the partial survey of the river 40 miles! This is all. My God. What will become of our appropriations if Congress knows of the follies of the Commissioner and his antagonists too."[49] Assistant Surveyor George Clinton Gardner, in a private correspondence, further attested to the rampant wastefulness. "The debts of the Commission out here are large and pressing," he wrote, "and will consume any amount that Congress will appropriate while the work will not be promoted one iota . . . the Commission is at an expense of some ten thousand dollars per month at this place [Frontera, Texas, north of Paso del Norte] with a great many doing nothing."[50] Gardner went on

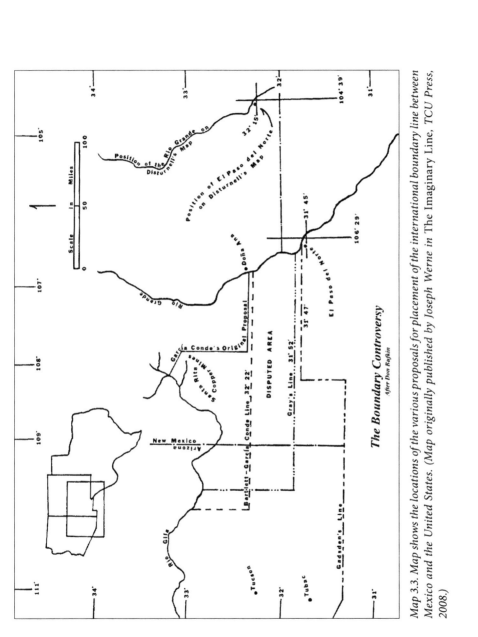

Map 3.3. Map shows the locations of the various proposals for placement of the international boundary line between Mexico and the United States. (Map originally published by Joseph Werne in The Imaginary Line, TCU Press, 2008.)

to state that he hoped Major Emory might command the survey in place of the spendthrift Bartlett. In their respective letters, Emory and Gardner touched upon every major shortcoming that had plagued the commission up to that point, and their prophecy of congressional appropriations being discontinued would not be long in coming.

Although Emory made few such claims during the time Bartlett held the position, he later publicly asserted that Bartlett, the eternal profligate, had pilfered the majority of the money appropriated by Congress on "a useless multitude of officers, quartermasters, commissaries, paymasters, agents, secretaries, sub-secretaries and whatnots."[51] Indeed, records indicate that Bartlett, while in charge of the boundary commission in 1851, had employed not only the necessary engineers and surveyors but also numerous secretaries, five carpenters, three blacksmiths, three wheelwrights, two harness makers, five tailors, four shoemakers, two butchers, nineteen laborers, six servants, and the list goes on.[52]

Furthermore, Emory believed that it would be virtually impossible to convince García Conde to withdraw from his agreement with Bartlett, which García Conde knew to be highly beneficial to the Mexican cause, and which, in the words of Emory, was "a great source of glorification for him."[53] At this juncture there existed no other clear alternative to the agreement, and it was eventually approved by both sides. Thus Mesilla remained an entity of the Republic of Mexico, and the smaller towns of Las Cruces and Doña Ana, east of the Rio Grande, remained in the United States.

Throughout the course of the boundary surveys, which limped along and cost the U.S. government hundreds of thousands of dollars in the process, Emory emerged as perhaps the most competent and dedicated person associated with the commission. Although spending only a minimal amount of time in the field with Bartlett, it owed in large part to his indefatigable labor and productive results that in 1854 Emory was chosen to head up yet another commission following the Gadsden Treaty.

In the meantime, with the Bartlett–García Conde compromise finally achieving bureaucratic approval on all fronts, the commissions could proceed beyond the Mesilla Valley with their surveys. The valley from El Paso northward to Doña Ana was surveyed by one of Bartlett's favorite and most capable assistants, Charles Radziminski, who incorporated the towns of Las Cruces and Doña Ana during that process. Radziminski completed the survey of the entire Mesilla Valley on June 6, 1852, and the matter of national sovereignty thereof finally came to a close. Bartlett was pleased with the outcome and with the work done by his assistant, which he said had been "executed in a highly satisfactory manner and accepted as the official Survey."[54]

The incidents surrounding the remainder of Bartlett's surveys from the Rio Grande to California are of little importance to the history of the Mesilla Valley and, voluminous as they are, cannot be discussed in detail here. After leaving the Mesilla Valley, Bartlett's commission set up headquarters at the abandoned buildings of the Spanish copper mines at Santa Rita del Cobre, where they spent several weeks surveying the surrounding countryside. This was, as Bartlett later described it, "a wild and barren region . . . destitute of inhabitants save hostile bands of Indians which roamed over the deserts or hid themselves in the fastnesses of the mountains."[55] Indeed, Apache depredations had a hamstringing effect on the commission during their time in the Rio Grande region. While stationed at Frontera, several miles north of Paso del Norte, George Clinton Gardner, a young assistant surveyor, noted that "we are not at peace on this frontier . . . for the Indians are daily committing depredations upon the different settlements on this river and some most daring murders have been committed within almost gunshot of the posts."[56] Hostile Indians were but one of many dangers with which the boundary commission had to contend.

The survey, as it pertained to the Mesilla Valley, had been completed, and now the boundary line could be drawn westward to a point on the Gila River, as stipulated by the Treaty of Guadalupe Hidalgo. Ironically, Pedro García Conde died of typhoid fever in mid-December 1851, about the same time that Bartlett was also stricken with illness. García Conde did not live long enough to see the completion of the Mesilla Valley surveys in June 1852, which would be carried out by his successor and former assistant, José Salazar Ylarregui. Had García Conde died sooner, it may have been possible for the United States to have refuted his claim in the agreement with Bartlett, and the matter might have continued on unresolved for even longer. García Conde lived just long enough to ensure that his compromise with Bartlett, in which he had taken a profound "sense of glorification," did survive the political maneuverings of scheming Washington bureaucrats.

Bartlett would never be afforded the opportunity to complete the survey all the way to California. Once again, the U.S. government stepped in and prevented any such progress from being made. The cause for this would be, not surprisingly, a change of heart on the part of U.S. lawmakers. The powers in Washington decided that despite its previous acceptance the Bartlett–García Conde agreement should once again be considered invalid. The underlying reason for this was the fact that the agreement excluded the desired railway route across southern New Mexico. A change in political leadership in Washington brought about by the 1852 election represented yet another cause. Bartlett's support as commissioner had been based primarily on his affiliation with the Whig Party, which lost the election in 1852 when Democrat Franklin Pierce assumed the presidency.

A mere two weeks after the newly elected administration took charge, Bartlett was removed as boundary commissioner, a further testament to the strong political ties that had affected his appointment in the first place. In his autobiography, written some fifteen years later in 1867, Bartlett dedicates only a few pages to his role as boundary commissioner; in the brief narrative that he does provide, Bartlett speaks only to his appointment and initial outfitting of the expedition, saying nothing whatever of the actual work he undertook after reaching New Mexico.[57] The fact that Bartlett relegates a pivotal component of his life story to a mere few pages and entirely omits any and all details of the work he conducted speaks to his long-lasting resentment over the outcome. Indeed, Bartlett would be lambasted for many years to come for his compromise with García Conde and for the resultant political controversies. It thus comes as little surprise that when writing his life story he would exclude the details of this unsavory part of an otherwise distinguished career.

Whatever the underlying causes may have been, in 1852, just as Lieutenant Emory had predicted would happen, Congress passed legislation blocking any further funding of the boundary commission until "it should be made to appear to the President of the United States that the southern boundary of New Mexico had not been established further north of El Paso than is laid down in the Disturnell map."[58] The spirited congressional charge to block the monetary flow to the commission was led by two senators in particular: Thomas J. Rusk of Texas and, not surprisingly, John B. Weller of California. Irony had once again caught up with the boundary survey. Weller, once fired from the position of commissioner, had resurrected himself in the more powerful role of U.S. senator and thereafter dedicated himself to evening the score for having being ousted. The debate in the Senate, which commenced on June 28, 1852, with the initial arguments being presented by Weller himself, was the final chapter in the story of Bartlett and his fabled boundary commission. Weller's proposed legislation, along with a report by Senator James M. Mason from the Committee on Foreign Relations charging that Bartlett had no authority to make the agreement with García Conde, succeeded in obtaining the majority vote necessary to block the $120,000 appropriation required to continue the survey.[59] Over four years had now elapsed since the signing of the Treaty of Guadalupe Hidalgo, and with all of these interwoven political maneuverings, the problem still had not been satisfactorily resolved.

The boundary question remained to be answered, the line being temporarily fixed at the point of Bartlett and García Conde's 1851 agreement until further negotiations should determine otherwise. George Clinton Gardner perhaps best summarized the debacle, writing to his father that "this Commission is the meanest affair that was ever got up under the Government. I only hope that after the whole affair has cost some $1,000,000 something will happen to make it of no account and compel them to do it over again."[60] The United States, discontented with the present boundary and desiring southern New Mexico's desert regions for the construction of a transcontinental railroad to California, began endeavoring to obtain that territory through alternate means. With this came the next major stepping-stone in Mesilla Valley history, the Gadsden Purchase.

CHAPTER 4

Enter James Gadsden

The boundary commissions of both the United States and Mexico had proven to be a dismal failure at best. After more than two years of continuous work in the field, the problem still had not been satisfactorily concluded. It had become clear that this particular method of ascertaining the placement of the international boundary line was not the correct one, and some other course had to be pursued. Quick and decisive action would be necessary if another war between the two nations was to be averted.

Contrary to the position taken by Mexican authorities at this point, the United States did not concern itself with a quick and easy solution to the problem. Diplomats in Washington concerned themselves with obtaining the desirable route for the transcontinental railroad, much more so than they did about possession of the Mesilla Valley. Bartlett's commission had been viewed as a failure primarily because he did not acquire this southernmost region of New Mexico during negotiations with the Mexican commissioner.

As early as 1845 James Gadsden had recognized the plausibility of building a railroad across southern New Mexico connecting Texas with California.[1] Gadsden suggested that the Gila River valley be used as a route, and Nicholas P. Trist, while negotiating the Treaty of Guadalupe Hidalgo, had orders from Secretary of State James Buchanan to include a clause giving this valley and the surrounding area to the United States.[2] Trist had only partially succeeded in doing this: he had secured the provisions of Article VI, which stated that "if, in the future, a road, a canal, or railroad should be considered which should run along the Gila River, within the radius of one marine league of either the right or the left bank, the two countries were to form an agreement as to its construction."[3] But the article provided no guarantee that the land would actually be turned over to the United States. Trist perhaps did not realize the importance of ensuring that the land for the railroad be obtained; to be fair, when the treaty with Mexico was signed in 1848, Trist could not possibly have prophesized that one year later the discovery of gold in the west would cause a massive influx of travelers. When the California gold rush of 1849 took the eastern part of the nation by storm and thousands of hearty pioneers struck out westward to try their luck, the need for the land and the railroad intensified.[4]

Trist and Bartlett had both failed in respect to the desired railway. Bartlett had favored the more northerly Gila valley route, which partially explains his negotiations with García Conde ceding to Mexico the more southern route (over which the railroad would eventually be built in 1880). Andrew B. Gray, ultimately fired from the commission, had favored a more southerly route, one that would more or less follow the present-day railroad across southern New Mexico. Surveyor Amiel W. Whipple, acting in Gray's absence, advocated a route that would have dipped south into Sonora, Mexico, before finally striking northward and reaching California. Obviously, there existed several possible locations for the railroad to be built. By the time the boundary commission disbanded in 1852, the differing opinions of these three men no longer mattered to Congress.

Before the U.S. government could take any official action, New Mexico territorial Governor William Carr Lane unwittingly stepped forward and intensified the matter. On February 28, 1853, Lane left Santa Fe and traveled south on the Camino Real toward the Mesilla Valley. Two weeks prior, on February 15, Lane wrote to his wife in St. Louis and foreshadowed the events to come: "be not surprised [sic] if I should take possession of the Disputed Territory, which I dare say I will find to be without adequate protection, against internal and external violence . . . be assured, that if duty calls upon me, to occupy & protect this country, provisionally, until the line shall be definitively established, I will do it."[5]

At that time no official boundary agreements with Mexico had been reached, the valley still being referred to as the "disputed area." When news spread that Lane intended to visit the region and forcibly take possession of it, the citizens and territorial legislature alike preached support for him. Prior to leaving Santa Fe, Lane called upon the department military commander, Col. Edwin Vose Sumner, for assistance in taking control of the Mesilla Valley. Sumner subsequently rebuffed Lane's request for military aid. Without the assistance of the military, Lane's support among the Santa Fe citizenry quickly dissipated. Undaunted by the lack of support from his counterpart Sumner, Governor Lane made the trip anyway and reached the village of Doña Ana with a small force of volunteers that he had raised himself. At Doña Ana, Lane issued a proclamation to the governor of Chihuahua, Ángel Trías. In his proclamation of March 13, Lane officially declared that the Mesilla Valley, in its entirety, belonged to the United States, proclaiming that he, as governor of the territory, "do hereby, in behalf of the U.S., retake possession of the said disputed Territory, to be held provisionally by the U.S., until the question of the Boundary, shall be determined, by the U.S. and the Mexican Republic."[6] Lane went so far as to stipulate that he would take it by force if necessary. To what force Lane referred is not known; he had no military troops to aid him in the conquest, only a small handful of poorly armed civilian volunteers from Santa Fe who would have been quickly routed by an army of Mexican regulars.

The indefatigable Lane further decreed that the Bartlett–García Conde agreement of the previous year was wholly invalid (a statement upheld by Congress), and should have no bearing on the rightful ownership of the valley. On a personal level, Lane had no respect for Bartlett and was especially bitter toward him for having made the agreement with the Mexican commissioner in the first place. "No doubt now remains, on my mind, that this quondam Boundary Commissioner, is both Fool & Knave," the governor confided to his journal.[7]

Mexican newspapers immediately rebuked Lane's claim to jurisdiction over the Mesilla Valley, with headlines as far south as Mexico City reading: "American Aggression in Chihuahua!"[8] A later Mexican newspaper article upheld their viewpoint that "La Mesilla has always been a part of Chihuahua, and was never understood to be a part of the lands ceded to our neighboring republic in the Treaty of Guadalupe Hidalgo," citing the earlier agreement between Bartlett and García Conde as evidence of this fact and noting that "both boundary commissions declared that Mesilla belongs to Mexico." The topic of rightful ownership of the Mesilla strip, along with Governor Lane's bold and offensive action, continued to appear in Mexican newspapers for several months. Governor Lane's proclamation was deemed "exceedingly offensive to Mexico . . . and the presumption upon which it is founded, constitutes an unnecessary and villainous injury."[9]

Chihuahua Governor Ángel Trías, dumbfounded by Lane's bold and unmitigated proclamation, immediately sent a dispatch to the Mexican president, Santa Anna, requesting orders on how to proceed in the matter. Trías was instructed to resist Lane through any means necessary, including military force. Armed with Santa Anna's support, Trías called Lane's proclamation a "manifest violation of international law" and informed the governor that he would "make use of all necessary means for the defense and preservation of the territory of La Mesilla in case of an attack, and the responsibility will rest exclusively on Your Excellency for the consequences."[10] Trías promptly led a large body of Mexican troops, numbering about 750 effective men, to a location on the Mexican side of the border at Paso del Norte. This command was soon reinforced by an additional 500 Mexican troops and four pieces of artillery from Zacatecas.[11] The U.S. consul in Paso del Norte, D. R. Diffendorfer, wrote an urgent letter to Secretary of State William L. Marcy, explaining that "the proclamation has created a great excitement in this place among both Americans and Mexicans, and at this moment much ill feeling exists against our countrymen." Diffendorfer went on to suggest that several companies of troops be stationed on the American side of the border, "to protect Americans and their property."[12] The Mexicans were prepared to fight it out with Lane, and for a brief few days it appeared as though the Battle of Brazito might have a sequel in the Mesilla Valley.

The issue became of such widespread importance, and the possibility of another war with Mexico appeared so imminent, that the state legislature of California organized a special committee to look into it. Plans were subsequently drafted by California's legislative body to call up ten companies of volunteer troops to march to New Mexico's aid if in fact a military engagement did occur in the Mesilla Valley. Luckily for all involved, it never came to that.

A day after issuing the proclamation at Doña Ana, and yet to receive Trías's response promising strong resistance to his claim upon the valley, Lane arrived at Fort Fillmore, commanded at that time by Lt. Col. Dixon S. Miles of the 3rd U.S. Infantry. Lane wrote unfavorably in his journal of the veteran colonel in command at the fort: "Made Ft. Fillmore [today], & was obliged, unwillingly, to quarter with Col. Miles, a walking sponge, martinet and a—."[13] Once there Lane called upon Miles to provide his garrison, consisting of several hundred infantry and dragoon troops, in case Governor Trías and the Mexican army did indeed make an attack. Lane and Miles came to an immediate disagreement over how to properly manage the situation. Miles had already been ordered by his commanding officer in Santa Fe, Colonel Sumner, not to assist Lane under any circumstances. This infuriated Lane, who, without the troops at Fort Fillmore, was powerless to enforce the provisions of his brash proclamation. The governor angrily penned a letter to Sumner, lamenting that, "had [Lt.] Col. Miles ordered a single company out of his cantonment of 350 men, who are not employed otherwise than upon ordinary camp and general duties, to have marched to Mesilla . . . not the slightest resistance would have been made."[14] Governor Lane's appeals fell on deaf ears in Santa Fe.

Army inspector Col. Joseph K. F. Mansfield visited Fort Fillmore in 1853, not long after Lane had been there, and made note of the situation in his final report to the War Department. Mansfield very directly addressed the issue: "It was at this post [Fort Fillmore] that ex-Governor W. C. Lane met with a refusal on the part of the commanding officer, Lt. Col. D. S. Miles, to take forcible possession of the Disputed Territory, the Mesilla Valley, on his requisition and in consequence accused 'some 350 U.S. troops who were unemployed and within 5 miles of the scene of action' of folding 'their arms in frigid tranquility and thereby sustaining the enemies of their country.' The propriety of the course of the commanding officer on this occasion cannot be questioned and the subject needs no further notice from me."[15]

The aforementioned letter from Governor Lane to Lieutenant Colonel Miles, written March 19, 1853, was indeed directly accusatory toward Miles for the events that had transpired. "As the army is subordinate and auxiliary to the civil authorities of the U.S.—in all the states and territories," Lane wrote, "the Governor of New Mexico is certainly not accountable to the army for his acts as civil magistrate. I therefore do not hold myself accountable to Colonel Sumner, or yourself, for what I have done, in relation to this disputed territory." Lane believed that he had acted appropriately given the circumstances, and continued to defend himself, stating, "I have acted under the best legal advice in the territory—and do not fear that my action will be disapproved, either by the President or the people. I have done my duty and nothing more; and if others have failed to do their duty, also let them take the responsibility of their ill advised acts." To conclude his letter, Miles cited the current state of affairs relative to the Mexican border crisis. He noted that Bartlett's original boundary line had been repudiated by the United States, that the boundary commission had long since dissolved, and "the authorities of the state of Chihuahua have usurped authority, in the acknowledged Territory of New Mexico, and trampled upon the rights of the citizens of the U.S." As for his own role, Lane upheld his course of action while condemning Miles, explaining that "the Executive Department of New Mexico (in the exercise of an undoubted right and plain duty) has asserted the rights of the U.S. and of the citizens, and some 350 U.S. troops, who are unemployed and are within 5 miles of the scene of action, fold their arms in frigid tranquility and thereby sustain the enemies of our country!"[16]

The governor was not pleased with the lack of support shown by other military and civil officials. By now Lane must have realized the futility of his pursuit and seems to have given up his claim on the Mesilla Valley. He left Fort Fillmore on March 29 and headed northwest to Fort Webster, near the old Spanish copper mines at Santa Rita del Cobre, where he shifted his efforts toward making a treaty with the Apaches in that vicinity. From Fort Webster the governor again wrote to his wife about the expedition, saying, "You are, I dare say, anxious about my health. I wish you could see me: you would begin to think, that my application for an extension of life, had been granted. I have neither ache, nor pain; & have never felt better, in my life. On my journey, I sometimes ride, in the carriage, & sometimes on horse back; & sometimes I walk, for recreation."[17] Lane later returned to Santa Fe to await word on the outcome of his actions in the Mesilla Valley; he must have suspected that the incident would not be perceived favorably by his superiors in Washington.

In a letter written from Washington, D.C. almost two years after the fact, in January 1854, Lane attempted to further justify his reasoning and actions in the matter. "When I went to New Mexico in the summer of '52," he wrote, "I was urged by the delegate from that territory to claim jurisdiction over the Mesilla district and take possession of it by force. For reasons that will be apparent . . . I declined to adopt this course, but as soon as I was informed that the government of the United States had repudiated Bartlett's line . . . I issued a proclamation and claimed jurisdiction of the country until the boundary line should be established by the two governments." Lane further explained that his actions had been met with direct military opposition by Mexican troops, "in which resistance I have reason to believe the authorities of Chihuahua were encouraged by certain officers of the United States army." Under these circumstances, Lane felt as though he had scarcely any other viable course of action than that of taking possession of the area in dispute, deeming it "advisable to attempt to take the

Figure 4.1. Territorial Governor William Carr Lane. (Courtesy Palace of the Governors Photo Archives [NMHM/DCA] Negative #9999)

country by force ... and restore our citizens to their rights of person and property in this district."[18]

Despite having backed down from his preliminary claims to jurisdiction over the disputed region, the ramifications of Lane's actions were severe. By occupying the Mesilla Valley and issuing his proclamation to Governor

Trías in Chihuahua, Lane had broken the fragile status quo agreement that existed between the United States and Mexico, which was supposed to remain in effect while further boundary negotiations with President Santa Anna proceeded. The New Mexico governor had muddied the waters in these negotiations, and matters only deteriorated from that point on.

Mexico's acting minister of relations to the United States, J. Miguel Arroyo, promptly addressed the situation in a correspondence with U.S. envoy to Mexico Alfred B. Conkling. "This territory [the Mesilla strip] has always been in the possession of Mexico," Arroyo claimed, "and is comprised within the boundary line drawn by the Commissions of the two countries according to the Guadalupe Treaty." He noted that President Santa Anna "has witnessed with surprise and dissatisfaction the highly irregular and reckless conduct of the Governor of New Mexico who, without orders from his government, assumes the grave responsibility of rendering himself the cause of war between two friendly nations."[19] The Mexican minister concluded his letter by urging Conkling to address a direct communication to Lane about the proclamation, which Conkling, realizing the potential for an outbreak in hostilities, agreed to do, telling Arroyo that he "considered the conduct of the governor rash and unwarrantable." In a private conversation with Conkling, Arroyo assured him "of the determination of the government [of Mexico] to resist the threatened movement of Governor Lane to the utmost extent of its power."[20]

In his letter to Governor Lane, dated August 8, 1853, Conkling reminded him that "the existing possession [of the disputed region] should be left undisturbed, until the question shall have been definitively settled by the two national governments, in favor of the United States." Conkling also stressed upon Lane the seriousness of the situation, warning him that "as you seem to contemplate the employment of military force, and are . . . in that case, certain to meet with resistance in the same form, I can but regard the affair as one of extreme gravity."[21] As an acting representative of the United States in Mexico, Conkling was more familiar than anybody with the reaction of the Mexican government, and his warning to Lane reflects the seriousness of the governor's proclamation.

Secretary of State William L. Marcy, while sharing Lane's opinion that the Mesilla Valley rightfully belonged to the United States, nevertheless condemned Lane for his use of a proclamation and threat of force in his

Figure 4.2. Territorial Governor David Meriwether. (Courtesy Center for Southwest Research, University Libraries, University of New Mexico. Keleher Collection ZIM CSWR PICT 742-0109)

attempt to take the valley. Lane defended himself against these and other allegations, saying that he had been "appointed governor of all New Mexico, and not a part."[22] The situation Lane had endured during his time in the territory was related in a letter written by himself on June 8: "On [the] 22d inst., it will therefore be 10 months, since I put my foot upon the soil of N. Mex.; and here have I been in N. Mex. squabbling & contending, ever since . . . I cannot say these 10 months have been happy."[23]

By the time these disputes were settled, Lane was no longer the governor of "all New Mexico," nor was he even governor of a part of it. Under intense scrutiny from Washington, Lane resigned his position as governor, his replacement being appointed by the president on May 22, 1853. The man taking his place was one well qualified for the job, and who had a great deal of prior experience and knowledge about the situation at hand. On

August 8, 1853, David Meriwether arrived in Santa Fe and assumed the office of governor for the Territory of New Mexico.[24] Almost simultaneously the controversial department military commander, Colonel Sumner, was likewise ousted and replaced by Gen. John Garland.[25] Together, these two men would work tirelessly to untangle the diplomatic knot that had been tied by Lane and Sumner during their administrations.

Meriwether was chosen to replace Lane for obvious reasons. He possessed a unique familiarity with New Mexico and the Mexican boundary dispute. In 1819, when New Mexico still belonged to Spain, Meriwether was taken prisoner in the territory and held in confinement at the Palace of the Governors, accused of being an American spy. Just nineteen years old when that happened, Meriwether never could have imagined that thirty-five years later he would return to the same building in which he had once been confined by the Spaniards. "It is worthy of note . . . that he who was a poor and unknown boy, and a prisoner in a foreign land, should, in the course of years, return with the power of the United States at his back to rule over the same people who had held him in captivity, and to administer laws in the very building in which he had been confined," commented a contemporary of Meriwether.[26] Several years after his release from captivity in Santa Fe, Meriwether became active in politics and eventually worked on a Senate committee dedicated solely to the issue of the boundary dispute with Mexico; it was Meriwether who had been called upon to draft the committee's report.[27] David Meriwether was probably more familiar with the particulars of the situation than any other man in America, making him the obvious choice of the president to fill William Carr Lane's vacated position in Santa Fe. He gave up his prized seat in the U.S. Senate and accepted the appointment as governor of New Mexico on one condition, that he "might be permitted to resign whenever this boundary question could be settled."[28]

Ex-governor William Carr Lane, while placing himself in an unenviable political situation, had succeeded in one thing: he had forced the United States and Mexico to take immediate action in order to bring about a peaceful solution to the boundary disputes. Lane's brute actions had, in a sense, necessitated the intensified diplomatic negotiations that were forthcoming in order to bring closure to the issue.

Now the issue would be left up to David Meriwether, and more particularly James Gadsden, to sort out. Secretary of State Marcy wasted no time in explaining the situation to Gadsden. "The late Governor of New Mexico [William Carr Lane], it seems, entertained an intention of taking actual possession [of the Mesilla Valley] and announced his purpose in a proclamation," Marcy edified in a letter to Gadsden, "but at the same time he declared that he was acting without instructions from his government. His intention was never executed, his purpose was disapproved, and Mexico was distinctly apprised that the United States will abstain from taking possession of the disputed territory in the belief that the difficulty will be settled by negotiation; and this government expects that Mexico will on her part take the same course."[29] Marcy was clearly frustrated with the actions of the previous New Mexico governor, his letter acknowledging that those actions would make Gadsden's negotiations all the more difficult.

Secretary Marcy, who favored the more southerly railway route proposed by Gray in 1852, provided Gadsden with a detailed description of the circumstances, directing him to begin his negotiations with Mexico accordingly. "You are therefore instructed," Marcy wrote Gadsden, "to ascertain whether there be on the part of Mexico a disposition to enter into an agreement embracing a final adjustment of all the matters to which I have alluded, *viz.,* a new line giving to this government additional territory for a feasible route for a railroad; a release from the obligations of the 11th article of the treaty of peace and limits; and a settlement of claims upon the respective governments by the citizens of each. For such an adjustment the United States would be willing to pay liberally."[30] If Gadsden could succeed in these things, a truly monumental task, he would effectively bring about a solution to all three of the major arguing points that had been created by the treaty. Gadsden had his work cut out for him.

When sixty-five-year-old James Gadsden took on the role of Envoy Extraordinary and Minister Plenipotentiary to Mexico in May 1853, he had already firmly established himself in the world of politics.[31] Gadsden had been a close friend of Andrew Jackson for many years, and his friendship with such an influential individual paid dividends. Jackson, who took an immediate liking to Gadsden, catapulted him to positions in government that far exceeded other positions filled by his peers. A prominent Florida politician from 1825 to 1838, Gadsden became president of the Louisville, Charleston and Cincinnati Railroad in 1840, an occupation in which he would continue for ten years.[32] Gadsden had political clout and a strong personal interest in railroads, both of which would be necessary for him to emerge successful in his negotiations with Santa Anna. Secretary of War Jefferson Davis recognized this and secured Gadsden's appointment as foreign minister.[33]

Arriving in the Mexican port city of Veracruz on August 4, 1853, Gadsden began what would prove to be months of negotiations with Mexico. On August 17 he held his first interview with Santa Anna, and he also met with Mexico's minister of foreign relations, Manuel Díez de Bonilla. Throughout Gadsden's time in Mexico it would be Díez de Bonilla, and not Santa Anna, with whom he worked most closely. By September 25, after several meetings among the representatives from the two nations, it was agreed that the disputed area, including the Mesilla Valley, should remain in status quo pending the outcome of their discussions. Gadsden thus eased the tension that had erupted earlier in 1853 when Governor Lane proclaimed the region to be a part of the United States.[34]

Gradually, as had been his intention from the beginning, Gadsden began hinting to Santa Anna that he should simply sell the disputed lands to the United States rather than spend several more years and millions of dollars on boundary commissions. It had already been proven that this method of solving the dispute was not the correct one, and both Gadsden and Santa Anna realized that a purchase of the land would be the easier and more beneficial solution for both sides. Interestingly, Gadsden had received instructions from his superiors in Washington that he should purchase only land suitable for the transcontinental railroad, and that the Mesilla Valley was of relative unimportance and need not be included in the purchase.[35] Time would ultimately prove the opposite to be true: when the government failed (until the 1880s) to build the desired railroad across southern New Mexico, possession of the Mesilla Valley ultimately became an important accomplishment of the Gadsden Purchase.

If, however, the Mesilla Valley did become an issue in the negotiations (which of course it did), Gadsden's instructions stated that he was to refute the Bartlett–García Conde agreement on the grounds that it was not legally binding because the U.S. government did not recognize A. W. Whipple's signature as surveyor ad interim. In other words, Whipple had not been authorized to sign the agreement, and it was therefore not binding upon the United States.[36]

To fully understand the reasons the purchase took place, it is necessary

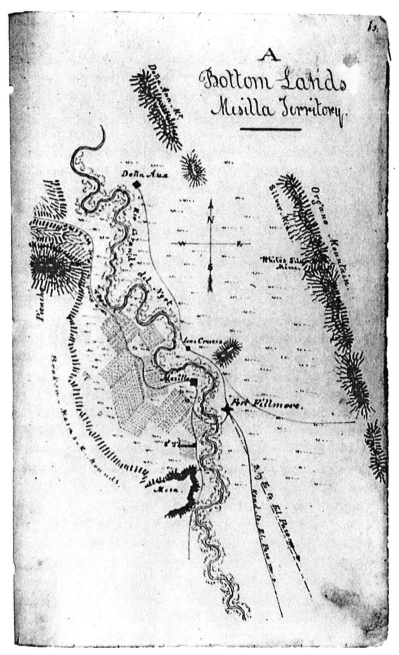

Map 4.1. Bottomlands of the Mesilla Territory, 1853, sketch by army inspector Joseph K. F. Mansfield. (From Robert W. Frazer, ed., Mansfield on the Condition of the Western Forts, 1853–54.*)*

to analyze the financial situation of Santa Anna's government in 1853. At the time, Santa Anna headed a virtually bankrupt regime, one in desperate need of money to avoid being overthrown by revolutionary elements within Mexico. When he took over as president of Mexico, the treasury had been nearly emptied by his predecessor, there was a deficit of some $17 million, and Mexico had accrued a monumental international debt that needed to be repaid.[37] Santa Anna needed money, and he needed it fast. To him, it made little difference how much land was swapped to the United States as long as the amount of money involved was sufficient to alleviate the predicament in which the Mexican leader found himself. Gadsden perhaps best described Santa Anna's Mexican regime, calling it "a government of plunder and necessity."[38]

By the time Gadsden began negotiating with Santa Anna and his minister, Díez de Bonilla, the threat of his government being overthrown was resounding. An observant Gadsden recognized this inevitability, in many instances rushing some of the negotiations in hopes that the entire ordeal could be concluded before Santa Anna was ousted from the presidential chair. It would be difficult for Gadsden to succeed if control of the Mexican government shifted midway through the process. The United States would be better off dealing with Santa Anna because of his desperation and dire need for money. Gadsden plainly understood that the megalomaniac Mexican president would undertake drastic measures, including the sale of a vast expanse of territory, to avoid being overthrown by demagogue revolutionaries. Another element that favored Gadsden was the fact that Santa Anna received no outside support from the powerful European countries. Already bankrupt, Mexico lacked the financial and military capability to fight another war with the United States, making the timing perfect for an exploitative Gadsden to step in and negotiate a deal favorable to the United States.

On October 22, 1853, Secretary of State Marcy dispatched Christopher L. Ward to Mexico with confidential instructions to Gadsden. Arriving there on the fourteenth of November, Ward delivered the secret message to Gadsden verbally (he had been required to memorize the orders so that no written document containing the information could be seized by Mexican authorities).[39] As a side note, it later came to the attention of officials in Washington that a profiteering Ward, seeking to advance his own personal agenda, had made self-serving alterations to the instructions before relaying them to Gadsden. At any rate, the most important information that Gadsden received from messenger Ward, as regards the actual procurement of territory, was a set of six possible options for purchase, which he would present to Santa Anna and open up negotiations thereupon.

The American president favored the first and most inclusive option; it included all of the northern portions of Chihuahua, Sonora, Coahuila, and the entirety of Baja California. For this, Gadsden was authorized to pay $50 million. If this option were chosen, the United States would also become the new proprietor of a seaport at the outlet of the Colorado River, further increasing the value of the purchase.

The second possibility presented to Santa Anna included substantially less land; it included Baja California and the port at the mouth of the Colorado River but contained a drastically reduced portion of the above-named Mexican provinces. For this the United States would pay $35 million.

Proposals three and four were more or less similar, the boundary lines differing only slightly from one option to the next. Both of these excluded Baja California entirely and generally accepted the Rio Grande as the southern boundary separating Mexico and Texas. For these, the prices offered were $20 million and $30 million respectively.

The final two possibilities would be the ones most closely taken into consideration by Santa Anna. Although Gadsden pleaded with the Mexican president to opt for the first of the six, which would have given the United States the most territory, Santa Anna refused and would only agree to proposal number five. Out of the six, this option ceded the least amount of land to the United States, with the amount to be paid set at $15 million. During the negotiations Santa Anna is said to have remarked, with a tone of both scorn and irony, that this amount equaled that paid by the United States in 1848 for the Mexican Cession lands, which deprived Mexico of one-half of its territory.[40]

Many people supposed that Santa Anna was wary of giving up too much land to the United States for fear of appearing weak to the European countries as well as to the revolutionary factions within his own nation. Newspapers in the east speculated as to Santa Anna's exact reasoning in making the agreement. The eastern population generally agreed that the Gadsden Purchase lands consisted of nothing more than a barren desert, essentially useless to Mexico anyway. The *New York Daily Times* wrote, "The territory [Santa Anna] has ceded away was overrun and desolated by the savages, and therefore, useless to Mexico, and . . . the railroad which we will probably run through the territory, and the American settlements likely to spring up along the line, will afford to Mexico an impenetrable defense against the Indians."[41] This sentiment represented that of many Americans during that time.

The treaty also included an agreement between the two nations concerning the abrogation of Article XI of the Treaty of Guadalupe Hidalgo.[42] "In freeing himself from the 11th article of the treaty of Guadalupe, Mr. Gadsden has got rid of an onerous duty," commented one newspaper.[43] It now appeared as though the United States would solve all of the problems arising out of the Mexican War at once. The railroad route across southern New Mexico would be secured, the Mesilla Valley would revert back to the United States without any additional boundary conflicts, and American troops would no longer be responsible for controlling Apache raiding in Mexico. If Gadsden's treaty could meet with the approval of an objective Congress in Washington, all of these things would be effectively accomplished.

As a final precaution the Mexican government took steps to protect the property of those already living in the Mesilla Valley in case need should arise after the finalization of the treaty. Anticipating the outcome of the treaty with the United States, the Mexican government granted formal title to the lands owned by individuals residing in the valley. This was done in part so that these people would not lose their homes and farms when the territory shifted to U.S. jurisdiction. The United States, as part of the Gadsden Treaty, agreed to honor all titles issued by the Mexican government, thereby assuring those living in Mesilla that despite their imminent change in citizenship their way of life would not be so vitally affected.[44]

The treaty conference between the leading diplomats was held in Mexico City beginning on December 10, 1853. Díez de Bonilla affixed his signature to the agreement on December 23 and Gadsden himself was quick to follow suit, doing the same on December 30. El Tratado de la Mesilla, as the Mexican government called it, needed now only to be ratified by the U.S. Congress in order to become law.

The ministers for both the United States and Mexico agreed to keep the signing of the treaty a secret until it was approved by their respective governments. Not surprisingly, the plight to maintain secrecy failed miserably; word of the treaty reached American newspapers before Gadsden even arrived back in Louisiana. The first such newspaper article speculating that the treaty had been concluded was published in the *New York Herald* on January 4, 1854, ten days before Gadsden set foot back in New Orleans. The treaty was evidently a great sense of pride to him, for, when passing through the customhouse there on January 12 and interrogated as to the contents of his suitcase, he replied, "Sir, I am General Gadsden. There is nothing in my trunk but my treaty."[45]

Propaganda spread quickly, and newspapers all around the eastern United States took an immediate partisan stance on the issue. In most cases, owing to the increasing severity of the slavery issue, sectional interests determined these stances. Southern newspapers generally praised Gadsden and the treaty stipulations because it would provide a transcontinental railroad route with a terminus in Louisiana, thus supporting southern industrial interests and the possible expansion of slavery into the western territories. The *Richmond Enquirer* summarized the elation of the South over the treaty: "The distinguishing merits of this treaty are, first, that it adjusts all the disputes between the United States and Mexico, and thus cements the amicable relations of the two governments; secondly, that it removes every inducement to filibuster invasions of Mexican soil; thirdly, that it secures the only safe and practicable route for a railway to the Pacific; and lastly, and chiefly, it gives the South a chance for two or three more slave states."[46]

Contrarily, most Northern newspapers strongly denounced the treaty; rumors began to circulate in the North that the entire thing had been an inside job, promulgated by conniving Southern sympathizers in Congress attempting to extend the institution of slavery to the newly acquired lands in the Southwest. Indeed, newspaper reports such as that out of Richmond regarding the possibility of additional Southern states seemed to support this claim. Others claimed that Santa Anna would use the $15 million to build up his army and declare war on the United States in an attempt to regain the land ceded following the Mexican War. The fact that Gadsden was a self-proclaimed Southern man and staunch advocate of secession did not help matters, nor did the fact that the leading topic on the congressional agenda in the spring of 1854 was the highly controversial Kansas-Nebraska bill.[47]

In spite of the intense speculation between the North and South sur-

rounding the potential outcomes of the Gadsden Treaty, the issue still had
yet to come before Congress. On February 10, 1854, the Senate finally addressed the issue but promptly tabled it again until March 13. It remained a
topic of debate in the Senate Committee on Foreign Relations for a considerable period of time, after which the treaty was finally presented on the Senate floor for ratification. A few minor alterations to the treaty's provisions
had been made by the committee and by President Franklin Pierce. Among
these amendments were a reduction in the size of the area to be purchased
by some 9,000 square miles, and a drastic reduction in the price to be paid
to Santa Anna, from $15 million to $10 million. On April 17 the Senate vote
came up three shy of the two-thirds majority required for ratification. After
additional minor amendments, another vote on April 25 resulted in the
treaty finally being passed.[48]

Both Gadsden and President Pierce were upset with the nature of the
Senate's amendments. Gadsden had taken great pride in his arrangements
with Santa Anna and found these alterations to be offensive. Pierce, who
had proposed some but not all of the amendments, felt that these changes
were not in complete accordance with his own ideas and was therefore also
discouraged by the Senate's actions in ratifying the treaty with the changes
that had been made.

Regardless of the feelings of certain individuals, the treaty had passed
in the Senate and was sent back to Santa Anna for his approval. When it
reached him, it is not surprising that his first inclination was to reject it because of the drastic 33 percent reduction in the amount of money to be paid.
Unfortunately for Santa Anna, rejecting the treaty was not a viable option.
By that time a revolution, known as the Plan de Ayutla, had broken out in
the Mexican State of Guerrero, and the money was too important for Santa
Anna to pass up. He approved the treaty in its amended version and returned it to the United States. Ironically, a short time later, the leader of the
revolution, Juan Álvarez, was successful in forcing Santa Anna to abdicate
the Mexican presidency. Had the Senate taken much longer in debating the
treaty, a new president would have been in place in Mexico, and the progress
of more than a year of negotiations would have been wasted.

Even with the approval of the Senate and Santa Anna, the treaty faced
yet another political obstacle before becoming law. On June 20, 1854, President Pierce presented the treaty to the House of Representatives, asking

Figure 4.3. James Gadsden, shown here in about 1820 in uniform as a military officer. (Courtesy State Archives of Florida, Call # Re07134)

them to approve it "as-is" and to appropriate the $10 million to pay Santa Anna.[49] Just as had happened in the Senate, the House struggled to come to an agreement on the adoption of the treaty. The final vote taken in the House of Representatives, after a full month of debate, was 105 to 63. Sectionalism and slavery proved to be the largest factors dividing this antebellum Congress on the issue; the controversy that had been portrayed by the newspapers for months had manifested itself clearly in the congressional debates. On June 29, after passing through the House of Representatives, President Pierce signed his name to the Gadsden Treaty and the seemingly endless political process of determining the boundary between the United States and Mexico finally concluded.

The following day, June 30, Pierce sent the first payment in the amount of $7 million to Santa Anna. Indicative of his personal character, upon receipt of the lump sum the wily Mexican leader wasted no time in pocketing

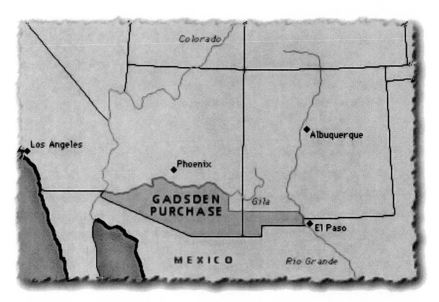

Map 4.2. Gadsden Purchase lands.

$700,000 to reimburse himself for monetary losses he claimed to have in-
curred at his private haciendas during the Mexican War.[50] The remaining
$3 million, according to the treaty, would not be paid to Mexico until the
boundary line was fully surveyed by an American commission.

The Gadsden Treaty, as ratified, contained ten articles. The first outlined the exact latitude and longitude of the boundary line. The United
States was careful to include exact figures in the treaty, so as to avoid conflicts such as those resulting from the Treaty of Guadalupe Hidalgo's use of
the erroneous Disturnell map several years earlier. Article V of the Gadsden
Treaty stated that all Mexican land grants in the purchased territory would
be recognized by the United States, provided that they had been previously
recorded and documented in the Mexican archives. Another article of the
treaty was dedicated solely to the abrogation of Article XI of the Treaty of
Guadalupe Hidalgo, so that the United States no longer held responsibility
for Indian incursions in the northern provinces of Mexico. Finally, each
country would once again appoint a boundary commissioner to stake out
the new international boundary line. This time, however, there would be
no disputing where the line was to begin and end. Once again, just as had
been provided for the last time the two countries made a treaty, the findings

of these commissioners would retroactively become a mutually recognized stipulation of the Gadsden Treaty.[51]

The area gained by the United States, for the amount of $10 million, comprised 29,670 square miles.[52] This included the Mesilla Valley and all land west from there to California's eastern boundary (the Colorado River). The two most important towns located therein were Mesilla and Tucson. With this, the international boundary between Mexico and the United States was finally settled, and to this day it remains unchanged. The residents of Mesilla, who only a half decade earlier had moved across the Rio Grande to remain Mexican citizens, now found no alternative to becoming Americans and submitting to the laws and regulations of that country.

The Gadsden Treaty, keeping with the tradition of years past, called for yet another commission to be raised to survey the new international boundary line. In this instance the importance was increased from Mexico's standpoint, because not until the survey was completed would they receive the remaining $3 million payment from the United States. With this incentive the Mexican government was eager to get the project under way. On the U.S. side, the importance of completing the survey lay with the potential transcontinental railroad that could be built once the boundary line had been permanently fixed. Because of Mexico's eagerness to complete the survey, cooperation between the two commissions far exceeded that which had occurred during previous attempts. In fact, the only delay in the work came when the Mexican boundary commissioner was imprisoned by his own government for a month, under suspicion of having antigovernment sentiments; he was soon released from captivity and was allowed to return to the commission.[53]

In August 1854 Gen. Robert Blair Campbell was chosen by the president to serve as boundary commissioner, and Maj. William Helmsley Emory (who had already served on the previous commission with Bartlett) was appointed as Campbell's chief astronomer and surveyor.[54] The line to be surveyed was 530 miles in length; it stretched from a point on the Rio Grande just a few miles north of El Paso, at the southern terminus of the Mesilla Valley, all the way across southern New Mexico Territory to California. To complete the work, Campbell and Emory received a congressional appropriation of $168,130, substantially less than Bartlett had received to conduct his commission's work.

TOWN AND VALLEY OF MESILLA
NEW - MEXICO.

Figure 4.4. An artist's rendering of Mesilla as it appeared in 1854. (Courtesy New Mexico State University Library, Archives and Special Collections. MS 0339)

Before the men got under way, Emory replaced Campbell, thus becoming the commissioner. On the Mexican side, the commissioner would be José Salazar Ylarregui, who had been Gen. Pedro García Conde's chief assistant during the 1851–52 surveys with Bartlett. Salazar Ylarregui assumed the position following the death of García Conde in December 1852 from typhoid fever.[55] The first meeting between the two commissioners transpired on December 2, 1854, six months after the Gadsden Treaty had become law.

The first objective would be to determine the starting point of the boundary line in the Mesilla Valley, and from that point proceed westward toward California. The point agreed upon by both commissioners was at 31° 47′ north latitude, several miles north of Paso del Norte on the Mexican side of the Rio Grande. On January 31, 1855, with numerous officers from the nearby military garrison of Fort Bliss in attendance, Emory and Salazar Ylarregui held a ceremony at the location and placed the first of many temporary obelisk-shaped monuments to mark the initial point of boundary.[56]

By October 14, 1855, the entire boundary survey from the Mesilla Val-

ley to California was finished. In a period of just ten months, Emory and
Salazar Ylarregui had completed what Weller, Bartlett, García Conde, and
others failed to complete in two years. Emory accomplished the task with
roughly one-third the amount of congressional appropriations as had been
afforded to Bartlett. One must take into consideration the fact that Emory
worked with a much more willing Mexican government, whose reliance on
a $3 million payment made the work flow more smoothly.

At the completion of the survey Emory immediately wrote to Secretary
of the Interior McClellan that the outstanding balance of $3 million should
be temporarily withheld until Mexican officials signed the agreement. If the
money was paid prematurely, Emory worried, Santa Anna would have less
incentive to sign, potentially forcing the two countries back to the negotiating table.

With the Gadsden Purchase lands now in the undisputed possession of
the United States, it became the duty of the War Department to garrison the
newly acquired area with troops to protect the citizens. In a region plagued
by Apache raiding, settlements and ranches were still few and far between.
Mesilla received protection from large-scale Indian incursions from nearby
Fort Fillmore, but Tucson was another matter of concern. For several years
prior to the Gadsden Treaty, Mexican troops garrisoned a small outpost at
Tucson, but those troops were removed on March 10, 1856, pursuant to the
Gadsden Treaty.[57] The U.S. War Department was slow in filling this void,
not sending troops to the region until November 1856, and only then follow-
ing numerous desperate protestations by those living there.[58]

On July 4, 1855, almost a year after the Gadsden Treaty had been signed
and approved by Congress and the president, Gen. John Garland and Gov.
David Meriwether traveled the Camino Real south from Santa Fe to take
part in an Independence Day celebration in Mesilla. This was perhaps the
first public display of pro-American sentiment ever shown in the town. Two
companies of U.S. dragoons from Los Lunas and Fort Craig, along with
two additional companies of infantry, took part in the parade. Bald-headed
Capt. Richard S. Ewell of the 1st Dragoons was placed in command of the
entire contingent.[59]

Arriving in Mesilla, Governor Meriwether held a meeting with Chihuahua Governor Ángel Trías, who finally consented to retract all Mexican
claims to the Mesilla Valley. In doing so, Trías, who so adamantly refused

Governor William Carr Lane's claim over the disputed region two years before, formally recognized the validity of the Gadsden Treaty and allowed undisputed American occupation of the entire valley for the first time in history. "The American flag was at once hoisted on the flag-staff so recently occupied by the Mexican flag," wrote one observer; "our flag was saluted with two pieces of artillery which we had brought across the river [from Fort Fillmore] with us."[60]

Governor Meriwether, in a moment resembling that which occurred when Gen. Stephen W. Kearny entered Las Vegas nearly a decade before, stood prominently atop an adobe roof and addressed the Mesilla citizens.[61] The governor later described the incident: "I told the Mexicans, through an interpreter, that by peaceful negotiations, the disputed territory had been transferred to the United States; that I hoped they would prove themselves loyal and law-abiding citizens . . . that any citizen who preferred the Mexican to the American government was at liberty to sell his possessions and move to the Mexican side of the line. . . . The Mexicans appeared to be satisfied with what I had said to them and applauded lustily, many coming to be introduced to me, and to whom I gave a cordial shake of the hand."[62] With this speech, those living in Mesilla, who had moved across the Rio Grande in 1848 to remain a part of Mexico, could now be sure of their status as citizens of the United States. Meriwether had succeeded in his purpose as governor. He had overseen the negotiations between the United States and Mexico, avoided any further unnecessary conflict like that which had occurred when William Carr Lane occupied the Mesilla Valley in 1853, and he was the first American government official to welcome the people living in the Gadsden Purchase lands to the United States.

On November 16, 1855, under orders from Governor Meriwether and military department commander Gen. John Garland, U.S. troops occupied the town of Mesilla.[63] Mexico at first denounced this action, under the premise that the final $3 million installment allocated by the Gadsden Treaty had not yet been submitted by the U.S. government, but their protests were without effect. The final payment was not issued until 1856, some time after the boundary commissions of Emory and Salazar Ylarregui had finished their work.[64]

James Gadsden, despite the importance of his successful negotiations with Mexico, did not receive the widespread acclaim that might be expected for such a noteworthy accomplishment. This owed in large part to the fact that now more than ever civil war was imminent in the east. A large portion of Northern sympathizers opposed the Gadsden Purchase because of Gadsden's well-known Southern roots. The procurement of the Gadsden Purchase lands, and the potential status of those lands as pro- or antislavery, had been a subject of controversy as a result of the intense sectionalism in the eastern United States at this time. Unfortunately, Gadsden's career and reputation were not immune to the negative effects that this brought about. On June 30, 1856, Secretary Marcy formally informed James Gadsden that he had been recalled from his position as minister to Mexico, and that his replacement was already on the way to relieve him. Gadsden's reward for acting faithfully was essentially nothing more than a slap in the face from the government he had served.

Ironically, the single most influential component in gaining the southern portion of the New Mexico Territory, the transcontinental railroad route, eventually turned out to be the last thing that received attention. Within a few years the region was opened up to miners who flocked to the gold fields at Piños Altos near the old Santa Rita copper mines, where gold was discovered in 1860. Settlers populated the Mesilla Valley with growing rapidity in the post–Gadsden Purchase years. But the transcontinental railroad of southern New Mexico was nowhere to be found. The Civil War imposed upon Congress's supposedly well-laid plans, and by the time that conflict subsided, a more northerly route across the Great Plains had been chosen for the railroad to California.

To be fair, the government did assign surveying teams to analyze southern New Mexico in the late 1850s. Lieutenant Pope, of the Army Corps of Topographical Engineers, surveyed the region from the Mesilla Valley eastward toward Texas beginning in 1855. Simultaneously, the Pacific Railway Surveys were being carried out farther to the north, and a dilemma arose when congressional leaders realized that there were several practicable routes for the railroad, not just the one proposed across the southernmost reaches of the Territory of New Mexico. Disagreements over the issue kept Congress entangled in indecision throughout the latter years of the 1850s. No course of action had yet been acted upon in 1861, at which point the secession of the Southern states demanded the undivided attention of Washington politicians. Not until 1881 did the railroad reach the Mesilla Valley, over twenty-five years after James Gadsden's treaty had been finalized.

The Gadsden Purchase signified the last U.S. acquisition of land in the Great Southwest. In essence, it represented the final chapter of the Manifest Destiny that had swept over the nation and maintained a firm grip on the imaginations of all Americans for the previous half-century. "We want the [rail]road, finally, to complete for us that *commercial empire* after which we have sighed—which has been indicated for us in every step of our progress, from the landing of the Pilgrim Fathers, and which appears to be *ours* by manifest and inevitable destiny," wrote John Reid in 1857.[65] His comment summarizes the beliefs of countless Americans during that time period.

With the finalization of the Gadsden Purchase, the contiguous United States would appear on maps as it still does in the present day, a vast nation stretching from one coast to another. Insignificant as it may seem on so grand a scale, the acquisition of the Mesilla Valley and southern portions of New Mexico and Arizona would be of incredible importance in the decades to come, as the region slowly became populated by adventurous Americans: miners, merchants, farmers, and ranchers who would soon call the region their home. James Gadsden had set the stage for the population boom in the Mesilla Valley that continues to this day.

CHAPTER 5

Fort Fillmore and the Apaches

Throughout the entirety of the period covered in this account, 1846–65, the people of the Mesilla Valley were continuously subjected to Apache raiding. Such had been the case for centuries, beginning with the initial settlement of the area by the Spaniards at Paso del Norte in the seventeenth century. In many ways dealing with the hardships presented by the Indians had simply become a way of life to which the residents had grown accustomed.

The Mexican government, which controlled the area during the period 1821–46, had done little to effectively prevent or even reduce Apache depredations. The single greatest obstacle to the tribe during that time proved not to be the Mexican troops but rather a few adventure-seeking scalp hunters, most notable of whom was James Kirker. But even these men, who succeeded in inciting an occasional sense of terror among the Apaches, had little positive effect.

Most early Mexican settlement in the Apache country had been hastily abandoned due to an inability to coexist with members of that tribe. First, the settlements near Brazito were established and then abandoned, along with the copper mines at Santa Rita del Cobre in 1804. In 1846, U.S. troops passing through Doña Ana recognized the helplessness of its citizens and left behind a cannon for protection against the Indians. All of this had inevitably led to a deep-seated, permanent hatred that was mutual between the Mexicans and the Apaches of southern New Mexico. Such was the scene upon which the U.S. government and its military troops entered when occupying the territory in 1846. Almost immediately government officials set out to bring greater protection to the inhabitants, chastise the Indians, and make the region safe for settlement and prosperity. This would be much easier said than done, as many army officers and Indian agents would come to find out in the upcoming years.[1]

Boundary commissioner John Russell Bartlett entered the Mesilla Valley in 1850 and quickly recognized that something must be done about the Apaches. He made several suggestions, some practical and some not, but his status as a civilian from New York who was unaccustomed to the rigors and customs of the Southwest negated the validity of his comments in the eyes of other officials. In his *Personal Narrative,* Bartlett commented:

> As the question has been repeatedly asked, what is to be done with the large tribes of Indians on the Mexican frontier? And as there is still a diversity of opinion on the subject, I shall take the present occasion to make a few suggestions, based upon what I have learned from personal observation, and my intercourse with the Indians. It is known that we already have along this frontier, but chiefly in the state of Texas and the territory of New Mexico, a large military force, embracing a full two-thirds of the army, which is supported at an enormous expense. Military posts have been established at various points on the Rio Grande and in the very heart of the Indian country in Texas and in New Mexico. Yet two of the largest and most widely spread tribes, the Comanches and Apaches, are as actively hostile to the Americans and the Mexicans as they were before the country occupied by them became a part of the Union. At no period have the incursions been more frequent, or attended with greater atrocities, than at the present time.[2]

Army inspector J. K. F. Mansfield, visiting Fort Fillmore and Mesilla in 1853, remarked upon the vast potential for growth in the region, but also noted that this would never come to pass as long as the Apaches roamed freely about the countryside and swooped down upon the settlements at their leisure.[3]

In 1849, with gold being discovered in California, the traffic across the California road (which passed directly through the Mesilla Valley) drastically increased, and the need to control Apache depredations became more apparent to those in power. Due in large part to the increased importance of this thoroughfare (later to become known as the Butterfield Trail), the U.S. Army permanently stationed troops in the area, both in Doña Ana at the northern terminus of the valley and in Franklin (El Paso) at the southern end. This marked the beginning of the army's presence in southern New Mexico, an occupation that would be perpetual throughout the upcoming decades.

The first permanent military presence in the Mesilla Valley came in

1848, two years after Kearny's occupation of the territory, when troops were stationed in adobe buildings at Doña Ana. Companies serving at Doña Ana, intermittently, included D, F, and H, 1st Dragoons and Company B, and 3rd Infantry.[4] Company H would be the first of these regiments to occupy Doña Ana, arriving there in January 1849 under the command of Lt. Delos B. Sackett, at that time filling in for Maj. Enoch Steen as commander. Subsistence for the troops would be drawn from distant Santa Fe, being freighted down the Camino Real to Doña Ana at considerable expense and inconvenience to the army. The government rented living quarters near the plaza for the two companies at an expense of $170 per month; by the time the army abandoned the post in the summer of 1851, the cost had jumped to $362 per month.[5] The living situation at Doña Ana was further described by Dr. S. W. Woodhouse, who noted on June 30, 1851, that he "arrived at Don Anna [sic] . . . here . . . the houses are miserable, even those occupied by the troops. . . . Maj. Sheppard [sic], who commands, Dr. Tenbrook, who is Surgeon of the post, & Lieut. O'Banion [sic] of the Infantry are the only officers at the post. Here we got a fine treat of some ice."[6]

Maj. Enoch Steen[7] arrived at Doña Ana in July 1849 to assume command of Company H, relieving Sackett and allowing him to return to his own company. Steen would immediately find himself immersed in problems at the post. Not only did Apache raids continue during this time, but also Steen's troops were ill equipped to fight them.

Major Steen received much praise as the commanding officer at Doña Ana. On October 10, 1850, army inspector Col. George A. McCall visited the post during his tour of New Mexico and reported the garrison at that time to consist of fifty-four men of Company H, 1st Dragoons, and forty-three men of Company B, 3rd Infantry. Furthermore, McCall added, "Major Steen has shown much zeal in the performance of his duties, particularly in several expeditions against Apache Indians in the Sacramento Mountains and on the River Gila, in which he had several engagements with them, and was once severely wounded." He also praised the conditions at the post: "Taken all together, it affords me pleasure to say that this company [H, 1st Dragoons] is in better order than any I have seen in this department."[8] Of all dragoon companies then stationed in New Mexico, Company H at Doña Ana maintained the best and most serviceable horses, according to the inspector. Even with this apparent advantage, the troops continually came up empty-handed against their Apache counterparts in the upcoming months and years.

For the soldiers in the Mesilla Valley, controlling the Apaches would be particularly difficult, the region being located directly between the homelands of two very distinct tribes, the Mescaleros and the Gilas. The Mescalero Apaches, living primarily in the Sacramento and Guadalupe Mountain ranges east of the Rio Grande, would be a continuous affliction upon the Mexican and American inhabitants in the upcoming years, and were frequently the target of military campaigns out of Doña Ana and Fort Fillmore. Likewise, the Gila Apaches (or Chihenne, as they called themselves), who made their homes primarily in the vicinity of the Mimbres and Gila River valleys west of the Rio Grande, would prove to be no less of a burden during the upcoming years. This continuously divided the attention of the military in two separate directions, undermining efforts to chastise them for raiding and plundering the Mexican settlements.[9]

The increasing population of the Mesilla Valley, coupled with the presence of American troops, gradually impacted some of the Apache subgroups. One of these small bands of Mescaleros, perhaps less prone to violence than other subunits of that same tribe, came into Doña Ana on December 9, 1849, to make a peace treaty with the government. They brought two captive Mexican boys for use as a bargaining chip in the negotiations. The Indians were in for quite a surprise, however. Upon entering the town two of the head chiefs, Santos and Buffalo, were immediately seized by the troops and held in confinement. The rest of the Apaches were told that before any peace talks could proceed and the two chiefs released, the captive boys and all stolen property must first be turned over to the military. On December 16, the Indians returned with the Mexican captives and several stolen articles. The two chiefs would eventually be released, although Steen made no treaty due to suspicions of them having a third Mexican boy they had not turned over.[10]

The first actual contact between American troops and Mescalero Apaches in the field occurred in the summer of 1850. On June 10 Major Steen led a detachment of thirty-two troops out of Doña Ana and into the Sacramentos. He suspected there to be some two thousand Mescalero warriors lurking in that vicinity, and, thinking himself greatly outnumbered, returned immediately to Doña Ana. What caused Steen to make this assertion remains unclear, as it was common knowledge that the Mescalero tribe could not muster more than a few hundred warriors; in fact, the entire tribe including women and children did not exceed two thousand.[11]

The Mescaleros were not the only Apaches committing depredations and causing headaches for Maj. Enoch Steen during this time. On February 2, 1850, having just recently returned from a scout of the Sacramento Mountains, Steen received news that a band of Gila Apaches had driven off livestock herds near Doña Ana and in the process had wounded four Mexican herders, one of whom later succumbed to his wounds. At least one Mexican boy had been carried away as a captive by the Indians. Company H, 1st Dragoons, immediately started in pursuit, along with a detachment of 3rd Infantry under the command of Lt. Laurence W. O'Bannon. The pursuit continued for some distance before finally being given up; however, when the men returned to Doña Ana, they had a surprise in store for them.

As soon as the troops had left the post at Doña Ana, thereby rendering the village essentially unprotected, another band of Gila Apaches swept down from the surrounding hills and drove off more livestock without fear of being chased by the troops, who were busy pursuing the decoy band of Apaches. Despite the efforts of Steen's dragoons, both raiding parties escaped successfully into the mountains without any loss. Steen was incensed. Writing about these embarrassing incidents to his commanding officer in Santa Fe, he raised several important points concerning the Apaches, and his concerns would remain relevant throughout the years to come. He wrote:

> I urge upon the commanding officer of the department the necessity of a campaign against these Indians, especially when Indians become so bold [that they] will come in broad daylight within a mile of a U.S. garrison where dragoons are stationed and drive off stock and murder the defenseless herders. . . . I think it becomes necessary to chastise them and this can only be done by a regular organized campaign against them . . . when these Indians start on a marauding expedition they come mounted on their best horses . . . and at the same time have relays waiting for them at 25 or 30 miles distant . . . and thus are mounted on fresh animals and can snap their fingers at us whose animals are broken down by the long chase; thus it is nearly impossible for any dragoons to overtake them and for this I

urge the necessity of an expedition against them. . . . I would suggest
that a depot be selected at or near the copper mines and that that be
established as the base of operations.[12]

Shortly afterward Steen appeased his curiosity on an exploring expedition into the Mimbres River country to reconnoiter a plausible location for
a military post in that vicinity. After returning to Doña Ana on March 23,
he wrote to Santa Fe: "For four days I examined the country about the mines
[Santa Rita del Cobre], in every direction, and in my opinion it is decidedly the best location for a post." Steen noted the site's central location in
the heart of the Apache homelands, the existence of buildings that would
be sufficient to quarter three companies of troops and that could easily be
repaired and made inhabitable in less than one month, and that water and
grazing for the dragoons' horses was "as good if not better than can be
found in any portion of New Mexico." In Steen's estimation, moving the
troops from Doña Ana to the Santa Rita copper mines would save the military department $15,000 annually, while increasing the potential effective-
ness of the troops by placing them directly among the Indians.[13]

Unfortunately for Major Steen his advice went unheeded by his superiors in Santa Fe. At that time, prior to the administration of Col. E. V. Sumner, common practice dictated that all troops be quartered in the Mexican
settlements. No major actions had yet been taken toward building military
forts among the Indians in their homelands. Steen's suggestion marked the
beginning of such a movement in New Mexico, and indeed, within a year
and a half, these changes would be implemented. But in the spring of 1850,
for the time being, the troops would remain stationed at Doña Ana.

In September 1850 Steen reported to the adjutant general in Santa Fe
that his men lacked proper clothing and uniforms, and by that time had
already been waiting nearly two years for replacement provisions. In fact,
many of Steen's troops had threatened to tender their resignation if they
were not promptly supplied with the necessary clothing and equipment.
Farther south, at Paso del Norte, U.S. troops found themselves in an iden-
tical dilemma, according to the commanding officer there. Interestingly,
in his 1850 inspection of New Mexico's military posts, George A. McCall
reported exactly the opposite, noting that at both Doña Ana and Paso del

Norte, "clothing and equipments are of good quality and sufficient for present wants."[14]

A significant event in 1851 brought about the permanent abandonment of Doña Ana as a military station. Not only Doña Ana but also nearly all settlements occupied by American troops were at that time abandoned by the military and the troops placed in more secluded, strategic frontier locations. In the summer of that year Col. Edwin Vose Sumner replaced Col. John Munroe as commander of the 9th Military Department of New Mexico, marking an ideological transformation in territorial military administration.

Colonel Sumner wasted no time in moving the troops away from the towns and villages, one of which he referred to as a "sink of vice and extravagance." The fact that the Mexican towns presented opportunities aplenty for the soldiers to indulge in immoral practices was well known. Col. Roger Jones, the army's adjutant general in Washington, wrote to Sumner shortly after he assumed command of the 9th Military Department and explicitly stated his desires: "There is reason to believe that the stations occupied by the troops in the 9th department, are not the best for the protection of the frontier against the inroads of the Indians. Accordingly . . . you will use a sound discretion in making such changes . . . you may deem necessary and proper." This order, coupled with Sumner's staunch predisposition to remove the troops from such vices, spelled the end of the soldiers' stead at Doña Ana, as well as most other previously occupied towns in New Mexico.[15]

In accordance with this order from higher command, and his own personal views as well, Colonel Sumner ordered the garrisons at Socorro, Doña Ana, El Paso, and San Elizario withdrawn, in addition to several other garrisons in northern New Mexican villages. This action did not pass without harsh criticism from the civil authorities in the territory who openly asserted that removal of these troops from the peoples' side essentially placed them in grave danger. Territorial Governor James S. Calhoun quickly voiced his disapproval of Sumner's actions. "The lives of the citizens of the Territory are in imminent danger if Colonel Sumner insists in carrying out his views to withdraw his main force from the settlements," the governor wrote. Needless to say, the general population backed Calhoun on the issue, and all across the territory people voiced their resentment over the removal of troops to more secluded frontier positions.

Nevertheless, many good reasons existed for placing the soldiers farther away from the Mexican villages along the Rio Grande. George A. McCall, inspecting the military posts in 1850, prophetically alluded to this necessity, writing in his final report that "the only way in which a military force can be advantageously and effectively employed to put an end to Indian spoliations in New Mexico is to post them, not in our settlements or on our borders but in the heart of the Indians, to punish them in their strongholds for the offenses they commit beyond their own boundaries."[16]

Other reasons for the eventual compliance with this recommendation by the military department included the numerous societal vices the towns readily made available to the troops. In each village there could easily be found, if one simply bothered to look, prostitution, gambling, and liquor. This was no secret to the military commanders, and it certainly influenced Colonel Sumner's decision to move his soldiers away from the settlements permanently and station them, in most instances, at locations several days removed from any town or village.

Doña Ana was thus slated for abandonment by the military and the troops would be withdrawn southward to select a site for a new military post. Several locations were considered, all of them along the banks of the Rio Grande between Doña Ana and El Paso. The site for the fort was selected on September 8, 1851, and on the fifteenth of that month Lt. Abraham Buford arrived there with the entirety of the former Doña Ana garrison of troops.[17] The official founding of the Mesilla Valley's new military post, to be called Fort Fillmore in honor of President Millard Fillmore, took place on September 23, 1851, with Lt. Col. Dixon S. Miles of the 3rd Infantry present to take command and oversee construction.[18] For the remainder of the decade, Fort Fillmore would play an important role in affairs throughout the Mesilla Valley.

At the time Fort Fillmore was built, the opposite (or western) side of the Rio Grande still belonged to Mexico. At this time the international boundary commission debacles were in full swing, and the matter had yet to be satisfactorily resolved. Accordingly, Fort Fillmore had to be located on the east bank of the river, therefore limiting the military department's choices of locations at which to build it. Not until the final days of 1853, with the

Figure 5.1. Lt. Col. Dixon S. Miles, 3rd Infantry, was the commanding officer at Fort Fillmore for many years. He is shown here in uniform as a Civil War officer. (Courtesy National Archives)

signing of the Gadsden Purchase, would the riverbank opposite Fort Fillmore revert to U.S. sovereignty. Thus for the first two years of its existence, Fort Fillmore was situated directly on the Mexican border.

Local Mexican citizens from the towns of Doña Ana, Las Cruces, and Mesilla were immediately hired to assist in building the fort, primarily in making adobes, an art in which the U.S. military commanders professed that they were entirely ignorant. Lumber was also used as a building material, being obtained by the soldiers from nearby Soledad Canyon in the Organ Mountains to the east.

Recognizing the potential usefulness of the local citizens as laborers at the post, the commanding officer wrote to Santa Fe requesting permission to hire civilians to work in the post farms, which at that time had not yet been planted. Having arrived at Fort Fillmore on September 23 with his Company K, 3rd Infantry, Miles admitted that the farming operation would likely fail if the soldiers tended the crops themselves, as only the Mexicans were familiar with the successful agrarian techniques employed in that region: "The making and management of acequias [irrigation ditches], all important to the raising of any vegetable or grain, is only understood by those raised in this country." Eventually, the troops were forced to do most of the work themselves, and as a consequence the Fort Fillmore farming experiment proved to be a complete failure by 1852. The Rio Grande, prone to frequent flooding, often ruined the crops, and the soldiers simply did not put forth the amount of time and labor necessary to make the farm a success.

Fort Fillmore, being situated along the eastern bank of the Rio Grande, was not nearly as secluded as many of the other New Mexico military posts during that time. Only a few miles to the north lay Mesilla with a population of nearly two thousand, and Paso del Norte was only about forty miles to the south. Excepting these primary population centers, however, there was little in between. A passerby in 1857 noted that after passing Fort Fillmore en route to El Paso, "the country is uninhabited until you arrive within four miles of the Pass, where you find three or four houses by the road side. There is evidence of former settlements along the valley, but the fields have gone back into a state of nature, the buildings tumbled down, and the acequias filled up, the whole having been laid waste by the Indians some years ago, and never resettled."[19]

One of the largest posts in New Mexico, Fort Fillmore frequently boasted a much larger garrison than its neighboring outposts (Forts Stanton, Webster, and Thorn). In 1857 one onlooker described it as being "a large and pleasant military post, and is intended to garrison a battalion of troops. . . . The buildings are adobes, but comfortable . . . there is also a well-selected post library for the use of officers and men, which is an evidence the government does not overlook the mental wants of her soldiers."[20]

Another observer, the wife of an officer stationed at the fort just prior to the Civil War, voiced much stronger criticism of the post. "Most dreary and uninviting did Fort Fillmore look to us as we approached it," she would later recall, "the stiff line of shabby adobe quarters on three sides of a perfectly bare parade ground suggested neither beauty nor comfort, and for once I felt discouraged when we went in to the forlorn house we were to occupy." After being shown her quarters, these too were found to be woefully inadequate for inhabitation by a lady, but were nevertheless typical of frontier military posts. "It was filthy, too," she continued, "and the room we chose for a bedroom must have been used as a kitchen. The great open fireplace had at least a foot of dirt in it, which had to be dug out with a spade before a fire could be lighted. . . . The woodwork was rough and unpainted; the modern method of oiling pine was not known in army quarters then."[21]

It was upon this important military post that the entire region would rely for support and protection from the plundering bands of Apaches during the next ten years. The fort's role was destined to be unparalleled in this regard, and throughout the 1850s the soldiers at Fort Fillmore constantly busied themselves pursuing hostile Apaches.

The Mescalero Apaches continued to be a burden upon the citizens, from El Paso all the way north to as far as Los Lunas. By the end of the decade several factors would lead to a decline in these habits: treaties, the construction of Fort Stanton, and the Bosque Redondo reservation; but at the time Fort Fillmore came into prominence in 1851, the Mescalero tribe raided the settlements in full force and commanded the immediate attention of the army.

On December 15, 1851, Lieutenant Buford left Fort Fillmore with all available men of Company H, 1st Dragoons, in pursuit of a small band of Mescalero Apaches who had reportedly attacked a government wagon train on the eastern slopes of the Organ Mountains about forty miles from the fort. In doing so, the Indians had made off with forty-four mules and three horses. Buford followed their trail until darkness prevented any further pursuit. The next morning the dragoons continued forward but eventually gave up the chase; the Indians by that time had more than a day head start on the troops and had already reached their mountainous haunts with their plunder. In his report, Buford related several items of interest, most notably recognizing the Apache's uncanny ability to escape their pursuers. "They could travel night and day, and I could follow only by daylight," a frustrated Buford wrote to headquarters, "I had only 20 men in the saddle with me . . . raw recruits that I have never had an opportunity to drill or instruct in the least consequence. With such a command as this I knew it would be folly in the extreme to enter the mountains with the view of carrying on war against the Indians."[22]

Buford cited a circumstance that was all too familiar to military officers throughout New Mexico at that time. The Indians consistently outwitted the military troops at their leisure, and there was often little that the civil or military authorities could do about it aside from venting their frustration in their written reports. Indian agent John Greiner, writing in March 1852, expressed his views on the apparent hopelessness of the Indian situation in the territory:

> There are 92,000 [estimated] Indians in this territory . . . we have not 1000 troops here under Col. Sumner to manage them. Our troops are of no earthly account. They cannot catch a single Indian. A dragoon mounted will weigh 225 pounds. Their horses are all poor as carrion. The Indians have nothing but their bow and arrows and their ponies are fleet as deer. Cipher it up. Heavy dragoons on poor horses, who know nothing of the country, sent after Indians who are at home anywhere and who always have some hours start, how long will it take to catch them? So far, although several expeditions have started after them, not a single Indian has been caught![23]

The Mesilla Valley region was not at all immune to the shortcomings cited by agent Greiner. With Apache raiding continuing virtually unhindered, the military finally deemed it necessary to establish another post, in addition to Fort Fillmore, that would hopefully act as a more effective deterrent to Indian raiding. On December 28, 1851, Bvt. Maj. Israel B. Richardson left Fort Fillmore with sixty-seven troops of Company K, 3rd Infantry, and marched for the old copper mines at Santa Rita del Cobre, west of the Rio Grande valley and in the heart of Gila Apache country. The fort, one of the first in New Mexico to be built directly among the natives in their homelands, utilized preexisting adobe buildings at the mines, the same buildings that had been used by John Russell Bartlett during his international boundary surveys of 1850–51. On January 23, 1852, the troops officially established their post at Santa Rita and work began on improving the dilapidated structures for habitation. Originally known as Cantonment Dawson, the name would soon be changed to Fort Webster.[24]

Although located a considerable distance from Fort Fillmore and the citizens of the Mesilla Valley, Fort Webster would play a critical role in Indian affairs throughout the ensuing two years; in conjunction with Fillmore, it would serve to minimize some of the Apache raiding that had been so prevalent during prior years. Because it was located in such close proximity to the Gila Apache homelands, Fort Webster would be the scene of numerous encounters between the white men and the Indians. Major Richardson had barely arrived at the copper mines when he almost immediately found himself and his soldiers in an unenviable predicament. Several of the Apache chiefs approached the military camp and received a less than amiable reception from the commanding officer. After being asked to leave, Richardson's troops fired upon them with their muskets and mountain howitzer, wounding several. From this point on, relations between the two parties would be tense.

A significant change in government administration in the territory occurred on September 13, 1852, when William Carr Lane arrived in Santa Fe to assume the role of territorial governor in place of the deceased James S. Calhoun. Almost immediately a feud developed between Lane and Col. Edwin V. Sumner, military commander of New Mexico, who had been acting as self-proclaimed governor following Calhoun's untimely death.[25] Governor Lane, during his relatively short tenure as territorial governor, played a critical role in the territory's Indian affairs. He promulgated numerous treaties, one of which was negotiated and finalized at Fort Webster though never ratified by Congress.

Despite the change in leadership in Santa Fe, the Apaches remained restless and continued, whenever possible and convenient, to raid the Mesilla

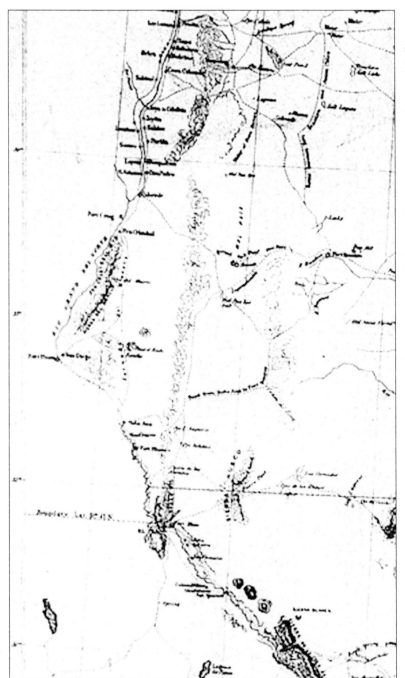

Map 5.1. Area of operations, Apache Country, 1857. (Courtesy New Mexico State University Library, Archives and Special Collections, G4030.1857.US 1900z)

Valley settlements. One of the early probate judges for Doña Ana County, Richard Campbell, at one point became frustrated with the Apaches and the continuous failure of the military to catch them. He issued a call to arms among the locals in Las Cruces, ordering that "all able-bodied men of Las Cruces capable of bearing arms . . . appear in front of the office of the Probate Clerk at 5 o'clock of the evening of the 3d of July inst. with such arms and accoutrements as they may have in their possession for the purpose of taking into consideration the propriety of forming an armed patrol for the protection against Indian depredations."[26]

While the presence of Fort Webster in the heart of Gila Apache country partially inhibited the tribe's raiding, there was no such military post in the homelands of the Mescaleros to act in a similar manner. Consequently, a large number of depredations continued to be carried out by that tribe. In February 1853, nine Mescaleros visited Lieutenant Colonel Miles at Fort Fillmore following an attack that had been made on them by the people of Doña Ana. By all available information the attack had been unprovoked, as the victims had been living peaceably in the area and trading with the Mexicans.[27] Miles accompanied the Indians back to Doña Ana, where, by his urging, the residents gave the Mescaleros various presents as recompense for the woman who had been murdered in the attack. While all seemed to have come out aright from this incident, the good tidings between the two races would be short-lived as usual. Several months later, in August 1853, the Mescaleros reciprocated by killing two Mexican men who had left Doña Ana for a salt lake, some eighty miles northeast of the village in the Tularosa Basin. Rumors abounded that these individuals had secretly taken whiskey with them to trade to the Apaches. The two were never again heard from, and thus was avenged the murder of the Mescalero woman at Doña Ana. This pattern, an eye-for-an-eye mentality that influenced the actions of the Apaches and the Mexicans alike, continued for many years and claimed the lives of countless individuals on both sides.[28]

Army officers at Fort Fillmore investigated the incident involving the two missing Mexicans, but to little avail. On August 18, within days of having received reports that the men were missing, ten Mescaleros came into Doña Ana, apparently unaware of the circumstances. A detachment of dragoons from Fort Fillmore was sent to the town, and afterward the Indians had a meeting with Lieutenant Colonel Miles and Indian agent Michael

Steck, but the Mescaleros did not divulge any information relative to the fate of the two Mexicans. Miles and Steck, both of whom were less than amused by the Indians' determination to withhold information, sent a messenger to their chief, Santos, informing him that "if he did not come in at once, we would come out and bring him in, and before starting, would hang those of his tribe we had."[29] Not surprisingly, Santos failed to appear at Doña Ana, and the incident finally blew over.

Col. J. K. F. Mansfield inspected Fort Fillmore in the autumn of 1853, reporting the post to be in a satisfactory state of neatness and that "the quarters of this post for both officers and men are the best in the Territory." Furthermore, the troops stationed there appeared to be well disciplined by their commanding officers. At that time four companies occupied the post: Company D, 2nd Dragoons, with sixty-one men; Company C, 3rd Infantry, with sixty-nine men; Company A, 3rd Infantry, with sixty-four men; and Company E, 3rd Infantry, with seventy-five men, bringing the total available force at Fort Fillmore to 269 soldiers plus eight commissioned officers. Mansfield praised Major Backus, the commanding officer, noting him to be "peculiarly well fitted for the command where so much discretion, as well as firmness, is necessary, within two miles of a Mexican population directly on the opposite side of the river at Mesilla."[30]

The conditions at Fort Fillmore represented the exception rather than the norm in New Mexico. Only a few months earlier, in April 1853, Lieutenant Colonel Miles complained that he had only thirty-five mounted dragoons available for duty, along with two mountain howitzers, but no powder to shoot them with. Shortcomings such as these, a lack of mounts for dragoons and a general lack of necessary supplies, continued to plague the army in New Mexico for many years. Mansfield himself referenced this, noting in his final report that "the supply of dragoon horses are quite too limited, being but 383 horses to 483 rank and file."[31]

On August 21, 1853, several Gila Apaches, led by their chief Cuchillo Negro, went into Mesilla and requested to make a treaty allowing them to trade with the surrounding population. The prefect of Mesilla, Domingo Cubero, vehemently opposed their professions of friendship and posted notices throughout the town stating that any person caught selling liquor or merchandise to the Indians would be fined twenty-five pesos. Undaunted, the small band of Apaches returned two more times to make similar requests, but in each instance were refused by the prefect and sent on their way. This is an interesting occurrence, for rarely did an Indian tribe approach a civilian population requesting a treaty; legally, these types of negotiations were limited to officials of the federal government. It is therefore not surprising that the Mesilla prefect so quickly denied Cuchillo Negro's requests.[32]

In December 1854, owing to friction between American and Mexican officials in the vicinity, a detachment of thirty-nine troops from Fort Fillmore was stationed in the small village of Santo Tomás, opposite the Rio Grande about three miles south of Mesilla, where they took up quarters in several small adobe buildings. The location was optimal because of its location on the Mesilla–El Paso wagon road, where it could provide protection to travelers and citizens from Apache raiding.[33] At any rate, the post at Santo Tomás would be short-lived; Miles ordered the detachment to return to Fort Fillmore on February 9, 1855.

In regard to relations with the troublesome Mescalero Apaches, 1855 proved to be an important year. In January an expedition of several hundred troops entered the Sacramento Mountains, where they fought the Indians at the mouth of James Canyon on the Rio Peñasco. The skirmish resulted in the death of three soldiers, one of them a highly regarded officer, Capt. Henry W. Stanton.[34] In April, with the death of Captain Stanton fresh on the minds of the military department, Miles again took the field with three hundred men of his 3rd Infantry in an attempt to vanquish Stanton's death. Stumbling upon a large Mescalero camp in Dog Canyon, on the western slopes of the Sacramento Mountains south of present-day Alamogordo, a headman of the tribe approached Miles and requested permission to make a treaty. Miles seems to have taken the camp almost entirely by surprise. "What a beautiful chance for a fight," he wrote, "the troops will never get such another. But they [Mescaleros] have met me in faith trusting to my honor." The colonel did not, however, conduct any treaty negotiations owing to the absence of several important chiefs, but he did promise to relay their desire for peace to both Governor Meriwether and Michael Steck, the Mescalero agent at Fort Thorn.[35]

Within a month of this expedition, the military department had decided upon the location of a permanent military post in the heart of Mescalero country, to be built on the banks of the Rio Bonito. The post would be named Fort Stanton, in honor of the recently fallen Captain Stanton.

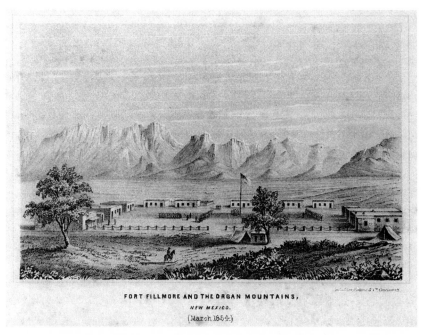

FORT FILLMORE AND THE ORGAN MOUNTAINS,
NEW MEXICO.
(March 1854.)

Figure 5.2. Fort Fillmore, looking east, as it appeared in 1854. The Organ Mountains are seen in the background. (Courtesy New Mexico State University Library, Archives and Special Collections, 03390019)

From this point forward, relations with the Mescalero Apaches veered in an entirely different direction. No longer could the tribe raid the Rio Grande settlements and escape to their mountainous haunts without risk of military action. The establishment of Fort Stanton in May 1855 can be viewed as the single most important action taken by the military department in preventing depredations by that tribe, and the post would continue to play a prominent role in Apache affairs for decades to come.

With the Mescalero Apaches having an incentive to cease their raiding habits, attention would turn again to the Gila Apaches west of the Rio Grande. In November 1855, a small band of that tribe raided Mesilla, in the process killing two Mexican herders and stealing several head of cattle before making their escape toward Cooke's Spring fifty miles to the west. According to Indian agent Michael Steck, this had purportedly been carried out as an act of revenge for some prior action taken by the Mexicans at Mesilla, the exact nature of which is not stated in the reports. This and several

Figure 5.3. Fort Fillmore as it appears today. Nothing remains but a few scattered adobe bricks. This view is looking east, and roughly corresponds to the view presented in the original 1854 drawing in figure 5.2. The Organ Mountains, not visible here, are directly behind the trees in the background. The flagpoles are located where the enlisted men's barracks were, on the southernmost side of the fort. The original parade ground was located where the grass is, behind the flagpoles and the metal building. The site is located on private property. (Photograph by author)

other raids in rapid succession during the latter months of 1855 resulted in an expedition into Gila Apache country led by Col. Joseph H. Eaton, the commanding officer at Fort Thorn.[36] Like most army excursions during this time, that of Eaton would prove to be fruitless; he returned shortly afterward to his post with nothing to report.[37]

Following the establishment of Fort Thorn in 1854 along the Rio Grande near present-day Hatch, New Mexico, Michael Steck came onto the southern New Mexico scene as an important figure, and would remain so well into the Civil War years. Steck was formally appointed Indian agent for New Mexico by Commissioner of Indian Affairs George W. Manypenny on May 9, 1854.[38] Steck, who would serve as agent for both the Mescalero and Gila Apache tribes, established his agency near Fort Thorn, thus locating himself only a short distance north of the Mesilla Valley and making himself available to nearby residents whenever necessary. Throughout his many years as Apache agent, Steck would prove to be an indispensable person, consistently making wise choices in regard to treatment of the Indians and acting equitably toward Indians and Americans alike. In many instances his quick, calm, and decisive actions prevented major outbreaks of hostility.[39] He would prove to be among the most effective, well-liked individuals to ever hold the position of Apache agent, commanding the sincere respect of the Indians with whom he worked.

On October 18, 1855, eighteen mules were stolen from Frank Fletcher's Mesilla Valley ranch located between Las Cruces and Doña Ana. Naturally in such cases, the Apaches received blame for the act. In this instance, however, the charge seems to have been misattributed. Shortly after the incident occurred, several Mescalero chiefs approached Fort Fillmore with friendly intentions, apparently unaware that the thefts had taken place and that their tribe stood as the accused. Colonel Miles informed the Apache leaders of the recent happenings, ordering them to return the stolen stock immediately or face military action. They claimed to know nothing of the thefts, but nevertheless, in order to avert any potential hostilities, agreed to send out a small party to search for the animals. Eventually, they succeeded in recovering all but four of the stolen mules and returned them to Fletcher's ranch.

The mules had been recovered not from another Mescalero band, but from Mexican citizens residing at Manzano, a small town east of Los Lunas. Miles himself admitted the mistake in blaming the Mescaleros for the depredation, stating, "From the direction of the trail and the place [camp] found, I believe [the Manzano Mexicans] to be guilty. I do not myself believe the Mescaleros stole the mules, or had a knowledge of the theft until I informed them—the chiefs deserve credit for the zeal displayed in recapturing them and shows most conclusively their desire to keep unbroken the treaty."[40]

This incident illustrates the propensity of the civil and military officials to immediately blame the Apaches for all crimes committed in southern New Mexico. However, this was sometimes not the case, as evidenced by the aforementioned situation. This failure of the Anglo-Americans to distinguish between guilty and innocent Apache bands often resulted in increased tension between the two cultures. In this instance the Mescaleros' friendly behavior and willingness to recover the stolen stock can perhaps be explained by the fact that only a few months earlier Fort Stanton had been

*Figure 5.4. Apache
Indian agent Michael
Steck. (Courtesy Center
for Southwest Research,
University Librar-
ies, University of New
Mexico. Keleher Collec-
tion ZIM CSWR PICT
000-742-0143)*

established in the their homelands; thus can be seen the almost immediate effect the new post had upon their behavior.

On March 8, 1857, following two recent failed excursions into the Apache country, Lieutenant Gibbs rode out of Fort Fillmore for a third time with a detachment of sixteen soldiers, pursuing a band of Gila Apaches who had run off several head of livestock belonging to Deputy Surveyor John W. Garretson near Robledo. Following the Indians' trail west for about fifty miles, the troops managed to catch up with them several miles past Cooke's Spring. The Indians, numbering seven in all, were immediately fired upon, and three of them were wounded in the first volley. As Gibbs approached the Apaches, the chief charged toward him and inflicted a wound with his lance, causing Gibbs to fall from his horse. A desperate struggle ensued. By the time he fell dead, the Apache chief had been shot ten times.

Gibbs, his lance wound having forced him to dismount, offered his horse to Corporal Collins who pursued the remaining three Apaches into the hills. Returning half an hour later, Collins reported that six of the Indians had been killed. A seventh one had been severely wounded and, although not captured, would likely perish. An express rider was sent posthaste back to Fort Fillmore to bring the assistant surgeon to care for Lieutenant Gibbs's wound. Shortly thereafter the detachment returned to Fort Fillmore, finally able to report something in the way of success against the troublesome Apaches.[41] The slain chief was thought to be Itán, although the accuracy of this assumption has never been fully determined. Instances in which the Apaches were caught by surprise and defeated were incredibly rare in the annals of southern New Mexico history, as they rarely acted as carelessly as this small band of seven apparently did.

THE MESILLA GUARD

The years 1857–58 witnessed the raising of an armed militia at Mesilla, known as the Mesilla Guard, to help combat Apache raiding in the vicinity. The area had been under the jurisdiction of the United States for ten years now, and still the Apaches plundered and pillaged the countryside with surprising impunity. The presence of troops at several area posts, specifically Forts Fillmore, Stanton, and Thorn, seemed to do little to deter the Indians from stealing along the Rio Grande. By 1857 a series of events had occurred that led to the people of Mesilla forming a civilian volunteer regiment dedicated solely to the task of chastising and punishing the Apaches.

In August 1857 there were thirty-eight Apache women and children being held captive at Fort Thorn, not far north of the Mesilla Valley settlements. During their first two weeks of captivity, five succumbed to illness. The commanding officer at Fort Thorn recommended that the prisoners be transferred to Fort Fillmore, where malaria was less prevalent, in order that further deaths might be averted. On August 16 troops escorted the remaining thirty-three Indians down the river to Fillmore, where they continued to perish at an alarming rate. Those still living made an escape attempt on the night of August 23, heading eastward into the Organ Mountains and scattering to avoid capture by the troops. Lieutenant Colonel Miles, commanding at Fort Fillmore, blamed negligence of the guard for their successful escape, although the report mentioned that the guardsmen, pitying the Indians for their desperate condition, might have been purposefully negligent.[42]

Not long afterward, in February 1858, some of these same Mescalero Indians, having returned to their respective bands, camped within about three miles of Doña Ana and were living peaceably there. This was the first instance in which the Mesilla Guard would make their appearance. Ignoring the fact that this particular band of Apaches was innocent of any wrongdoing and camped there solely for the purpose of trading with the inhabitants of Doña Ana, the Mexican volunteers attacked them, killing three. They then rode into the plaza, where more Indians were found bartering with the townspeople. The Mesilla Guard began shooting these Indians "indiscriminately," killing a total of eight or nine and wounding several more; among those killed was Chief Shawono.[43] Historian Edwin R. Sweeney appropriately observed that "this pernicious attack would prove to be a foreshadowing of relations between the inhabitants of Mesilla and Doña Ana and the Apaches in the years to come. It was one of the most fearful atrocities in the history of southern New Mexican relations between Apaches and Whites."[44] Rafael Ruelas, prefect of the county and a resident of Mesilla, did not sympathize with the Apaches. In response to a terse inquiry from Dr. Steck, Ruelas wrote, "it seems very strange that the Indians are at peace with the people of Doña Ana . . . yet they are stealing from the inhabitants of La Mesilla. In other words, they are at peace with one side of the river and war with the other. . . . Now if you in Doña Ana begin to protect the thieving Indians when they have broken every peace treaty they have made . . . we do not esteem you in Doña Ana [for] treating us [in Mesilla] as savages and barbarians for having done our duty."[45] There appears to have been a serious point of contention between the residents of those two towns in regard to their respective relationships with the Mescalero Apaches at that particular point in time, with the Mesilleros ultimately opting to take matters into their own hands.

Whether the residents of Mesilla felt justified in their actions or not would prove to be inconsequential. This treacherous and unprovoked attack guaranteed an immediate response from the Mescaleros, who seldom failed to avenge such an atrocity. Within a few days more than one hundred warriors from that tribe, led by Chief Gomez, had congregated in the vicinity of Doña Ana. Lieutenant Colonel Miles sent a messenger to the Indian agency at Fort Thorn asking agent Michael Steck, perhaps the only man these Mescaleros trusted, to come to Doña Ana to "pacify the Indians." Exhibiting his remarkable capabilities as an Indian agent, Steck succeeded in convincing the Mescaleros to return to their homelands and await the decision of a U.S. District Court on the matter. The agent informed the Indians that if they went into Mesilla to avenge the deaths of their kin, the troops at Fort Fillmore would "carry the war into their country."[46]

Miles fully expected an attack on Mesilla. Writing to the assistant adjutant general, he warned, "From the numerous signal fires around the mountains . . . [there is] not a doubt but the Apaches are collecting to take revenge, and a terrible bloody retribution will follow . . . this act will bring the entire Mescalero nation into active hostility."[47] Indeed, under normal circumstances, this is precisely what would have transpired; Steck's presence was the only factor that prevented it.

Writing to the prefect of Doña Ana County, Rafael Ruelas, Lieutenant Colonel Miles urged the citizens of Mesilla to return a Mescalero boy who had been taken captive during the attack at Doña Ana. Miles warned of the retaliatory measures that could be expected if they failed to return the boy to his tribe. "It would be well for you [the prefect] to warn the inhabitants of the impending storm . . . that will break soon over them," Miles wrote. However, the army officer also pledged his support to the residents of Doña Ana County in general: "At any alarm of danger I will come to your assistance with whatever troops I can spare from this fort—you know I have but two foot companies . . . I can defend, but I cannot pursue with any probability of success in overtaking."[48] As was so often the case, the garrison at Fort Fillmore was depleted, and as Miles revealed in his letter, there were not enough troops at the fort to effectively pursue or chastise such a large band of Indians.

Gen. John Garland, commanding the military department, was not amused by the actions of the citizens of Mesilla. It was supposed to be the responsibility of the military to handle the Indians, and officials in Santa Fe heavily frowned upon any independent action taken by civilians. Garland threatened to permanently abandon Fort Fillmore, the only source of military protection in the Mesilla Valley, if any further attacks occurred. His threat, so pertinent to the general welfare of the people, did not go unnoticed. People living in Mesilla wasted no time in drafting a petition to Garland requesting that he reconsider his proposal to abandon Fort Fillmore. The people, as an excuse for having raised their own volunteer regiment, cited the fact that no mounted troops occupied Fort Fillmore, and accordingly they saw fit to organize their own primitive cavalry regiment "to pursue and chastise the marauding Indians." Furthermore, the Mesilleros "felt it imperatively necessary to form a company of mounted men." They claimed the Doña Ana incident to be "grossly exaggerated and false," asserting that both Miles and Steck had submitted falsified and embellished reports. Their final plea to Garland read: "There is no county in the territory more exposed, or more in want of military protection than Doña Ana . . . if you adhere to your intention of evacuating Fort Fillmore, the result will be disastrous not only to the residents of the county but to the travelers over the roads."[49]

If Garland would agree to reinforce Fort Fillmore with a company of mounted troops, the Mesilla residents promised to disband their volunteer regiment. The Mesilleros, however, did not stand in any position to attempt to negotiate with the commanding officer of the military department; their actions blatantly and unquestionably contradicted what was considered lawful behavior on the part of the territory's citizens. General Garland, while ultimately deciding against the abandonment of Fort Fillmore, warned the people of Mesilla that "those of our citizens who perpetrate acts of violence and outrage . . . have no claim to the protection of the military and will receive none."[50]

In an attempt to further explain the actions taken by the Mesilla Guard, the alcalde sent a letter to Colonel Miles claiming that several skulls of dead Mexicans had been placed atop a large pole near the town, probably in an attempt to frighten the inhabitants. The alcalde requested that Miles send troops to find the guilty parties for this misdeed, but he declined. The army officer never investigated, so whether or not there was any truth behind the claim of the Apaches having committed this atrocity remained undetermined.

According to Miles the Mesilla Guard was composed of approximately one hundred men, all landholders from Mesilla and the immediate vicinity.

However, if these individuals chose not to actively serve in the regiment, they could send one of their peons or laborers in their place. These peons, who in reality constituted almost the entirety of the Mesilla Guard, were mostly either deserters from the Mexican army or laborers who had run away from ranches in Mexico. In the attack on the Mescaleros at Doña Ana, those familiar with the incident believed that only about five actual land-holders played an active role. However, this would be of no consequence whatsoever if the Indians did attack the town, as they would make no dis-tinction between landholders and peons. "Should this independent action of the inhabitants of Mesilla continue," wrote Lieutenant Colonel Miles, "the Indians will to a certainty unite . . . by wiping this town out."[51]

Lt. J. W. Alley of the 3rd Infantry, also stationed at Fort Fillmore, con-ducted a further investigation of the attack made by the Mesilla Guard. In his final report Alley described the general nature of the militia: "This Mexican band is held in high esteem by the people of Mesilla; a party seems to be constantly held in readiness to pursue Indians, retake stolen property from them, and when not employed on active service of this nature, en-joying certain civil privileges in that town; they are known as the 'Mesilla Guard.'"[52]

Following the attack at Doña Ana and the widespread pandemonium that resulted, local military officers believed that the pointlessness and fu-tility of taking such action had been fully impressed upon the citizens at Mesilla. "I do not think [we] will ever hear again from the action of their volunteer company," Miles predicted.[53] But this would not be so. The army's threat of abandoning Fort Fillmore, the tense situation arising when over one hundred Apaches congregated in the valley prepared to lay the town of Mesilla to waste, and the general discontent throughout the territory with the Mesilla Guard's actions, did nothing in the way of deterring them from taking further unprovoked action against the Indians.

On April 17, 1858, the Mesilla Guard, consisting of thirty-six men led by Juan Ortega, openly attacked yet another Mescalero Apache camp, this time near Fort Thorn some forty miles to the north. The camp, consisting entirely of peaceful Indians who were living in that vicinity and drawing rations from Steck at his agency, were caught completely unsuspecting. The Guard swept down upon the camp, killing seven and wounding three more;

the murdered Apaches were later buried behind the Fort Thorn cemetery.[54] No viable motive could ever be ascertained for the attack.

This time the culprits did not make it far before being apprehended. Lt. William H. Wood of the 3rd Infantry, assisted by Lt. George Washington Howland of the Regiment of Mounted Rifles, arrested the entire group of thirty-six men about half a mile from the fort. The attack had occurred so close to Fort Thorn that not only the gunshots but also the cries of the Apaches could be heard by the troops inside the walls of the post. The guilty parties were subsequently confined in the guardhouse to await trial.

Steck, who had been absent on official business at the time of the attack, arrived at Fort Thorn the following day and learned of what had happened. Steck praised the two army officers: "The conduct of Lieut. Wood merits the highest praise. But for his promptness and energy the bloody work might have continued much longer. In fifteen minutes from the time he received information of what was doing he rushed into the midst of the outlaws, drew his pistol and demanded of their leader immediate surrender. The prompt action of this officer has had a most excellent effect upon the Indians, many of whom saw him make the capture. . . . So far as I can learn there had been no cause for this cowardly and murderous attack. . . . This is the same party of men who committed the outrageous murders in Doña Ana."[55]

Another unlikely source provides additional insight on this attack at Fort Thorn. Lt. William W. Averell, an army officer on active duty at the time, was passing through the area transporting money to the paymaster at Forts Bliss and Fillmore. He arrived at Fort Thorn the day after the attack, where he found "intense excitement prevailing." The Mexican prisoners had been "brought into the garrison, disarmed and placed under a strong guard." Parties were then sent out to retrieve the bodies, and the three wounded Indians were placed in the hospital at Fort Thorn. In addition to these three, Averell feared that more might have been killed or injured in the melee and had not yet been found. "Some of the Indians who had escaped under pursuit to the river bottom to hide among the trees and shrubbery were yet unaccounted for," wrote Averell, "and it was feared that some of them had been wounded or killed. One of the women had been pursued and killed within five hundred yards of the Fort to which she was running for refuge . . . the boy that was killed was a favorite of the garrison, and after killing him the Mexicans had ridden around his body and expended some of their surplus ammunition by shooting his head to pieces."[56]

The soldiers at Fort Thorn had been well acquainted with this particular band of Indians, who had been living in that area on peaceful terms. Many of them, including the murdered boy referred to as a "favorite of the garrison," were held in high regard by the troops for their peaceable disposition. In his report Lieutenant Wood wrote, "This affair is but a repetition of the horrible massacre perpetrated at Doña Ana . . . these Indians for the last four or five months have been at peace . . . have been daily in and about this garrison, quiet and well behaved and I sincerely believe have given no cause for this cowardly outrage."[57]

Consequently, "Lieutenant Wood was obliged to exercise immediate watchfulness to prevent the soldiers from putting the Mexican fiends to death. We were all half inclined to think that he had made a mistake in capturing them when he had the chance to wipe them off the face of the earth. Had the enormity of the outrage been fully known to the soldiers when they captured them, there would have been no subsequent proceedings in which these miscreants would have felt any interest, and the government would have been saved some expense." The following morning Averell carried Lieutenant Wood's official report to Santa Fe, where Judge Kirby Benedict promptly issued a warrant for the arrest of the thirty-six Guardsmen. Not long afterward, the prisoners were transported under a heavy guard consisting of forty-four men of the Regiment of Mounted Rifles to Fort Craig, and then on to Socorro where they would await their day in court.[58]

All thirty-six men accused of murdering the seven Mescaleros appeared in a Socorro courtroom on October 12, 1858, for trial in the case *United States vs. Juan Ortega et al.*[59] Their confinement in prison had been brief, their families having collected the $5,000 necessary to bail them out until the trial date.[60] In a case such as this, the victims being Apaches and the jury being composed of the guilty party's peers, there existed little chance that justice would prevail. This was precisely the case; the jury wasted little time deliberating, promptly acquitting the members of the Mesilla Guard of all charges and setting them at liberty. Many of those who had been present that fateful day at Fort Thorn and witnessed the actions of these men were appalled by the outcome. One man who sided with the Mexicans in this matter, interestingly enough, was territorial Governor Abraham Rencher, who declared the attack to be "worthy of imitation."[61] Lieutenant Averell described the trial in succinct detail:

> Judge [Kirby] Benedict held the court . . . the court in session was something worthy of contemplation. The public interest reached its climax when the case of our prisoners was closed, and the Judge charged the jury with sonorous declamation, "Senores Caballeros," and a dozen Mexicans arose to their more or less bare feet from the jury benches. . . . All wore the serape. . . . The cigarillo solaced their arduous mental strain. They could have said unanimously to the prisoners, "Estamos hermanos" (we are brothers), and appearances would have sustained the statement. . . . The Judge went on to state that there was no doubt that the crime of murder had been committed, it was not denied and there was no defense nor mitigation offered. . . . The Judge called upon them to do their duty as citizens of the greatest republic on earth, and to show that they themselves were worthy and capable of self-government. . . . The Senores Caballeros endured it patiently and shuffled out when it was concluded and returned as soon as they had smoked another cigarillo with a verdict of "not guilty," and the prisoners were discharged.[62]

Averell's description of events in the Socorro courtroom that day is indicative of the times: the men in the jury hated the Apaches just as much as the men accused of killing them, and there was never any doubt that the jury would acquit them of the charges. With this the matter came to a close. Following the acquittal, many feared that the Apaches might attempt to enact their own form of justice and begin attacking the settlements; the military stationed small detachments at several locations for a brief period in order to protect the people in the event that the Indians did in fact seek revenge.[63]

Amazingly, having made two unprovoked attacks on peaceful bands of Apaches, and having gotten in trouble with the civil and military officials on both occasions, the Mesilla Guard failed to retire to their homes and hang up their arms. In March 1860, agent Steck reported that the Guard remained active; they had recently chased a band of Apaches westward into the Florida Mountains and then crossed the international boundary south into Mexico. The Guardsmen, numbering about thirty according to Steck, thought better of their plight when they suddenly stumbled upon a camp of some 380 Apaches in northern Chihuahua, easily enough to annihilate the small group of Mexicans. They returned to the Mesilla Valley, where they went to Fort Fillmore and requested that troops be sent out, but their pleas fell upon deaf ears at the post.[64]

In May 1861, with a Confederate invasion imminent and widespread paranoia prevalent throughout the area, the Mesilla Guard still clung to life. The townspeople held a meeting during which they authorized Capt. George Frazier "to raise a company of rangers to chastise the Apaches for their late outrages. The command at Fort Fillmore makes a liberal offer of ammunitions and provisions to the company."[65] In the fall of 1861, after Colonel Baylor's Confederates had taken possession of Mesilla and made it their seat of operations in "Arizona," another volunteer regiment, consisting of two units, was mustered to protect the citizens and alleviate the Confederate troops from some of these duties. The *Mesilla Times* reported on a meeting during which Colonel Baylor commissioned Isaac Langston as captain of one company, and Anastacio Barela and Pablo Melendres as co-captains of the other company.[66]

It should be noted, however, that these last two Mesilla volunteer regiments raised by Baylor cannot technically be considered the original Mesilla Guard. That regiment, first raised in 1857, had consisted solely of civilian peons commissioned to fight in place of their owners. These final two regiments, raised during the onset of the tumultuous Civil War period in New Mexico, were not created by an independent action of the citizens, but rather out of military necessity due to the events occurring at that time. One of the two 1861 Mesilla volunteer regiments was led by an Anglo-American (Langston), and many of the men fighting were Confederates of similar ethnic descent.[67]

In some ways one cannot blame the citizens for finally taking matters into their own hands; after all, the military had been permanently stationed in their backyard for close to ten years and little had been done to deter the Indians from raiding the towns. However, where the Mesilleros went wrong was not necessarily in the fact that they raised their own militia, but in the fact that they acted haphazardly and irresponsibly, perpetrating numerous atrocities against peaceful bands of Apaches rather than hostile bands.

Were it not for these deplorable actions, the Guard might have been viewed as a success and perhaps even as a model for neighboring towns wishing to discourage Indian raiding.

On July 17, 1861, only a few days before the invasion of the Confederate army and subsequent abandonment of Fort Fillmore, Apaches attacked the fort's hay camp, in the process killing one local Mexican and taking another boy captive. The following day, July 18, the Indians struck again, this time at the small village of Santo Tomás three miles south of Mesilla. In this raid, two more people were killed. Later that evening, the same band of Apaches descended upon the town for a second time and killed two Mexican sheepherders before running off a sizable portion of the herd. All of this occurred within a short distance of the Fort Fillmore garrison, and yet somehow the military never learned of the circumstances in time to take action.

The editors of the *Mesilla Times* were less than amused by the ease with which the Apaches murdered the citizens and made their escape. "These sheep were stolen and men murdered within a mile and a half of a company of U.S. infantry," read the newspaper's column, "and within five miles were eleven companies of Regulars both mounted and foot."[68] The reason for this apparent negligence by the Union garrison at Fort Fillmore, while never actually stated, likely related to the fact that the Confederate army was fast approaching from the south and preparations were being made to resist any attack that might be made on the fort itself. In the eyes of the commander at Fort Fillmore, and much to the chagrin of the locals, the threat posed by the Confederate army far exceeded the importance of quelling Apache raids.

The same issue of the *Mesilla Times* addressed recent Apache depredations and observed that the problem had consistently worsened during the preceding months. According to the newspaper, the Apaches became bolder with each passing day, the troops having been withdrawn from many of the more secluded military posts and congregated at Forts Fillmore and Craig along the Rio Grande. The *Times*, speaking no doubt for the majority of the Mesilla Valley's citizens, expressed frustration with the general nature of things in the summer of 1861:

> The rumors of Apache depredations and of Apache murders come to us from all sides and quarters. They . . . have been allowed to go on unchecked for so long a space of time, they grow bolder

and bolder at each successive stage. They think they have driven off the Overland Mail and compelled the United States troops to abandon their forts and leave the country. They have compelled the abandonment of mines and mining districts, of ranches and whole valleys, and nothing seems to limit their daring. They will soon get some understanding of the war movements now going on amid the whites, and when they once appreciate these difficulties their operations will be incessant and unrestrained, and a few weeks will wipe out the progress of civilization of years. The situation of Arizona is gloomy in the extreme.[69]

The prediction that the Apaches would learn of the U.S. Army's dilemma in resisting the invading enemy force proved entirely correct. The Apaches watched from the nearby hills as the military department abandoned its frontier posts and removed the troops to the Rio Grande valley. In southern Arizona, Forts Buchanan and Breckenridge were almost simultaneously abandoned in the summer of 1861, leaving that area entirely destitute of military protection.[70] Fort McLane, near the Santa Rita copper mines, was likewise abandoned and the troops concentrated at Fort Fillmore. To the Apaches, this large-scale movement of troops out of their homelands was perceived as a surrender by the U.S. government. Apache agent Michael Steck, in an 1863 report to the commissioner of Indian affairs, noted, "The condition of the territory shows that it has not fully recovered from the effects of the Texan invasion. During the occupation by the insurgents all intercourse with many of the Indian tribes was entirely broken up. The military force was necessarily withdrawn from the frontiers to defend the territory against the invaders, and the Indians were thus left without the controlling influence of its presence. This at once led to evil consequences, which still exist to a greater or less extent today."[71] The Apaches thought they had finally driven the white man out of their country and would no longer have to fear being pursued or engaged in battle by the soldiers. Consequently, Apache raiding during this brief period increased dramatically, and the residents of the Rio Grande settlements could do little more than attempt to defend themselves to the best of their ability.

Fort Fillmore was abandoned and its entire garrison captured by the invading Confederate army in July 1861. This left the Mesilla Valley under the complete control of the Confederate army and their commander, Col. John R. Baylor. This officer promptly established a Confederate government in Mesilla, naming himself governor and Mesilla the capital of the "Confederate Territory of Arizona." In taking this action, Baylor also assumed the responsibility of protecting the people from the Apaches, something that would prove to be no small task, even for a veteran frontier Indian fighter like Baylor. Matters would not get any better under the Confederate governor; Apache raiding continued almost unimpeded. On September 30, five Apache warriors swooped down upon the village of Picacho, north of Mesilla, and stole some two hundred head of cattle. "To show the audacity of these Indians, we will add that the stock was stolen within five miles of a camp of 650 soldiers," lamented the local newspaper.[72]

In October 1861, three months after Baylor took possession of the area, the staunchly pro-South *Mesilla Times* wrote, "Nineteen Twentieths of the Territory of Arizona is under their [Apaches] undisputed control."[73] In response to this, the *Santa Fe Gazette,* a pro-North newspaper, sarcastically remarked that "one-twentieth of the Territory therefore remains in the possession of the Texans. That leaves a small field for the army of occupation to operate in, and proves the Indians to be quite as good, if not better, at conquest than the Texans. . . . The Apaches have fully united their tribes, and the war which they wage is one of extermination. The unprotected ranch and the towns fare alike."[74] For once officials in Santa Fe approved of Apache raiding, which served to frustrate the Confederates and inhibit their progress northward to meet the Union troops.

The Confederate army would ultimately be driven from New Mexico a year later, the last Rebel troops leaving the Mesilla Valley in the summer of 1862. At about the same time, Maj. James Henry Carleton took command of the military department, bringing with him a stubborn personality and a ruthless ideology on how best to deal with the territory's urgent Indian problem. His policies were frequently disagreed with by the majority of the territory's officials, and considerable controversies arose as a result. Carleton's plan, essentially one of extermination of the Apaches, had unfortunate ramifications that the major did not foresee.

The army, pursuant to their new commander's orders, continued to wage a war of extermination upon the Apaches for the duration of Carleton's incumbency, all the while managing more than anything to irritate

the Indians and bring about numerous brutal acts of reciprocity upon settlers throughout the territory. Judge Joseph Knapp of Mesilla, constantly
at odds with Carleton for more reasons than one, wholeheartedly opposed
Carleton's Indian management policies. On February 4, 1865, Knapp wrote
to Commissioner of Indian Affairs William P. Dole criticizing the army officer. "General Carleton . . . commenced a war of extermination against the
Apaches in this Territory and Arizona," he wrote. "The cry was no quarter
for the Apache, and the people are now suffering the consequences . . . the
'plan' as Gen. Carleton calls it, has now been in force [for over two years]
and though he himself reports that we have peace and safety throughout the
land, the Indians in scattered bands are roving everywhere, and the property and lives of the people have to suffer for it." The "plan," as conceived
by Carleton and carried out under his orders by his subordinate officers
throughout the territory, was "executed by killing every one which can be
seen—a war of extermination, reaching to the women and children. The
Apache on his part returns life for life, when the soldier cannot be taken the
citizen is taken . . . the consequence is that the Indians have much the best
of the contest, and the citizens are the sufferers."[75]

Judge Knapp did not stray far from the truth in his observations of current events in southern New Mexico. Hundreds of innocent civilians would
be slain by the Apaches during the 1860s, the vast majority of these murders
coming as a direct result of similar atrocities perpetrated upon the Apaches
by Carleton's troops and by miners who had moved into the Apache country in droves. It was much easier and safer for the Apaches to attack and
kill civilians than the heavily armed soldiers. The eventual result would
be the complete failure of Carleton's Indian policies and proposed war of
extermination, and eventually Carleton himself became an object of such
immense controversy that he would be removed from his position as military commander.

The Apache wars continued for more than two decades after the end of
the Civil War. It would not be until 1886 that the last Apaches, led by Man-
gus and Geronimo, surrendered to the military, doing so in September of
that year. The Apaches, among the most versatile, enduring, and swarthy
Indians on the continent, held out far longer than many other tribes across
the American West. But in the end, civilization simply overwhelmed them.
During the 1850s the region remained somewhat sparsely populated, al-

lowing them to operate and raid with relative impunity. As the years progressed, all that began to change. The discovery of rich mining districts in the Apaches' favorite mountainous haunts brought thousands of enterprising, wealth-seeking men to the territory, and innumerable disputes resulted. It simply became impossible for the free-spirited Apaches to roam at will as they had for centuries before, the result being their eventual surrender and removal from New Mexico entirely.

CHAPTER 6

Separatist Movements in Mesilla

No sooner had Mesilla become a part of the United States than the residents there began taking strides toward change. That they were American citizens could no longer be debated; however, the territory within the United States to which they would belong was an altogether separate issue, one that certain Mesilleros intended to address. Due in large part to the great distance separating Mesilla from the northern New Mexican settlements, most importantly Santa Fe, a general sense of separation and detachment quickly developed in the Mesilla Valley. The political maneuverings and the ensuing endeavors of Mesilla to secede from New Mexico during the latter half of the 1850s did not at all lack in complexity.

From the time of its founding by several dozen free-willed Mexican families from Doña Ana in 1850, Mesilla bore the distinction of being the most populated and most important place in the area. The town was still located in the disputed region when the New Mexico territorial legislature created the county of Doña Ana pursuant to an act of July 10, 1851, with the smaller village of Doña Ana being selected as the county seat.[1] Mesilla's location in the region under dispute between the United States and Mexico prevented it from being the county seat, despite the fact that it boasted a considerably larger population than that of Doña Ana and Las Cruces combined.[2]

Doña Ana County was named the third judicial district of the Territory of New Mexico in January 1853, whereupon President Franklin Pierce appointed Kirby Benedict to preside as judge there.[3] Throughout his career as a judicial official in southern New Mexico, Benedict frequently became involved in controversial regional and national issues, including the claim Texas made to the Mesilla Valley prior to the Gadsden Purchase.[4] Benedict would be the first of many important political figures who proved to be a determining factor in the region in the upcoming years.

Along with Benedict, Richard Campbell was appointed to serve as the first probate judge of Doña Ana County in 1853, pursuant to the Territorial Organic Law of 1850, which implemented the institution of the prefect system in New Mexico. As a probate judge, Campbell held both legislative and executive jurisdiction in the newly created Doña Ana County. In one

of his amusing actions as probate judge, he issued the following order on
September 17, 1853:

> Ordered by Richard Campbell, Probate Judge in and for the
> County of Doña Ana and Territory of New Mexico, that the holes
> made in the streets of the town of Las Cruces for the purpose of
> making adobes and for other purposes be filled up within thirty days
> from the issuing of this order with the posative [sic] assurance that
> all those who made such holes and do not fill them up or comply
> with this order within thirty days from the date hereof will be finded
> [sic] and legal steps taken to compel the payment of such fines.[5]

Because of the control the probate judge held over local and state elections, these positions were among the most sought after political offices in
the territory. His successor as probate judge was Pablo Melendres, former
alcalde of the village of Doña Ana, who assumed the position in 1855. In
these early years of Doña Ana County's existence, the Gadsden Purchase
still lay in the future; therefore the town of Mesilla was not considered a part
of the county, instead remaining uninvolved in these political proceedings
until 1854.

From a political standpoint, a general lack of organization prevailed in
Doña Ana County. All government proceedings up until the end of the
Civil War were held at various locations throughout the county, depending
on availability. As a further inconvenience, the county had no permanent
courthouse or offices for elected officials. It was not until 1865 that two local
men, Thomas J. Bull and Daniel Frietze, began plans for the construction of
a sorely needed courthouse and jail in the town of Mesilla.[6] Until that time
court would be held at irregular intervals, further stifling the growth of the
valley and inhibiting political recognition by other, more well established
portions of New Mexico.

Doña Ana and Las Cruces, the first two seats of the newly created Doña
Ana County, lacked flamboyance and were less than attractive from an
outsider's point of view. One passerby in the mid-1850s, W. W. H. Davis,
remarked on the region with minimal enthusiasm. "The famous Mesilla
Valley . . . has caused such a hubbub in the political world," he wrote. "The
glowing accounts that have been written about the beauty and fertility

of the Mesilla Valley are not sustained by the reality, and were gotten up by those who were entirely ignorant of the subject. The population is much less than represented. At the first election held after the Gadsden Purchase the number of votes polled was two hundred and thirty-five and at the Congressional election in 1855 the number was between five and six hundred, making the population, at the highest estimate, not more than about twenty-five hundred. . . . I would not exchange a good Pennsylvania farm of a thousand acres for the whole valley for agricultural purposes."[7] Clearly, the region for which the United States had fought so hard to obtain did not much impress the visiting Davis, or others for that matter.

The smaller village of Doña Ana was "a modern-built Mexican town, with a population of some five hundred; the river bottom . . . broad and fertile, and well watered and cultivated."[8] Less than a decade later, a California newspaper described Doña Ana as a town "built of adobe, with a woebegone appearance, and altogether the wreck of what it was ten years ago."[9] From these observations, it is easy to surmise that the entire region had been hyperbolically romanticized, and a false impression of its importance therefore bestowed on the outside world. The region was by no means an industrialized urban center like the sophisticated municipalities back east, yet it was equally as important to its surroundings as any major city in the nation. Whether the settlements in the Mesilla Valley could truly be considered woebegone or not was a matter of opinion. At any rate southern New Mexico occupied the full attention of the territory in the upcoming years, continually making a name for itself through its tireless pursuits for political independence from the Territory of New Mexico.

Once Gadsden's treaty had been signed by both countries and approved by each respective government in 1854, Mesilla, the nucleus of the region's population, became the seat of Doña Ana County. It retained that position continuously for the next twenty-seven years. But the political turmoil that came about as a result of Mesilla's designation as the seat of government was considerable, and in the 1850s and early 1860s the residents there found themselves almost daily embroiled in heated exchanges of secessionist sentiments. In the upcoming years Mesilla would become, in a sense, the Richmond of the West. The town first attempted separation from New Mexico, and when the Civil War loomed on the horizon, it diverted its efforts to separation not only from New Mexico but also from the entire Union.

Beginning as early as 1854, even before Mesilla became the county seat, residents of Doña Ana County began taking steps toward separating from the Territory of New Mexico and creating their own independent territory. James A. Lucas,[10] a clerk of the county probate court, became a member of the New Mexico territorial legislature and petitioned Congress to create a separate territory out of Doña Ana County. Lucas introduced this measure to the legislature on January 23, 1855, but it was promptly tabled and never voted on, due mainly to the northern New Mexico counties who at that time possessed firm control over the legislature. As a result the petition never reached Congress.[11] Despite his initial failure, Lucas would go on to become a prominent figure in pre–Civil War Mesilla Valley politics, never straying from his goal of an independent territory for the Gadsden Purchase lands.

In the summer of 1856 Lucas tried his separation plan again, this time joining with Charles D. Poston and U.S. Attorney William Claude Jones in writing another petition. Signed by some 260 prominent Mesilla citizens, it advocated the formation of a separate governing body for the lands acquired by the United States through the Gadsden Purchase. In the document subsequently created, the name "Arizona" was purportedly used for the first time in history, and thus began the movement to establish a Territory of Arizona.[12] The citizens of the Mesilla Valley, opting to memorialize Congress for their own separate territory, selected Nathan P. Cook as their delegate and sent him to Washington to advocate for the creation of an Arizona Territory, with Mesilla as the proposed capital. Once again, despite the increased level of organization of Lucas and others, the attempt failed. The Congressional Committee on Territories rejected the idea, citing the very small population of the region as a reason for refusing the request.[13]

Resilient in their efforts, leading Mesilla citizens convened on August 29, 1856, to hold the first Arizona Territorial Convention, despite their lack of political recognition by any outside governing bodies. This convention, the first of several to come, was attended by such men as Mark Aldrich, the mayor of Tucson; James Douglas, a former chemistry professor from Quebec; Granville H. Oury, a well-known southern sympathizer and Arizona pioneer; along with Ignacio Ortíz and José M. Martinez representing the Hispanic contingent of the population.[14] Whether or not this meeting had much, if any, influence in Washington was never fully determined, but in 1857 the advocates of separation succeeded in gaining the attention and support of President James Buchanan.[15] Among other things, the president recommended that Congress create the requested Arizona Territory, incorporating along with it "such portions of New Mexico as they may deem expedient." His recommendation initially being ignored by Congress, President Buchanan stated on December 6, 1858, that "the population of that territory [Arizona] numbering as alleged, more than 10,000 souls, are practically without a government, without laws, and without any regular administration of justice. Murder and other crimes are committed with impunity. This state of things calls loudly for redress, and I therefore repeat my recommendation for the establishment of a territorial government over Arizona."[16] With this the radical movement undertaken first by James Lucas and subsequently joined by leading Mesilla citizens achieved national recognition.

The Mesilla Valley and its surrounding region quickly progressed in political importance. The population of Doña Ana County, estimated to be 8,660 in 1858, represented a considerable increase from pre–Gadsden Purchase times. This estimate was significant in that it proved Doña Ana County to have a larger population than all other New Mexico counties except three: Taos, Rio Arriba, and San Miguel. Of those 8,660 inhabitants, 3,100 of them lived in Mesilla, 823 in Las Cruces, and 300 in the distant, newly sprung mining camp of Piños Altos near modern-day Silver City. In a countywide vote for the separatist movement, 2,897 individuals voted in favor of the creation of a new territory. It is not known what percentage of the total population actually exercised their right to vote, although it would seem likely that this number must have represented a vast majority of the total votes cast.[17]

The allusions to murder, lawlessness, and a lack of "administration of justice" made by President Buchanan in 1858 were generally true. The Mesilla Valley did in fact suffer from a higher rate of crime and overall lack of law enforcement due to its seclusion from the other New Mexico population centers in the northern part of the territory. It was these northern New Mexico counties that possessed control over the territorial legislature and continuously promoted self-serving legislation whenever possible. Despite the fact that Doña Ana County had a higher population than most others in the territory, it was still allowed only one member in the House. Contrarily, Bernalillo County (including Albuquerque), with a population considerably less than Doña Ana, had three members. Frustrated by this lack of recognition, Doña Ana County did not even bother to send a representative to the legislature on six separate occasions between the years 1851 and 1861. Furthermore, early territorial legislatures were detrimentally partisan; James L. Collins, a prominent merchant and Indian agent, remarked in the 1850s that "the legislature is in session but they are so completely under the influence of party that they are likely to do little."[18] As a result of these self-promoting ideologies in the legislature and the staunch unwillingness of Doña Ana County to participate in territorial politics, those living in southern New Mexico essentially had little voice in most issues.[19] Not surprisingly, this was among the primary instigating factors mentioned in support of their attempts to create a separate territory.

Mesilla held an Arizona Territorial Convention on September 3, 1858, with the prominent Sylvester Mowry in attendance to support the cause. By now the separatist movements began to garner serious attention in northern New Mexico newspapers. "Lieut. Mowry has been through here raising the devil about the Territory of Arizona," editorialized one Santa Fe newspaper. "He has persuaded the people of Mesilla to hold no election under the laws of New Mexico, and to pay no attention whatever to the courts."[20]

Yet another convention convened less than a year later on June 19, 1859. The most important and consequential resolution made at this gathering, pursuant to Mowry's proclamations as reported by the *Santa Fe Weekly Gazette* a year earlier, decreed that Doña Ana County and the extralegal Territory of Arizona would no longer take part in New Mexico's elections from that point forward.[21] This bold declaration caught the attention not only of the New Mexico legislature but also the U.S. Congress. Other resolutions made at the June 19 convention included one stating in part that "the people of Arizona residing on the Rio Grande address the refusal of the [U.S.] Congress to provide for the proposed territory of Arizona"; another one recognizing the failure of the Territory of New Mexico to regularly hold court south of the Jornada del Muerto (in the Mesilla Valley);[22] and that the proceedings of the convention be published by major eastern newspapers in cities such as St. Louis, New York, and Washington, D.C.[23] On July 3, 1859, yet another convention, held in Tucson, adopted many of these same resolutions.[24] Clearly, Doña Ana County had become fed up with the lack of recognition from its northern New Mexico counterparts.

Interestingly, while citizens in the Mesilla Valley continued to seek admission to the Union as a territory, those citizens of "Arizona" residing farther west expressed somewhat different views. The *Weekly Arizonian,* published in Tubac south of Tucson, editorialized, "It is our candid belief . . . that the scheme of a separate Territorial government for us, at this time, has been sufficiently tried to demonstrate its impossibility. For several years that portion of New Mexico called Arizona has had a delegate at Washington asking for a Territorial organization, but without success, or even the expression of a decided intention on the part of Congress to organize a government."[25] The residents of this portion of "Arizona" seemed to employ a more realistic vision of the territorial movements, recognizing the futility of the efforts. Nevertheless, conventions would continue to be held and delegates sent to Congress.

At the territorial convention of June 19, 1859, an infamous pro-South man, Sylvester Mowry, was selected to serve as Arizona's delegate to Congress. Mowry is a figure well known to Arizona history, and he got his start with the Doña Ana County separatist proceedings of the late 1850s. A graduate of the military academy at West Point, Mowry resigned his commission in 1858 as a lieutenant in the 2nd Artillery to pursue a career as a miner and merchant in the Tucson area. He was among the first to recognize the potential mineral wealth of the region, dedicating many of his business ventures to exploiting the riches of what would soon become the Territory of Arizona. Naturally, with such strong business interests in the area, he became heavily involved in local politics. Mowry served as Arizona's delegate to Congress three times before the Civil War, despite the fact that Arizona had not been incorporated as an official U.S. territory at that time. When the Civil War reached the Mesilla Valley in 1861, Mowry became embroiled in that debacle as well. He would continue to play a dominant role in southern New Mexico/Arizona events for many years to come.[26]

By 1860, mainly as a result of intense political strife in the area, Mesilla had its own newspaper, its primary purpose being to promote secession and the creation of an Arizona Territory. The newspaper would be used by individuals in the area as an outlet to draw attention to the cause and to inform the people of the advancements being made by those orchestrating the separatist movement. On September 20, 1860, the governor of the artificial Arizona Territory, L. S. Owings, issued a proclamation in the *Mesilla Times* calling for an election to be held on November 6 for delegate to the

Figure 6.1. Sylvester Mowry, ca. 1864. (Courtesy Arizona Historical Foundation. 627-N-68 [Box 11, Folder 1])

second session of Congress, "to fill a vacancy caused by the resignation of the Honorable Sylvester Mowry."[27] Mowry, for personal reasons, recanted his position as congressional delegate, although he by no means departed from the southern New Mexico political arena.

The issue arising from Mowry's resignation was an important one, as Arizona had not yet been incorporated as a U.S. Territory by Congress, and they needed a competent and dedicated delegate to ensure the greatest chance of success in their endeavor. The election called for by Owings did indeed take place on November 6, and two days later the *Mesilla Times* carried a portion of the results from the precincts nearest Mesilla. The nominees for the position had been Dr. Michael Steck, Apache agent at nearby Fort Thorn, and Edward McGowan, a citizen of western Doña Ana County (modern Arizona). The first four precincts reporting were Las Cruces, La Mesa, Doña Ana, and Mesilla, with a result of 741 votes for Steck and just 63 for McGowan. The Rio Grande valley region heavily favored Steck, whose selection would have been a good one, as he was well acquainted with politics, and the local population already knew and respected him for his benevolent work as an Indian agent over the previous six years.

The *Santa Fe Weekly Gazette,* learning of the initial reports from the first four precincts, printed an editorial condoning Steck's election as congressional delegate, calling him "a useful representative." A couple of weeks later, when the remainder of the precincts submitted their election results, the findings were quite the opposite. Steck's support began and ended with the Mesilla Valley, as the entirety of western "Arizona" voted for McGowan. At the mining camp of Piños Altos, for example, the lopsided vote was 668 for McGowan and just 10 for Steck. The outcome of the election essentially boiled down to one simple factor: Steck was a Northerner from Pennsylvania and vehemently opposed secession, whereas the miners and frontiersmen of western "Arizona" were, for the most part, ardent Southern sympathizers. As the final tally of votes indicated, McGowan received the majority of the vote and became the next congressional delegate. By this time the Civil War loomed on the immediate horizon and the blatantly pro-South *Mesilla Times* openly supported McGowan's selection as Mowry's successor. The new delegate's future role for Arizona would be simple: "Should the South separate, he [McGowan] is instructed to attend the Southern Convention and pledge the Territory [of Arizona] to the Southern Confederacy, and, to ask for a Territorial organization under that Confederacy."[28]

It became clear in towns and cities across the west that Mesilla and the fictitious Arizona Territory of which it served as capital staunchly supported the Southern secession movements. The nation was divided against itself, and if a war between the North and South did indeed break out, it became clear where the Mesilleros and Arizonans stood on the issue. There was little doubt that a Confederate Congress, if created, would be eager to expand geographically and would happily incorporate Arizona as one of its territories.

The aggressive movements in Mesilla to support the Confederacy began long before the firing on Fort Sumter, South Carolina, on April 12, 1861. By the early part of 1860, the groundwork for the future Confederate Territory of Arizona had already been laid out by the region's Southern sympathizers, with the *Mesilla Times* boldly leading the charge.

CHAPTER 7

Mesilla: Capital of the Arizona Territory

The latter months of 1860 were a trying time for the United States. The North and South still clung together, but only by a thread. The presidential election of 1860 featured Abraham Lincoln as the Northern antislavery candidate and John C. Breckenridge and Stephen A. Douglas as the primary Southern proslavery candidates, with the nation violently divided on the issue. Mesilla, despite being thousands of miles away and not taking an official part in the voting, was no exception to the prevailing sentiments of vehemence. The residents there, whether just for entertainment or to prove a point, held their own mock presidential election on the town plaza. First reported on by the *Mesilla Times,* other newspapers around the country quickly picked up on the absurdity occurring in the Mesilla Valley. The *San Francisco Herald* of November 20, 1860, noted that "though, under the circumstances, the people [of Arizona] had no vote in the election for President, it seems the citizens were determined to give expression to their sentiments on this important subject. A ballot box was obtained by Capt. Hawley and a direct vote taken for president and vice president with the following result: Breckenridge & Lane, 40; Bell & Everett, 7; Lincoln & Hamlin, 5; Douglas & Johnson, 3."[1] The *Mesilla Times,* incessantly printing pro-South propaganda, sarcastically remarked on the election that "though we believe it is impossible to find an individual in our midst who will say publicly he is a Lincoln man, it seems there were 5 in town day before yesterday."[2] Farther south, in El Paso County, Texas, the outcome differed little: 1,052 votes for Breckenridge, 11 for Lincoln. Army surgeon James Cooper McKee, upon arriving at Fort Fillmore remarked, "I found the garrison and people in the neighboring towns of Mesilla, Las Cruces, and Dona Ana in great excitement and agitation at the near approach of hostilities between the North and South, on account of the election and inauguration of Mr. Lincoln to the Presidency."[3]

Ultimately, the votes in El Paso and Mesilla were inconsequential; in the face of staunch Southern objections, Abraham Lincoln was sworn into office as president of the United States in March 1861. Pro-South residents of the Mesilla Valley were taken aback by the result of the election, and the

Mesilla Times echoed the widespread disappointment. "We have about 1000 American, or 'white,' population in Arizona," read the newspaper's fiery editorial, "and nine-tenths of that number favor a disruption of the Union; since the disastrous election news that has reached us from the Northern States . . . we are utterly astonished at the vote that Lincoln has received in [California]. It has been all along supposed that California would go for Breckenridge."[4] Indeed, California had surprisingly come out in favor of Lincoln in the election. Nevertheless, Arizona Territory remained steadfast in its pro-South convictions, determined to remain loyal to the Southern cause at all costs.

As they had done in years past, leaders in Mesilla and throughout Arizona quickly called together conventions to address the issue of subscribing to the Southern Confederacy. On March 4, 1861, the mining camp of Piños Altos hosted the first such convention, where the potential admittance of Arizona as a state in the Confederacy commanded the delegates' attention. Such a prospect appealed to many Arizonans. In fact, public sentiment so outwardly favored the Southern cause that anybody opposing that point of view received threats. "The Chairman [of the Piños Altos Convention] . . . warned the convention against the selection of delegates who were not known to be thoroughly Southern in sentiment."[5] With intimidations such as these, few individuals spoke out in opposition of the majority.

Two weeks later, on March 16, Mesilla held its own Confederate convention. With James Lucas once again presiding, officials were selected to serve in the various necessary capacities.[6] An issue of the *Times* printed the very same day as the convention notified its readers that polls would open at the local precincts on April 2 in order that the people might "vote for the ratification or rejection of the resolutions" passed at the March 16 convention.[7]

In April 1861, about the same time that Fort Sumter was being shelled by Confederate artillery off the coast of South Carolina, Tucson and Mesilla united in their efforts to achieve status as a new state in the Confederacy. Yet another convention convened, this time comprised of leading men from each of the two towns, who collectively pledged their undivided loyalty to the South in hopes of achieving immediate statehood in the Confederacy. The men comprising the legislature made no secret of this underlying motivation. In a letter to Confederate authorities several months later, on June 6, 1861, James Lucas wrote, "We [Arizona] desire above all things a Territorial organization by the Confederate States of America . . . all this may be done without any conflict with the U.S. troops now here [at Fort Fillmore], unless it should be desired by the Confederate States of America."[8] Lucas's letter seems to have insinuated that those living in the Mesilla Valley would not have objected to taking forcible measures against the nearby Union outpost of Fort Fillmore, a suggestion that reeked of treason and would doubtless have made any Northerner cringe.

Another less dominant reason was the general feeling of frustration with the U.S. Congress over the past several years, which, in failing to incorporate Arizona as a territory, had alienated the citizens and turned local opinion against the North. Congress had treated southern New Mexico in much the same marginalized manner in which the New Mexico territorial legislature had treated it, and the citizens now endeavored to find acceptance with the Confederacy.[9]

Acting as a single Territory of Arizona, the two towns of Tucson and Mesilla agreed to "ordain and establish" their own provisional government with elected officials. Towns represented at the convention included Mesilla, Santa Rita del Cobre, Las Cruces, Doña Ana, La Mesa, Santo Tomás, Picacho, and Amoles in New Mexico, and Tucson, Arivaca, Tubac, Sonoita, Gila City, and Calabasas in Arizona. The thirty-one delegates in attendance at the convention selected Dr. Lewis S. Owings to continue in his office as governor.[10] Additionally, Ignacio Orrantía of Chamberino was chosen to serve as lieutenant governor, and Granville Oury received the nod to become chief justice of the Arizona Supreme Court. Sam Bean, brother of famous western lawman Roy Bean, would serve as marshal for the territory.[11] A territorial militia, to consist of several hundred volunteer troops, was also established under the shared command of W. C. Wordsworth and Palatine Robinson. Initially, this militia was mustered in order to defend against Apache incursions in the area, but with the onslaught of the Civil War in southern New Mexico, they would take on the additional role of aiding the Confederate troops.[12]

In order to split the jurisdiction of their newly created territory, the convention mapped out the country into four separate counties. The preexisting Doña Ana County retained mostly the same boundaries, but would now be part of Arizona instead of New Mexico. In addition, the delegates also created three other counties: Mesilla, Ewell, and Castle Dome.[13] On the one

hand, Mesilla and Castle Dome Counties received their names from prominent geographical locations; Ewell County, on the other hand, was named
for Capt. Richard S. Ewell of the 1st U.S. Dragoons, a staunch secessionist
and adamant lifelong supporter of slavery and the Southern cause. Ewell,
a veteran Indian fighter who had already spent years in New Mexico, went
on to become a Confederate general in the Civil War. Those in attendance
obviously thought his personal convictions toward the South to be praiseworthy, as he was the only individual for whom the delegates named any of
their new counties.

Rather than write their own set of laws, the convention elected to adopt
the laws of New Mexico, which were to be immediately applicable to the citizens of their newly created territory.[14] Arizona's territorial legislature would
be composed of nine senators and eighteen representatives. Governor Owings's inaugural address, as well as the territory's newly written constitution, were both printed in Tucson and distributed throughout the towns.[15]

One particularly defamatory resolution stemming from the April convention caught the attention of New Mexico leaders and placed added strain
on an already tense situation. In resolving to permanently alienate itself
from New Mexico, the representatives at the Arizona convention wrote that
"we will not recognize the present Black Republican Administration [of the
Territory of New Mexico] and . . . we will resist any officers appointed to
this territory by said administration with whatever means in our power."[16]
Matters had truly reached the boiling point in southern New Mexico, where
the Civil War would initiate an incredible chain of events in the upcoming
months of 1861.

The *Mesilla Times* issue of March 30, in anticipation of the April conventions and desirous of promoting an outcome favoring the personal view
of the newspaper's editor, stirred the blood of the citizenry and called upon
the delegates to do their civic duty. "Gentlemen of the Convention: choose
ye North or South—now or never!" proclaimed the *Times,* "There are anarchy, misrule, blights, neglect and ruin, northward; while to the southward, freedom, equal rights, and the blessings of a government beckon us."[17]
Clearly the newspaper hoped for an annexation into the Confederacy and
held no reservations about stating this in their publication for all to see.

Indeed, Mesilla's solitary newspaper proved to be a controversial publication from its first issue to its last, frequently printing items that infuriated

those who remained loyal to the Union. In being so openly secessionist, the editor of the *Times* likely helped sway the public opinion in Mesilla, and all of Arizona for that matter, against the Union. After Abraham Lincoln's election to the presidency in November 1860, an editorial published in the *Times* boasted that a public meeting had been held on the Mesilla plaza in which "a resolution was adopted pledging life and fortune to prevent any official, civil or military, appointed under Lincoln's administration from exercising jurisdiction in Arizona."[18] The newspaper hailed the secession of the Southern states as heroic and praised the creation of the Confederacy and the beginning of the Civil War. One San Francisco newspaper, reporting on conditions in Arizona, informed its readers that "the news of the taking of Fort Sumter was received in Mesilla with enthusiastic cheers, and occasioned much excitement among the population."[19]

The *Times* no doubt had an effect on the sentiments of the poorer population, many of whom had been Mexican citizens for most of their lives and understood little about the conflict raging in the eastern United States. While many of these early citizens of Mesilla and Arizona spoke only Spanish and were also illiterate, it is still likely that the secessionist ramblings of the *Times* reached these people through word of mouth.[20] The remainder of the English-speaking population was, by and large, very outspokenly pro-South. In February 1861, two months before the Civil War began, one observer wrote that "the mass of the [Mesilla] Mexicans, I feel certain, and more particularly the wealthy and intelligent classes, are decidedly in favor of the institution of Slavery, and this sentiment has been steadily growing ever since the enactment of our Slave Code."

Dozens of wealthy and prominent white businessmen lived in Mesilla and El Paso, and with few exceptions these men proclaimed their loyalty to the Confederacy as well. These individuals possessed the monetary and economic means by which the Southern cause could be most readily supported, and they had a great impact on public sentiment in the Territory of Arizona. Two such men were James W. Magoffin, famous El Paso pioneer merchant and ardent secessionist, and Simeon Hart, a wealthy mill proprietor who pledged thousands of dollars from his own pocket in support of the Confederacy. El Paso, being located in Texas, was already a part of the Confederate States by this time, and the feelings of those living there, including Magoffin and Hart, drifted northward up the valley and doubt-

less had an effect on the Mesilleros. Others who publicly voiced support for
the Confederate cause included the entirety of the newly created Arizona
territorial legislature, including Governor Owings and ex-congressional
delegate Sylvester Mowry, many of the U.S. officers stationed at nearby Fort
Fillmore, and of course the notorious *Mesilla Times*.

For those remaining loyal to the North (and these were few and far between) matters reached desperation. These men, if they spoke aloud their
true feelings, risked imprisonment or even death. One such individual was
Lorenzo Labadie, an Indian agent in New Mexico who would later be associated with the Bosque Redondo Reservation debacle. In June 1861, Labadie, a self-proclaimed Northerner, visited Mesilla on official business and
received a less than cordial reception from the Southerners there. After arriving in Mesilla he complained that "they have desired to compel me to
depart from within the limits of the Territory of Arizona, and have given
me to understand that if I do not comply voluntarily they will drive me out
by brute force—that they have at hand a fine barrel of tar, into which they
will put the first officer appointed by President Lincoln, feather him, and
start him out to fly."[21]

Nor did a U.S. tax collector, Samuel Wood, encounter much in the form
of an amiable welcoming party when he entered Mesilla in June 1861. Arizona was not yet a Confederate territory, but the sentiment was already
there. The *Times* gleefully reported his coming and the potential results of
his visit: "Mr. Samuel Wood has been appointed by Mr. Lincoln as Collector
for the District of Paso del Norte, New Mexico. This district includes the
whole of Arizona. We would suggest to Mr. Wood that he reflect upon the
dangers of acclimation in Arizona, that sudden changes in climate often
prove fatal to persons of certain tendencies. We can assure Mr. Wood that
he will meet with a warm reception—much warmer than he expects—one
of the warmest kind."[22] There is no evidence to suggest that Samuel Wood
did in fact receive the "warm" reception promised by the secessionist newspaper, yet it is certain that his efforts as tax collector within the boundaries
of Arizona were unsuccessful. In 1861, to enter Mesilla as a known supporter
of the North was a dangerous and daring act.

One of the few self-proclaimed Union supporters in the Mesilla Valley,
W. W. Mills of El Paso, understood the biases of public sentiment and did
not hesitate to voice his disapproval. In June 1861, just a few weeks before

the impending Confederate invasion of New Mexico, Mills wrote to a friend about the unfortunate situation in Arizona, specifically the town of Mesilla: "I find matters here in a most deplorable condition. A disunion flag is now flying from the house in which I wrote, and this country is now as much in the possession of the enemy as Charleston [South Carolina] is. . . . The Mesilla Times is bitterly disunion, and threatens with death anyone who refuses to acknowledge this usurpation."[23]

Mills did not stray far from the truth in his observations. Many of the army officers at Fort Fillmore did in fact support the South and preached hatred for the North to their enlisted men on a daily basis. Many of these officers would soon resign their commissions in the Union Army and travel back east, where they promptly enlisted as officers in the Confederate Army. This lack of loyalty to the Union would be among the causes of the downfall of Fort Fillmore in the near future. Mills also mentioned the *Times* being "bitterly disunion," a comment that despite being bluntly derisive was still an understatement. Finally, Simeon Hart of El Paso did indeed involve himself in scandalous activity at this time, lending his full support to the Confederacy. Rumors abounded that Hart had offered payments in gold to local Union officers in exchange for their defection to the Confederacy. Clearly, with so many conspirators in the grand scheme, the situation in the Mesilla Valley became intensified with each passing day.

As all of this transpired, the Confederate government plotted an invasion of the Territory of New Mexico, hoping to seize control and expand the institution of slavery as well as the Confederate empire. With sentiment in the Mesilla Valley in their favor, and promises of protection and assistance from those living in that area, the Confederate Congress was further reassured of the prospects for success of such an invasion. They knew that the invasion point affording them the greatest chances for taking New Mexico would be up the Mesilla Valley toward Santa Fe. That is precisely what the Confederate Army did in the summer of 1861.

CHAPTER 8

The Confederate Invasion

Following the Mexican War the United States possessed a standing army of about 10,000 men; a decade and a half later, just before the Civil War broke out, that number had increased only slightly to 16,000. Of those 16,000 troops, a considerable percentage of them, 2,466, were stationed at the nine military posts in the Territory of New Mexico.[1] During the first months of the war a large number of regular army soldiers in New Mexico received orders reassigning them to the east. Pursuant to these orders, only five companies, one of mounted riflemen and four of dragoons, were to remain in New Mexico to defend the inhabitants from Indian depredations. Ultimately, the department commander, Col. E. R. S. Canby, procrastinated in sending the troops off and the majority of them remained in New Mexico. Even with this considerable number of federal troops, the territory became a target for another force, one that greatly outweighed the threat of Indians. At the onset of the Civil War, the attention of the newly formed Confederate States of America was diverted toward the far-distant western territories, including New Mexico. One Confederate officer, after learning that many of the soldiers had been ordered out of New Mexico, commented, "New Mexico can now be easily taken."[2]

Indeed, the Territory of New Mexico was of paramount importance to the Confederacy at the onset of the Civil War. The potential strategic importance of New Mexico was well known to both the North and South, and consequently both sides aimed to control the territory. For the North, the important issue at stake was preventing the spread of slavery to yet another territory. For the South, economic considerations formed the predominant cause for the movement to take New Mexico by force.

Throughout the Civil War, the Confederacy suffered from its economic situation. Food, supplies, weapons, ammunition, and money were all scarce in the South. Before the war even began, many of the leading Confederate officials recognized that if they could take control of New Mexico, they would have a clear road to the California gold fields and ocean ports, and could thus fund their war effort and at the same time have a hamstringing effect on the economy of the North. President Abraham Lincoln, well aware

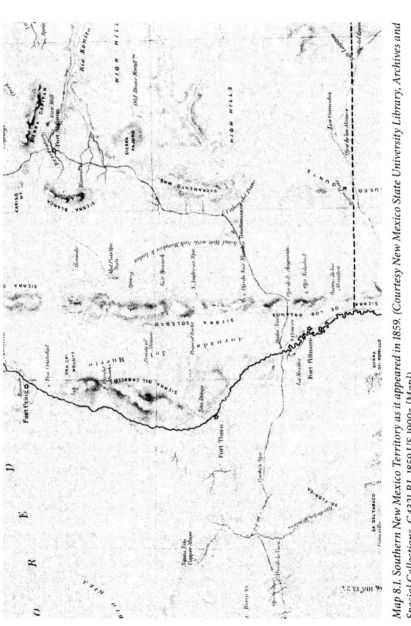

Map 8.1. *Southern New Mexico Territory as it appeared in 1859. (Courtesy New Mexico State University Library, Archives and Special Collections. G4321.R1.1859.US 1900z [Map])*

of the wealth coming into the nation from California, went so far as to deem the gold fields there "the lifeblood of our financial credit."[3]

Control of New Mexico would have meant several things for the Confederacy, which sought to annex not only that territory but also the northern Mexican states of Sonora and Chihuahua. This would have given the Confederacy another coastline, and three good ports from which to import and export goods. Such an advantage would dramatically increase their trading potential not only with the western territories but with foreign countries as well. Possession of New Mexico would have also meant that the South would have a direct, uninhibited overland route to California.

A wagon road already existed from Texas to California. The first wagon road through the Gadsden Purchase lands, this route had been laid out in 1856–57 and would become known as the Butterfield Overland Mail Route.[4] The Confederates could have utilized the preexisting Butterfield Trail as a convenient means by which to conquer California. If this could be achieved, then Confederate leaders in Richmond believed that they would attain support from several major European powers in their war effort against Abraham Lincoln and the North. Clearly, the South had much to gain by taking New Mexico. No sooner had the war begun in the East than the Confederate Congress began to set in motion their far-reaching plot.

Some people believed that the Southern scheme to take New Mexico and California began long before the Civil War broke out. There is evidence to suggest this may have been the case. The president of the Confederacy, Jefferson Davis, had served as U.S. secretary of war in the 1850s, during which time he may have nonchalantly advanced the Southern cause in preparation for a conflict he knew was inevitable. William Need, a pro-North man in New Mexico during the Civil War, waxed metaphoric in his accusations of such a long-running scheme by the South. "With an eye that never winked and a wing that never tired has Jeff. Davis for more than ten years past turned his thoughts and desires to the Mexican line for indefinite expansion," wrote Need, "his military prototypes and protégés, Ewell, Fauntleroy, Steen, Loring, Longstreet, Crittenden, Grayson, Rhett, Reynolds, etc.—were placed here purposely to second and forward his ulterior designs."[5] Indeed, all of these high-ranking army officers had been stationed in New Mexico during the 1850s, all of them staunchly advocated the Southern cause, and all played active roles in the Confederacy during the Civil War.

Another key premeditator of this scheme was Miguel A. Otero, New Mexico's congressional delegate just prior to the breaking out of the Civil War in 1861. According to one historian, Otero acted "hand in glove with the secession leaders of the South and [was] an active party in the conspiracy hatches in the nation's capital whereby the army officers in New Mexico military posts were to make it possible for the Confederacy to secure possession of all forts and munitions of war throughout the Southwest frontier. He secured the distribution of an address, in Spanish and English, throughout the territory inciting the people to rebellion, believing they would follow his leadership."[6] It would seem, then, that the future president of the Confederacy, aided by territorial officials, might indeed have promoted the cause in New Mexico before the Civil War ever even began.

Once the Civil War actually broke out in 1861, the North quickly realized that their Southern foes had ulterior designs on southern New Mexico. Many Northerners were mistaken, however, in their assumption that southern New Mexico, or "Arizona," was a worthless tract of land and would afford no benefit to the Confederacy. "What the devil do they care for Arizona without 100 souls in it, and nothing worth having there?," wrote one Northern sympathizer in 1861. His question was a rhetorical one. He continued: "They wish to march into Sonora as is intimated from many sources, and take quiet possession ... if they once get possession of this State and its posts, the North may just as well give up the complete line through from the Gulf of Mexico to Gulf of California, and it will require a superior effort then to rout them."[7] In other words, the Southern scheme to take "Arizona" merely veiled their grander scheme to annex northern Mexico, where valuable ocean ports were located. The South could not achieve this without first taking possession of New Mexico and forcing the Union troops out of the territory.

From the onset the South underestimated the enormity of the task upon which it embarked. Gen. Henry Hopkins Sibley, a former Union officer who had accepted a commission in the Southern army at the beginning of the Civil War, typified the relaxed sentiment that prevailed throughout the South's government at the time. Writing to Maj. Trevanion Teel before the invasion of New Mexico, Sibley remarked that "the objective, aim, and design of the campaign [is] the conquest of California, and as soon as the Confederate army should occupy the Territory of New Mexico, an army of advance would be organized, and 'On to San Francisco' would be the watchword."[8] Sibley obviously thought that routing the Union troops in New Mexico and marching onward to California was a task his Confederate troops should experience little trouble in achieving. Reality would prove otherwise.

One of the leading causes for this misconception in the South was the reports being received from several western newspapers, one being the *Mesilla Times*. If one believed the contents contained within the pages of that newspaper, every soul in New Mexico favored the South and eagerly awaited the day the Confederate Army would come to rescue them from the brutal, dictatorial rule of the Northern political and military officials in the territory. According to the newspaper, the Territory of Arizona, with Mesilla as its capital, was even more staunchly pro-South, and would aid the Confederate troops in any manner that the situation might necessitate. Southern newspapers back east took notice and began calling on their government to proceed with the invasion, which, according to the *Mesilla Times,* would go forward without a hitch.

The *Santa Fe Gazette* and the *Tucson Arizonian* (once owned by Sylvester Mowry) also expressed pro-Southern sentiments, serving to further reinforce the claims of anti-Northern sentiment printed in Mesilla's short-lived newspaper. In June 1861, only a few weeks before the Confederate Army arrived in the Mesilla Valley, one of the few northern sympathizers remaining in the area accurately remarked that "the Mesilla *Times* is bitterly disunion, and threatens with death anyone who refuses to acknowledge this usurpation."[9] A May 1861 issue of the *Times* boasted a drawing of the Confederate flag, accompanied by the poem "Dixie Land."[10]

Despite the proclamations of the newspapers, it was never fully known where the loyalties of the Mexican population truly stood. The newspapers, with few exceptions, were published by white men with only a nominal understanding of the prevailing sentiment in the small Mexican communities across New Mexico. What they printed was, in most cases, merely speculation. None of the leading officials in Santa Fe knew for certain how the Mexican population would react if indeed the Confederates did invade the territory. Most of the people of Spanish descent living in the northernmost communities of New Mexico were widely believed to support the Union, while those living in the southern regions, namely the Mesilla Valley, were believed to be pro-South. W. W. Mills, writing from Mesilla in June 1861, suggested that despite what appeared in the *Mesilla Times* there remained "a latent Union sentiment here, especially among the Mexicans, but they are effectually overawed."[11] Territorial Governor Abraham Rencher and future Governor Henry Connelly both accurately believed that the northern population of New Mexico would maintain their loyalty to the Union cause. Because the territory consisted of such a staggering majority of Hispanic residents, the Northern cause depended upon these people remaining loyal. In the long run, it would be these very men, Hispanic residents of northern New Mexico, who would form volunteer regiments and assist in thwarting the impending Confederate invasion.

Ultimately, the continued reassurances of full-fledged support by the populace of the Mesilla Valley and Arizona resulted in the Confederate Congress mustering a group of Texas troops to invade and conquer New Mexico. In addition to this, Henry Hopkins Sibley,[12] freshly appointed a general in the Confederacy after resigning his commission with the U.S. Army in April 1861, had traveled to Richmond and conferred with Jefferson Davis on the topic. Sibley possessed an immense firsthand knowledge of New Mexico, having served with the army there for several years and also having acted as commanding officer at Fort Union for a brief period. Sibley's reports agreed with those of the secessionist territorial newspapers: New Mexico could be taken with relative ease.[13]

With Colorado (which also remained loyal to the Union) bordering New Mexico on the north, it seemed only natural that the invading Confederate troops would be coming from Texas; the geographic position of that state essentially made it the only Confederate possession from which an attack could be strategically made with any prospect of success.[14] Accordingly, plans were made by the Confederate government in Richmond to go ahead with the invasion.[15] Although the Canadian and Pecos Rivers in eastern New Mexico were initially considered as points of entry, ultimately the Confederates chose the Rio Grande valley as the point at which to enter the territory.

Lt. Col. John Robert Baylor[16] was placed in command of the 7th Texas Mounted Volunteers, assigned to take and maintain possession of the southernmost portions of New Mexico in advance of a larger body of Texans still being mustered. Baylor's regiment consisted of a mere 258 men, an astoundingly small number for the enormous undertaking they were ordered to fulfill. The soldiers gathered in San Antonio, Texas, in the spring months of 1861 with plans to march westward toward New Mexico in July of that year. The preparations made by the troops and their officers provide further evidence of their lack of preparedness for the endeavor upon which they embarked. Nearly the entire invading rebel force was poorly armed with obsolete rifles and muskets, and were inadequately clothed and equipped for the journey through the desert. With only a small number of the Confederates even wearing uniforms, they no doubt resembled a ragged-looking lot of men marching across the Texas desert from San Antonio to El Paso.

Baylor's Texans also underestimated the ferocity and tenacity of the Apaches in the area surrounding the Mesilla Valley. As the men trudged northward from El Paso, they came to know firsthand the difficulties with which they would have to contend over the upcoming months. Several small Confederate detachments, sent north ahead of the main column for reconnaissance purposes, were repeatedly attacked by these Indians, who succeeded in running off several of their horses and further depleting their already minimal amount of supplies and provisions.[17]

By the time Baylor's troops reached Fort Bliss at El Paso, their intentions and movements were well known to Union commanders in New Mexico, including Maj. Isaac Lynde in the Mesilla Valley. One of the few remaining loyal men in the El Paso area, W. W. Mills, continuously wrote to the authorities in Santa Fe keeping them informed of the proceedings at that location.[18] On July 5, 1861, having arrived with his troops from nearby Fort McLane, Lynde assumed the role of commanding officer at Fort Fillmore. Located several miles south of Mesilla, this fort would serve as the first point of Federal opposition to Baylor's force as they proceeded up the valley.

Remarkably, despite indisputable evidence of what was about to occur, Major Lynde took very few precautionary measures in preparation for the oncoming rebel invaders. Some of Lynde's subordinate officers recommended that fortifications be built and reinforcements brought in, but these suggestions seem to have gone unheeded by their commander. The wife of one of Fort Fillmore's officers, present at the post during this time, wrote, "Of course, every day all sorts of rumors were brought in of intended attacks on the post by Confederates, and caused a good deal of uneasiness among us all." Department headquarters had even authorized Lynde "to call into the service of the United States two or more companies of volunteers from the neighborhood of your post."[19] Interestingly, a communication between

Figure 8.1. Lt. Col. John Robert Baylor. (Courtesy Center for Southwest Research, University Libraries, University of New Mexico. Keleher Collection, ZIM CSWR PICT 000-742-0014)

Lynde and the assistant adjutant general seems to imply that this authorization was rescinded just days prior to the arrival of the Confederate troops.[20]

Major Lynde seemed utterly oblivious of the danger and took no means to strengthen the post or to put his small force where it would be most efficient in case the Texans carried out their plans to raid the garrison. "Officers loyal to the United States grew restless under Lynde's command . . . there could not have been a better man in command to help the Southern cause, nor a worse for the government, than Major Lynde."[21] Assistant surgeon James C. McKee related similar sentiments relative to Lynde's indifference in commanding the Union troops. "An enemy was advancing on us, over a public highway running through the fort, and not a picket out for our security to prevent a surprise," McKee lamented. "Not even an addition made to the ordinary routine sentinels on post duty, viz., one at the guard-house, one at quartermaster's corral, and one over the commissary store-house. Nothing was done, and no measures taken to guard against surprise, either by night or day. Was there ever such another instance in all history of such imbecility, neglect, or criminal indifference?"[22]

Maj. Isaac Lynde, who figured prominently in the ensuing events, was described as having gray hair and a gray beard, "giving him a venerable appearance; he was quiet, reticent, and retired, giving the impression of wisdom and a knowledge of his profession. I looked up to him with more than ordinary admiration and confidence, thinking and reasoning . . . [that he] could be depended on to defend the honor of the flag."[23] The author of this description, surgeon McKee, would ultimately find his initial impression of Lynde to be woefully ill founded.

While some of Lynde's officers pleaded with him to prepare for an attack, others professed their feelings of approval for the Confederate cause. "A number of the officers of my command were Southern men who did not conceal their sympathy with the seceded states," Lynde later wrote.[24] Thus Lynde faced an enormous challenge in that it sometimes proved difficult to discern where a person's sympathies lay.

By the time Lynde took command of Fort Fillmore in July 1861, twenty-four privates had already deserted that year, in addition to two officers, Captain Garland and Captain Jones, who had disappeared when the Civil War broke out.[25] W. W. Mills would later note that when passing through the fort many of the men were afraid to speak with him about the war. One Dr. Alden, at Fort Fillmore during that time, arranged to meet with Mills at Mesilla rather than the fort; "such was the feeling against the Union men that this United States officer [Alden], almost under the guns of his post, did not dare speak to me on the street, but beckoned me to an outhouse," Mills wrote.[26] Clearly there existed considerable tension among the men and officers at Fort Fillmore as the day of reckoning neared.[27]

On July 6, the day after Major Lynde took command of the federal troops stationed at Fort Fillmore, the *Mesilla Times* reported that the soldiers had "commenced fortifying the post . . . a picket guard is kept out some three miles . . . the concentration of so large a force at this point, the receipts of supplies, and every preparation apparently being made to permanently locate them here, excites considerable anxiety in the valley."[28] This would suggest that Lynde did in fact take some measures of precaution as the Confederates advanced toward him; however, the actions he took were minimal and insufficient at best. The force at Fort Fillmore, consisting of several hundred effective Union troops, was deemed sufficient by the leading men of the military department to thwart the advancement of the invading Confederates.

Major Lynde soon realized that Fort Fillmore lay in a poor defensive position and would be highly vulnerable to an attack by artillery. The fort had been constructed in 1851 for the sole purpose of controlling Apache depredations and therefore little thought had been directed toward the post's location from a defensive standpoint. Just prior to the post's abandonment, Lynde wrote that "the fort was so placed as to be indefensible against artillery, being commanded on three sides by sand hills within easy range of a six-pounder."[29] With the Confederate troops expected to be approaching from the south at any time, Major Lynde found himself in quite a predicament.[30]

On the morning of July 25, a deserter from Lieutenant Colonel Baylor's army approached Fort Fillmore and informed Major Lynde that the Confederates, numbering about three hundred men total, were marching up the Rio Grande toward the fort. The Confederates approached unnoticed to within approximately six hundred yards of Fort Fillmore the previous night, July 24, and encamped there awaiting the opportune moment for an attack upon the garrison.[31] The attack might have been a complete surprise but for the deserter, whose timely arrival caused a prompt call-to-arms of the entire garrison. Indeed, assistant surgeon James McKee had no doubt that the Union forces would have otherwise fallen. "The Texans . . . intended to surprise us at daylight, on the morning of the 25th, kill or capture the officers in their quarters, and then take the men prisoners in their barracks. A perfectly feasible plan, as the men, without any officers to give orders, would have readily submitted. Luckily for us, one of the Confederate pickets . . . deserted from their posts, came in, and alarmed the garrison."[32] Baylor himself reported this incident, writing that "the surprise of the enemy would have been complete but for the desertion of a private from Capt. T. F. Teel's company, who reported to Major Lynde our strength and position."[33] With the element of surprise now lost, Baylor, with a force half the size of that quartered within the walls of Fort Fillmore, had no choice but to bypass the fort and go directly to Mesilla.[34]

Accordingly, the Texans crossed the Rio Grande and at daybreak on July 25 passed through the village of Santo Tomás, opposite Fort Fillmore, without opposition. Two companies of U.S. troops from Fort Fillmore had previously garrisoned the small Mexican settlement, but these had been withdrawn several days before to strengthen the garrison at the fort.[35] The Mesilla newspaper reported that the Rebels took eight Union soldiers as prisoners at Santo Tomás, but set them at liberty after they swore not to take up arms against the Confederacy.[36]

Around 10 A.M. on the morning of July 25, Baylor's troops marched into Mesilla, "and were received with every manifestation of joy by the citizens."[37] Baylor's force at that time consisted of 303 Confederate troops.[38] The *Mesilla Times* was not at all discreet about its position on the matter. The headline for July 27, two days after Baylor's occupation, read "Arizona Free at Last." The people, too, evidently exulted in the long-awaited arrival of the Confederacy, to whom the Territory of Arizona had pledged its full support. As the gray-coats marched into the plaza, "Vivas and Hurrahs . . . [gave] them a welcome from every point."[39] With the Confederate army at Mesilla, and the Union army just a few miles away at Fort Fillmore, the stage was set for the first clash of these opposing forces in New Mexico.

Around 3 P.M. on the afternoon of July 25, a force of 380 Union troops, composed of two companies of the Regiment of Mounted Rifles, six companies of the 7th Infantry, and four howitzers, left Fort Fillmore and marched up the Rio Grande toward the Confederate stronghold at Mesilla. Only one company of the 7th Infantry, along with the regimental band, stayed behind at Fort Fillmore. "It made my despondent heart glad as I rode along and looked at the glittering array of muskets, well-drilled men, and trained horses," recalled assistant surgeon McKee. "Now, I fondly hoped, we would at last certainly redeem ourselves, and make a successful blow for the honor of the old flag, which fluttered in the breeze at the head of the column."[40] McKee's elation, however, proved to be short-lived.

"At about five o'clock the clouds of dust indicated the enemy were advancing towards the southern part of the city," reported the *Times*. "The whole [Confederate] force was moved to that point and every preparation made to give them the warmest of receptions."[41] As the Union soldiers approached the town of Mesilla, they "were drawn up in line of battle between two cornfields. . . . The citizens posted themselves on the tops of the houses on the principal streets prepared to render their assistance."[42] Thus it would seem that the bulk of the Mesilleros had pledged their support to the Confederate army, preparing to assist the Rebels in any way possible in thwarting the Union cause.

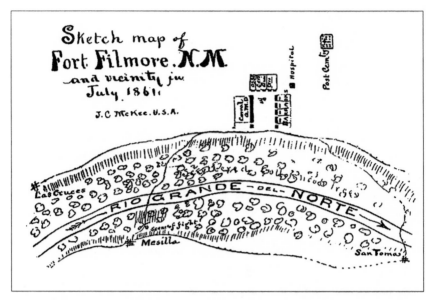

Map 8.2. Map drawn in 1861 by Assistant Surgeon James Cooper McKee who was present at Fort Fillmore during the Confederate invasion. The map shows the location of the fort in relation to Mesilla, San Tomás, and Las Cruces. (From James Cooper McKee, Narrative of the Surrender of a Command of U.S. Forces at Fort Fillmore, New Mexico in July A.D. 1861.*)*

The Confederates, preparing for the ensuing battle, concealed themselves on the southern end of the town behind whatever cover they could find, mostly corrals and brush. "Several of the principal streets in Mesilla converge at the southern end of town . . . the proximity of the corn fields make the position very advantaged to defend. Two companies were ordered to take their positions on top of the houses on the main plaza," reported the *Santa Fe Gazette.* Only one company, under command of Captain Coopwood, remained mounted for the fight.

Maj. Isaac Lynde, commanding the forces from Fort Fillmore, sent Lt. Edward J. Brooks and assistant surgeon James C. McKee in advance of the main column, under a flag of truce, to demand an unconditional surrender from Baylor and the Confederates.[43] Lynde's only advantage was numerical; in terms of defensive positions and the sentiment of the local people, Baylor enjoyed the advantage. As Brooks and McKee approached Mesilla, they were met south of the town by Maj. Ed Waller Jr. and Maj. P. T. Herbert of the Confederate Army, who provided Baylor's response to the request for an unconditional surrender: "If you wish the town and my forces, come and take them."[44] With both sides determined to stand steadfast behind their respective causes, there would be no peaceful resolution to the situation.

Having received Baylor's response, Lynde pressed onward toward Mesilla. The *Times* reported that "the enemy advanced to within 500 yards of our position and halted and formed in line of battle with two howitzers in the centre and the infantry, and on the wings cavalry, the whole force appearing to be about 500 men."[45] At this juncture, with his troops now less than half a mile away from the enemy, Major Lynde ordered his artillery to fire two rounds into the Confederate positions. This would prove to be a controversial decision, given the presence of civilians throughout the town and the inherent danger in which this placed them. The editors of the *Times* deplored this action by the Union commander, claiming that no notice had been given to the noncombatants, and that Lynde took the action with no consideration of their safety. The artillery rounds struck some of the adobe buildings on the southern end of the town, "fortunately without doing any injury to a single individual. . . . The first shell thrown struck on the top of a building on which was stationed a portion of Captain Teel's company and exploded."[46] Thus began the Battle of Mesilla, the first Civil War battle fought in the Territory of New Mexico.

The Union infantry now formed skirmish lines on either side of the artillery, but due to the cornfields through which they had to march in order to reach the town their lines quickly became broken up and staggered. At this point, with the Confederates remaining concealed in and around the town, and the infantry advance being slightly dismembered by the thickness of the cornfields, Lynde ordered his cavalry (in this case, mounted riflemen), commanded by Lt. C. H. McNally, to lead the attack on Mesilla.[47]

Here Lynde made a tremendous logistical blunder. "Instead of throwing out Infantry skirmishers in the cornfield to feel the enemy and protect his column," wrote McKee, "he ordered Lieut. McNally to deploy his [cavalry] company mounted in *front* of the infantry, with the result of making the mounted men conspicuous targets for the Texans."[48] The blunder would have severe ramifications for the Union cavalry. One Confederate soldier wrote, "After they had shot with their cannon the command was given to the cavalry and infantry to charge. The order was obeyed and they had advanced to within 250 yards when Baylor told one or two good shots to fire at the leader of the cavalry Lieut. McNally."[49] This statement is in general agreement with the later reports filed by Union officers, and McNally was in fact shot in the chest at the onset of the futile charge. The young lieutenant was the first man wounded during the battle, and it would thus seem likely that he had been picked off from a distance by enemy sharpshooters, as the Confederate witness suggests.

With their commander now fallen, the Union cavalry nevertheless continued forward. When they reached the concealed positions of the Confederates on the immediate southern outskirts of the town, of which they seemed to have had no prior knowledge, the Rebels arose from their hiding places and unleashed a volley into McNally's cavalrymen. This, the first Confederate volley, had the result of killing one and wounding at least three more. This action by the Confederates frightened and confused their enemies: "The order was given [by McNally] to charge four times to no purpose and they retired in confusion carrying with them the dead and wounded. . . . They were disheartened by their ill success in the charge, and as night was falling they drew off their whole force in good order, in the direction of Fort Fillmore."[50]

The utter confusion that now prevailed throughout the Union lines caused a major gaffe, one that almost cost the lives of many of McNally's retreating cavalrymen. The soldiers of the 7th Infantry, having formed skirmish lines some distance south of the town, mistook their retreating comrades for the enemy and fired into their ranks.[51] Wrote one soldier, "Our own infantry opened a perfect volley on our own cavalry—by mistake, it was said." By this time, the sun had gone down and darkness was fast approaching. With the Union defeat now apparent, "a few shots were fired by the artillery, when the whole command was ordered to retreat back to the post," where they finally arrived at about 9 P.M.[52] Upon receiving the order to retreat, "my soul sank within me," recalled surgeon McKee, "had any of the senior officers present at the time stepped forward, put Lynde in arrest, and taken command, his fortune would have been made."[53]

Baylor ordered several men to hide among the corn stalks and fire at the Union soldiers as they made their way back to Fort Fillmore, but beyond this the Rebels offered no pursuit. In this Major Lynde had been fortunate; Baylor mistakenly thought the retreat to be a ruse by the Union commander

to lead the Confederates into an ambush and thus did not pursue the army
as they hastily retreated to Fort Fillmore. "Fortunately they did not follow
us to the river. Had they done so, I verily believe Lynde would have surrendered us at that time," McKee later wrote.[54] The surgeon's disappointment
in his commander, Lynde, cannot be overstated. "The grand old 'Organ
Mountains' to the east loomed up in all their magnificent majesty," he lamented, "their rugged, clear-cut sides stood out in bolder relief than usual,
as if in mockery at the pitiable military farce going on at their base."[55]

Union losses at the Battle of Mesilla were three killed (Privates Lane,
Jenkins, and Sherwood), and six wounded.[56] In his report, Lynde erroneously exaggerated the strength of the Confederates, stating, "They were at
least 550 strong at Mesilla, while I had only about 500 all told."[57] The Confederates emerged victorious over a superior enemy force, due in large part
to the questionable decisions, tactics, and leadership exhibited by Lynde. To
be sure, the Rebels occupied the more favorable position, but nevertheless,
the Union soldiers, outnumbering Baylor's command and possessing a clear
advantage in artillery, should have exhibited a much more impressive and
spirited display.

One final spectacle occurred that fateful summer evening in Mesilla,
and brings with it a sort of comic relief. The story was recalled some months
later in the *Mesilla Times:*

> As in incident of the Battle of Mesilla, worth remembering, when
> the U.S. forces, under Lynde commenced bombarding the town of
> Mesilla . . . the Alcalde, became very indignant and angry, and pro-
> nounced the proceedings a "disorden grande," and said he would go
> out at once and put a stop to the row. He mounted his horse, put on
> his big spurs, and went cluttering down the streets to the scene of
> war, where he was saluted with a round of grape and the whistling
> of small-arm shot. Wheeling his horse . . . he came back at a terrible
> rate, saying he had given orders to stop, but nobody paid any atten-
> tion to them.[58]

With a little imagination, one can easily envision the Mexican alcalde
riding angrily into the midst of a Civil War battle under the false premoni-
tion that his order to cease firing would be obeyed by both sides. Obviously,

his pleas fell on deaf ears, and the mayor was fortunate to escape back into the Mesilla plaza with nothing injured, except perhaps his pride.

With Major Lynde's troops defeated and on the retreat back to Fort Fillmore, Baylor clearly held the advantage, and the aggressive Confederate commander would not let the opportunity pass him by. Rather than engage his troops in another skirmish, Lynde opted to abandon Fort Fillmore entirely and attempt to reach Fort Stanton, some 140 miles to the northeast, before being captured or defeated by Baylor. It was a fateful decision, one that would plague both Lynde and the Union army for a long time to come.

Around one o'clock in the morning on July 27, Major Lynde issued the order to abandon Fort Fillmore. The withdrawal of troops and supplies was conducted in great haste with the hope of maintaining secrecy to allow their safe retreat to Fort Stanton. "The time allowed was so short," wrote Captain Crilly, "that few stores could be destroyed, except the ammunition, which was entirely destroyed. . . . The officers left their personal property in their houses; very few of the officers knew of the destination of the command, and no particular preparation was made by the Company officers for a long march without water."[59] Additionally, the hospital and its supplies were thoroughly destroyed by surgeon McKee and others. "All the iron bedsteads [were] brought out and broken with sledge hammers, then all the mattresses, blankets, sheets, etc. piled upon the debris ready to be fired," McKee wrote.[60] Indeed, before the final abandonment of the post, the troops destroyed as much property as possible to prevent it from falling into the hands of the enemy. Much of the equipment and ammunition was either burned or buried; with so little time, some of the more important items were probably tossed into the latrines, under the assumption that surely the Confederate troops would not fish them out for their own use.

Dr. Morgan W. Merrick, who accompanied the invading Confederate force, arrived at Fort Fillmore the following morning and recorded the destruction in his diary. "They had left the place in a topsy-turvy stat[e]," he wrote. "The Q. M. D. was a confusion of boxes, barrels, paper, etc. At the hospital they had thrown the beding [sic] in a pile & emptied and broken bottles of medicin [sic] over them, had pulled or turned over the shelving in the dispensary into the middle of the floor, making a fine mess."[61] The fort itself, however, remained almost unharmed and might have been occupied by the Confederates had Baylor elected to do so. According to reports, nearby citizens set upon the fort like vultures the following morning, picking up everything they could carry and returning to their homes with the abandoned Union supplies before finally being run off by Confederate troops arriving to salvage any remaining supplies.[62]

Major Lynde's reasoning in this maneuver was simple. "If I remained, the troops and the public property would fall into the hands of the enemy," he explained to his department commander. "If I abandoned the post, the troops, it was hoped, would escape capture and the public property be destroyed."[63] As it were, neither proved true. Much of the supplies and provisions at Fort Fillmore were gathered up, both by the local people and the Confederates.[64] Nor did Lynde's troops, by abandoning the post, save themselves from capture. The ensuing events soon became notorious across the country; Lynde's retreat seems to have been doomed from the beginning and the events played out in such a disgraceful manner that Lynde's military career would never recover.

As previously noted, the abandonment and withdrawal from Fort Fillmore began at about 1 A.M., under cover of darkness. All went well until the sun came up. Southern New Mexico is known for scorching hot summer temperatures, and July 27, 1861, was certainly no exception. "As early as nine o'clock the extreme heat of the sun, made doubly hot reflected from the sand, and want of water, caused many of the men to fall out of ranks, exhausted, to seek the shade of the bushes, which were so small as to cover scarcely their heads," wrote Captain Crilly, "about 12 noon the whole Infantry Command can hardly be said to have had an organization; it was stretched for miles along the line of march, each man trying to save himself from the terrible heat."[65] Before traveling more than a dozen miles from Fort Fillmore, the command was in total disarray, and perhaps for more reasons than just the summer heat.

For years the supposed role of whiskey in the retreat has been among the most conjectured-upon components of the entire episode. Many have argued the case; numerous firsthand accounts of the incident vary in their particulars, and in some such accounts there is no mention whatsoever of excessive imbibing on the part of the troops. Yet other sources clearly state that this caused their dismemberment and subsequent capture. What is known for certain is that there was a large quantity of liquor kept on hand at Fort Fillmore, and it was frequently made available to the troops. This was the case at many frontier forts. It has often been asserted that prior to leaving Fort Fillmore for the last time many of the soldiers opted to fill their canteens with whiskey rather than water.

The matter demands even greater interest, however, when one considers the pro-South sympathies of Fort Fillmore's sutlers just prior to and during the Confederate invasion. On September 20, 1860, Samuel J. Jones, an outspoken supporter of secession, had been appointed to the position. On July 20, 1861, less than one week before Baylor's occupation and victory in the Battle of Mesilla, two new sutlers, Tully and Ochoa, replaced Jones. Once again, both of these men ardently supported the Southern cause and made no attempt to conceal the fact. The widespread Southern sentiment in the Mesilla Valley, coupled with the fact that plans for the invasion had been in the works for quite some time, invokes a certain amount of curiosity as to why the Union army would appoint two Southern men as sutlers at a Union fort.[66] If nothing else, this raises the question of whether these two post sutlers might have purposely supplied the bluecoats with copious amounts of spirits just before they marched out of the fort on the morning of July 27. Both Tully and Ochoa would have known that such an action would assist Baylor and the Confederates. Seven hundred men marching drunk in triple-digit temperatures through a barren, waterless desert spelled complete disaster, and in fact that is what happened. Did Tully and Ochoa premeditate the plan to distribute the liquor to the troops to prevent their safe march to Fort Stanton? This may never be positively known, but the idea should not be discounted.

Another aspect of the supposed drunkenness involves the treachery of many of the Union officers at Fort Fillmore. With the exception of only a couple, all other officers at Fort Fillmore during this period openly favored the Confederacy and preached their feelings almost daily to their troops. W. W. Mills, a prominent citizen of the El Paso area and a staunch supporter of the Union cause, protested bitterly against the anti-Federal sentiment throughout the valley, and he was particularly dumbfounded by the officers at Fort Fillmore. In June 1861, a month before Baylor's conquest, Mills wrote, "All the officers of Fort Fillmore, except two, are avowedly with the south, and are only holding on to their commission in order to embarrass our Government, and at the proper time to turn everything over to the South . . . the soldiers at Fillmore, in defiance of the teaching of their officers, and the offer of gold from [Simeon] Hart, are yet faithful."[67]

Given the fact that these officers were known to have anti-Union sentiments, it would not seem unlikely that many of them secretly *wanted* to surrender to Baylor. Thus it might not have been out of the question for the officers to allow the whiskey to be supplied to their troops just before embarking on the march to distant Fort Stanton. The fact that this might have occurred is supported by one participant's subsequent comments, published in a Midwest newspaper several weeks later:

> At half past ten [on July 26] an order was given to evacuate that night. The Commissary was ordered to roll out the whiskey, and the infantry were allowed to drink it and fill their canteens. No water was furnished for the hot march before them. The march was undertaken in the most irregular manner, and before we had gone ten miles, men were dropping from the ranks and falling down drunk. At two in the afternoon, Texan troops were seen advancing on the Las Cruces road. Our Adjutant, on being informed of it, made no preparation to resist an attack, but said "They have nothing to fear from us." Of the seven companies, so many had been left drunk and captured that no more than two companies went into camp.[68]

As the troops gradually began staggering into camp at San Augustine Springs on the eastern slopes of the Organ Mountains, it became evident to the Union commanders that their time was limited. Baylor's soldiers had left Mesilla in pursuit around sunrise, as soon as they learned of the evacuation of Fort Fillmore. According to Baylor, on the morning of July 27, "a little after daylight, my spies reported a column of dust seen in the direction of the Organ Mountains, distant 15 miles, on the Fort Stanton road. I could from the top of a house with my glass see the movements of the enemy. I immediately ordered the command to saddle and mount, for the purpose of intercepting them at San Augustine Pass."[69]

With the Union troops spread out for miles along the trail and with no means of defense, it would prove to be remarkably easy for Baylor to conquer the last remaining Northern contingent in the Mesilla Valley. One solitary Union soldier along the route openly resisted. "Crazy from thirst, fatigue, and undoubtedly despair, [the private] fired his musket at Colonel Baylor . . . and was immediately shot down by him," recalled one witness.[70]

Baylor overtook the entirety of the command, including Major Lynde, at San Augustine Springs; in doing so, the Confederate officer swayed south of the main wagon road through San Augustine Pass, pursuing a rougher but more direct route to the springs, through what would come to be known as Baylor Pass in honor of the conquering Rebel officer.

When the first Confederates rode toward the Union camp east of the Organ Mountains, there were not more than one hundred soldiers present; the remainder, strung out along the road, had already been captured. Nevertheless, under Lynde's orders, the remnant of the Federal force took up the line of battle and made ready their single remaining howitzer. According to the local newspaper, "Men were taken prisoners and disarmed in squads; the artillery was captured and a greater portion of the Infantry were taken before the main command was reached."[71] When Major Lynde finally announced his intention to surrender the whole of his command without resistance, only two of his fellow officers, Captains J. H. Potter and M. R. Stevenson, are said to have protested the decision.[72] This, however, is contradicted by reports of other officers, most notably surgeon J. Cooper McKee and Capt. Alfred Gibbs, who maintained that they and others among the officers present had adamantly opposed Lynde's decision, but their outspoken oppositions had been in vain.

In a moment not unlike that which occurred in 1846 when Mexican Governor Manuel Armijo surrendered New Mexico to General Kearny without resistance, Maj. Isaac Lynde capitulated his entire command to the Confederacy without firing a single shot. The Union troops outnumbered those of the Confederacy by a ratio of more than two to one, yet through blunders of planning and leadership failed to offer even the slightest resistance to their foes. Eleven officers, two surgeons, 399 troops of the 7th Infantry, ninety-five troops of the 3rd Cavalry, and over one hundred horses were captured by the Confederate commander.[73] At the time this constituted almost one-quarter of the Union regulars stationed in New Mexico. Writing to the assistant adjutant general a week later, Lynde explained the circumstances in which the surrender had taken place:

It was reported to me that a part of the teams had given out and could not be brought up, and that large numbers of the infantry had become totally overpowered with the intense heat. At this time an express from Captain Gibbs reported that eight companies of mounted men, supported by artillery and a large force of infantry, were approaching our rear guard. I had the "Call to arms" sounded, and found that I could not bring more than 100 men of the infantry battalion on parade. Captain Gibbs, with a mounted force, now rode into camp, and stated to me that eight companies of mounted Texans (supported by a regiment of Infantry, more or less) were approaching; that they had driven in or captured our rear guard and the men that had given out in the rear. Three of the four mountain howitzers that we had with us were with the wagons in the rear and captured.[74]

The *Mesilla Times,* always quick to provide commentary on the success of their esteemed Baylor, wrote, "In brief . . . 700 effective men surrendered to 280 Confederates. . . . The men and officers were disappointed in one thing alone—that the victory was so easily won. . . . All these important movements and the great success, have been made and gained without the loss of one drop of blood in the Confederate side."[75]

"The surrender of the troops at Fort Fillmore was one of those unaccountable events," wrote Capt. J. F. Crilly, present at the time of the surrender, "resulting from a combination of circumstances happening in quick succession, until the unfortunate affair itself was the climax."[76] One California newspaper with pro-North leanings reprinted the Mesilla Times' coverage and lamented as highly unfortunate the entire debacle, expressing discontent with the episode."[77]

Capt. Alfred Gibbs, of the 3rd Cavalry (formerly the Regiment of Mounted Rifles), further described the event:

I heard Major Lynde say "I agree to these terms," and I called to some of the officers to come up. When we came up, all the officers being present, I think, Major Lynde said: "Colonel Baylor, to avoid bloodshed, I conditionally surrender this whole force to you, on con-

dition that officers and their families shall be protected from insult
and private property be respected." Nearly every officer protested
earnestly, and even violently, against this base surrender; but Major
Lynde said: "I am the commander of these forces, and I take upon
my shoulders the responsibility of my action in the matter."[78]

The prisoners were almost immediately paroled, for at least two reasons.
First, Baylor's small army was in no way prepared or equipped to maintain a
prisoner-of-war facility in which to detain the Fort Fillmore troops. Second,
Capt. Isaiah N. Moore was on the march toward the Mesilla Valley from Fort
Buchanan with several companies of Union troops and posed an imminent
threat. "I could not guard the prisoners I had and meet the coming forces,"
Baylor wrote.[79] The entire Union force was therefore paroled by the Confederates and set free, "the men on oath, the officers on honor—not to fight
against the Southern Confederacy until duly exchanged. . . . The prisoners
paroled were allowed to take their departure for New Mexico, which they
did in two divisions, the cavalry companies in one, the infantry companies
in another."[80] Those of the Federal troops who resisted did not fare so well:
"Fourteen privates refused to take the oath, and are now at Fort Fillmore, doing good work for the Southern Confederacy, in the shape of hard work."[81]

To their credit the Confederate victors generally treated their captured
Union counterparts with dignity and honor. After surrendering, surgeon
McKee wrote, "they were considerate and kind to all and behaved like soldiers in all respects."[82] Major Lynde similarly noted that "the Texan troops
acted with great kindness to our men, exerting themselves in carrying water
to the famished ones in the rear."[83]

The reputation of Maj. Isaac Lynde would never fully recover from this
humiliating and demoralizing defeat by a far inferior force under Baylor.
"Whatever the truth, history has treated him on a par with Benedict Arnold,"
wrote one historian.[84] The commander of the military department, Col.
E. R. S. Canby, ultimately chose not to court-martial Lynde, but only due to
the fact that not enough officers present at the time could be counted upon
to testify against him. Nevertheless, formal charges were proffered against
Lynde by some of those under his command, including Captain Potter of
the 7th Infantry, who had been one of the few officers to protest Lynde's
decision to surrender. On November 25, 1861, pursuant to orders from the

Map 8.3. Map showing the appearance of the Southern Confederacy, denoted in black, as it existed in August 1861, following the admittance of Arizona as a Confederate Territory. (Courtesy John P. Wilson, Las Cruses, N.M.)

president, Major Lynde lost his commission in the army "for abandoning his post and subsequently surrendering the command to an inferior force of insurgents." Ultimately, Lynde would formally request to be reinstated to his former commission, and, following an investigation by the secretary of war, he was indeed restored, first to his former rank of major, then to lieutenant colonel, before being formally retired on November 27, 1866.[85]

With the surrender of Lynde's troops, the Federal government no longer controlled the Mesilla Valley. Lt. Col. John R. Baylor, in the name of the Confederate States of America, had invaded the region and taken charge of it, bringing the area under complete Confederate jurisdiction. Baylor wasted no time in establishing a new Confederate government in Mesilla, simultaneously recognizing the "Territory of Arizona" as an entity of the Southern Confederacy.

CHAPTER 9

The Confederate Territory of Arizona

With the garrison of Federal troops at Fort Fillmore no longer an imminent threat, Lieutenant Colonel Baylor turned his attentions elsewhere. Much work remained to be done; indeed, the Confederate commander had only taken the first small step toward the ultimate goal of controlling the Territory of New Mexico. Baylor now began to concern himself with more important regional matters: the creation of the Confederate Territory of Arizona (with himself as governor), the marauding Apaches, and plans for the remainder of the Confederate scheme to take New Mexico. He clearly had his work cut out for him.

The *Mesilla Times,* true to form, lavishly praised Baylor for his defeat of the Union army and encouraged their new leader to continue the "good fight." The *Times* edition of July 27, besides spewing its typical share of pro-South editorials recounting the Battle of Mesilla and the defeat of Major Lynde at San Augustine Springs, recalled with enthusiasm the events of the past week in the Mesilla Valley:

> The excitement of the last five days leaves our citizens in a general glow of joy and congratulation. The rapid movements of Lt. Col. Baylor and his Command, has changed our position from one of fear and anxiety to wild enthusiasm—the dread of armed oppression and outrage give place to the brightest hopes and most confident security. The transition from darkness to light has been sudden, skillful, and glorious. We are now delivered from the hands of our enemies, and our most sanguine expectations realized. Our seven-starred banner, instead of being trampled in the dust by the minions of an Abolition despot, is bathed in new glories. Arizona has thrown off the chains which have so long bound her. . . . The present Confederate Congress will give us a territorial organization; the gallant Confederate troops have given us freedom from oppression; they will in proper time scurge [sic] our fair land of Indian marauders; the capital of the country will receive new impulses; every field of labor will feel the invigorating influence; the immense resources of the country

will be developed; and a golden age of prosperity and progress will be our heritage, instead of studied neglect and a continued series of misfortunes. Well may our citizens rejoice: 'tis a full theme of joy and congratulations. We have changed from sorrow to gladness, from death to life.[1]

The profound anti-Federal sentiment that obviously prevailed in Mesilla, and throughout the valley, cannot be understated. All throughout New Mexico, even before the Civil War broke out, political leaders and average citizens alike had expressed concern about the area as a potential safe haven for ill-intentioned advocates of secession. This had provided a tremendous boost of confidence to the Confederate invaders who knew they would be surrounded by friendly compatriots.

On August 1, 1861, Baylor issued his famous proclamation establishing a provisional Confederate government in the Territory of Arizona, with Mesilla to serve as the capital. "The social and political condition of Arizona being little short of general anarchy, and the people being literally destitute of law, order, and protection," Baylor wrote, "the said Territory, from the date hereof, is hereby declared temporarily organized as a military government until such time as Congress may otherwise provide."[2] With this general statement, the people of Mesilla, Tucson, and everywhere in between finally received what they had so long desired: recognition as their own sovereign territory. The organization as such, however, did not come under the banner of the United States of America, as they had originally requested beginning in 1856, but rather under the flag of the newly created Confederacy. For many of the leading citizens, this was even better than they had hoped for; they not only achieved their long-sought political recognition but also received it under the auspices of the South, whose cause they had so openly espoused.

According to Baylor, who used the proclamation to appoint himself governor and vest within himself nearly all political powers and privileges possible, Arizona would consist of "all that portion of the recent territory of New Mexico lying south of the thirty fourth parallel of north latitude." In other words, the Confederate Territory spread from the Rio Grande westward to the Colorado River, covering all of the southern portions of present-day New Mexico and Arizona, with the northern boundary just south of the town of Socorro, New Mexico.

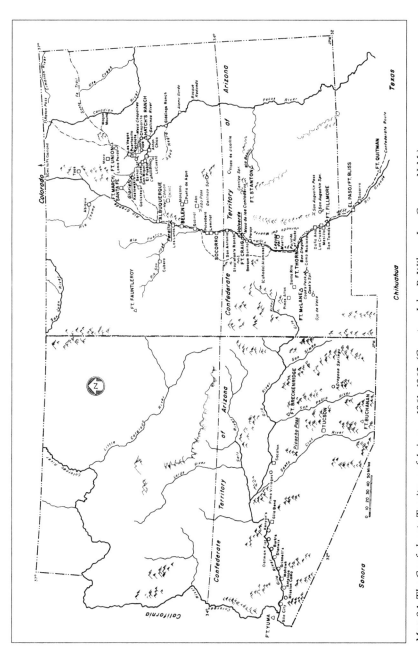

Map 9.1. The Confederate Territory of Arizona, 1861–1862. (Courtesy John P. Wilson, Las Cruces, N.M.)

All of the laws of New Mexico previously in effect would remain applicable, in addition to the laws and regulations of the Confederate States of America, in order to maintain a smooth transition in leadership and government. This policy was to remain effective "until such time as the Confederate Congress may otherwise provide." Baylor established just two branches of government for the territory (executive and judicial), rather than the familiar three branches composing the Federal government. As far as the districting of the territory, Baylor wrote that "the judicial districts of the Territory shall be divided as follows: The first district shall comprise all the portion of Arizona lying east of the Apache Pass, the district and probate court whereof shall be holden at La Mesilla. The second judicial district shall comprise the remainder of the territory. The district and probate courts shall be holden at Tucson."[3] Baylor's action placed all political power in the towns of Mesilla and Tucson, at that time the only settlements of any considerable size and importance located within the Confederacy's jurisdiction.

On the day following the issuance of his proclamation, Baylor announced his appointments to the various territorial offices. James A. Lucas, with whom much of the original work toward the creation of an Arizona Territory had begun, was enlisted to serve as secretary of the territory. Marcus H. MacWillie would fill the role of attorney general, H. Apperstein would serve as treasurer, George Frazer as marshal, and Frank Higgins would be probate judge in the first judicial district of Mesilla. In addition, as prescribed by the terms of Baylor's proclamation, each town was to have a justice of the peace. All appointees were ardent Southern enthusiasts, committed to working side by side with Baylor to ensure the successful outcome of the Confederate invasion and the proper maintenance of the newly established Arizona Territory.

The Confederate courts that Baylor established levied taxes on fandangos, or dances, as well as theater performances in Mesilla.[4] Numerous common, everyday things were outlawed by the court, which failed to recognize the cultural differences existing between the Mexicans of Mesilla and the newly arrived Southerners. Washing clothing outdoors in the acequias, or irrigation ditches, which had been a common practice in Mesilla as well as most other Mexican settlements, was strictly forbidden by Higgins's successor in the office of probate judge, J. Peter Deus. "It is ordered that from and after this date all Persons are forbidden to wash their Clothing or other dirty Articles in the Acequias and Water Holes within the limits of the towns of this County," he announced on March 3, 1862; "any person violating this order to be fined in the sum of Five Dollars to be collected by the Justice of the Peace of the Precinct in which the offense is committed."[5]

Many other common Mexican practices, which were openly abhorred by the newcomers from the Confederate States, were also ordered to be done away with. The probate court, in addition to outlawing the cleaning of clothes in ditches, further ordered on September 7, 1861, that "no person shall be allowed to deposit Wood or other Fuel upon the streets or plaza of this Town for sale under the penalty of Twenty Five Cents for each offense." Additionally, the court ordered that "the practice of butchering Animals upon the streets or plaza of the Town for sale is prohibited and a fine for each breach of this order is assessed at fifty cents," and finally, the judge ordered that "the Rendering or Frying out Tallow and Lard upon the streets and plazas is declared to be a Public Nuisance and a fine of fifty cents shall be collected from each offender against this ordinance for every violation of the same."[6] If nothing else, these decrees would serve to improve sanitation in and around Mesilla.

The Confederate Congress eventually passed Baylor's acts, for the most part, on January 18, 1862 (by that time, Baylor had been replaced by General Sibley as commanding officer at Mesilla). One of the few changes made by the Congress was to create three districts, rather than the two (Mesilla and Tucson) proposed by Baylor. Naturally, the institution of slavery received protection in Arizona, and future governors of that territory would serve six-year terms.[7] The governor received a salary of $1,500 per annum, plus an additional $500 for his dual role as commissioner of Indian affairs. The Confederate Congress further decreed that all legal proceedings in Arizona were to be conducted in English rather than the familiar Spanish. Finally, the territory was allowed one delegate to the Confederate Congress, to be paid eight dollars per day for his services, plus an additional ten cents for every ten miles traveled while engaged in his official duties.[8]

Baylor's success in capturing Fort Fillmore and establishing a Confederate government in southern New Mexico created a widespread hysteria across the territory. Still, in some instances news spread slowly, especially to the west, where several companies of Union troops had remained stationed at Forts Buchanan and Breckenridge (both in present-day Arizona). During the first week of August, these troops abandoned their posts and marched east across the Butterfield Trail toward Mesilla, still unaware of the Confederates' capture of Major Lynde's entire command. An express rider rode from Fort Craig in hopes that he might overtake the Union troops and warn them before they suffered the same fate as those at Fort Fillmore a week and a half before. The rider intercepted the command at Cooke's Spring, a mere sixty miles west of Mesilla, whereupon the commanding officer, Lt. Isaiah N. Moore, ordered all of the wagons and excess provisions burned and his troops to march posthaste to Fort Craig, arriving there safely a day later.[9]

Baylor had been well aware of the approach of these Union troops from the west and had prepared accordingly. "Several companies of Confederate troops had been encamped for several days at the village of Picacho, the point where the California road leaves the Mesilla Valley," wrote the *Mesilla Times*. "Cannon were planted, and every arrangement made to receive the United States forces under Lieut. Moore, who were abandoning western Arizona. This force consisted of four companies, two of the 2nd Cavalry and two of infantry. Scouts reported them advancing leisurely, unaware of any war movements in the territory." Baylor would likely have scored another victory had the express from Fort Craig failed to reach Lieutenant Moore's command in time. As it was Baylor had no chance of overtaking the soldiers after they left the Butterfield Trail and struck northward toward Fort Craig. "Before the condition of affairs could be known by our scouts, and expressed to the command at Picacho, they had many hours the start, and it was useless to follow them," noted the *Times*.[10]

Just as the Union posts in far western New Mexico were being hastily abandoned, so too did the troops abandon Fort Stanton northeast of the Mesilla Valley. Fort Stanton had been Major Lynde's intended destination just a week earlier when retreating from Fort Fillmore. Because he failed to reach that place, the garrison there remained too small to thwart a possible attack by the Confederates, and the troops were pulled back to the more northerly posts in the territory.[11] The Union troops had "hastily abandoned the fort after having destroyed a considerable portion of their supplies and Government property . . . all would have been destroyed but for a storm of rain which extinguished the fire intended by the enemy to destroy it."[12] The pandemonium at Fort Stanton consequent to Baylor's successful occupation of the Mesilla Valley also received mention in a *Times* issue of August 10. The abandonment, they noted, "occurred shortly after the surrender of San Augustin; two fugitives from Lynde's command fled to this post and gave information of that affair. The garrison was panic stricken, and, supposing the whole Confederate forces would be down upon them, immediately evacuated the fort . . . not one federal soldier is now left on the soil of Arizona."[13]

Despite his unhindered success up to this point and bright prospects for more of the same in the future, Baylor wrote to his commanding officer, Gen. Earl Van Dorn, on August 12 requesting a leave of absence in order that he "may be allowed to go to Virginia to defend the graves of my ancestors, and I ask for a leave of absence for two months . . . as there is nothing to do here, I would like to go where I can render some service to our country. I ask that some competent man be sent to relieve me."[14] The fact that Baylor, a mere two weeks after his defeat of the Union forces and establishment of a new government of which he himself served as governor, would make such a request is somewhat baffling. Van Dorn refused to grant the leave of absence, and it would therefore be Baylor's personal misfortune to remain in the Mesilla Valley for several more months awaiting further orders from headquarters.[15]

With his request for a transfer back east denied, Baylor reluctantly turned his attentions to the issues facing him as self-appointed governor of Arizona. Just as had been the case throughout the decade before his arrival, the Apaches continued to cause hardships for the people of the Mesilla Valley and Arizona, and it now became Baylor's responsibility to curb these depredations. Baylor's men continued to have skirmishes with hostile Apaches, during the course of which several Confederate troops lost their lives. As a result of these continued struggles, Baylor requested reinforcements from General Van Dorn for use in suppressing Indian depredations. He found it nearly impossible to simultaneously operate against the Apaches and advance northward to face the Union forces.

Baylor did not immediately receive the reinforcements and, as a consequence, he authorized the raising of four companies of local troops "to hold the territory and afford protection to the citizens."[16] These volunteer troops came to be known as the Arizona Guards, and their most important duty as such, according to Baylor, was to "reopen the road between Mesilla and Tucson [the Butterfield Trail], [and] especially to rout the savages from Apache Pass."[17] Many of the local citizens serving in the Arizona Guard likely served in the Mesilla Guard several years prior, as they were always willing to take up arms against the Apaches whenever the opportunity arose.

The Arizona Guards, led by Capt. Thomas J. Mastin, were mustered into the service of the Confederacy in August 1861, and were thereafter thrust into action against the Apaches. Several small skirmishes occurred between Mesilla and Tucson, most notably a fight in the Florida Mountains with eight Indians reportedly being killed by the guards. However, Captain Mastin would not remain long at the helm of his volunteer Southern regiment; on October 7, 1861, during a fight with Apaches at the gold mining camp of Piños Altos, Mastin received wounds from which he shortly thereafter succumbed.[18]

Throughout his short stead as governor, Baylor came to know intimately the previous fifteen years of hardships endured by the people and soldiers of New Mexico in regard to the Indian raiding and warfare that plagued the area. On the morning of September 27, between 250 and 300 Apaches attacked the town of Piños Altos. The front page of the *Times* featured a description of the incident, accompanied by a cry for assistance in defending against the Indians. "The Apaches seem to have united, and their tribes have gathered in hosts and commenced a war of extermination against the whites," the article began. "In such formidable numbers they have never assembled before on the war scout, and never before have they . . . evinced such boldness as to attack a town of two or three hundred houses in open daylight. . . . The slightest journey must be performed in numbers, and with armed bodies of men . . . every day brings from the east, west, north and south, appalling additions to our black list of Indian murders." The situation appeared bleak, with destruction having been wrought across the landscape. "Homes deserted, friends fallen victim to the savage foe," the *Times* lamented. "Added to this the scourge of war, and our situation is most piteous and most unfortunate. In our very midst is a multitude of friends [the Confederate troops], willing and ready to render assistance, but prevented by the presence of another foe [the Union troops to the north]."[19]

Baylor struggled to solve the problems presented almost weekly by the Apaches, and his predisposed enmity toward all Indians, regardless of tribal affiliation, did not help matters. Baylor, a seasoned Indian fighter from Texas, showed little remorse for the starving and destitute Apaches. In an infamous letter written to Capt. Thomas Helm, Baylor advocated genocide, which would ultimately lead to controversy for the commander of Arizona. His orders to Captain Helm came to be abhorred by most who read the letter, even those whose sentiments toward the Apaches agreed with Baylor's. He concluded his instructions to Helm by saying that "you will therefore use all means to persuade the Apaches or any tribe to come in for the purpose of making peace, and when you get them together kill all the grown Indians and take the children prisoners and sell them to defray the cost of killing the Indians. Buy whiskey and such other goods as may be necessary for the Indians . . . and have a sufficient number of men around to allow no Indian to escape."[20]

Confederate Gen. Henry Hopkins Sibley, who disliked Baylor (a personal feud existed between the two), submitted copies of the order to newspaper editors in Texas, whereupon the contents were published and the editors openly denounced Baylor's Indian policy as cruel and barbarous.[21] Baylor, not to be outdone, wrote a terse editorial in a Houston newspaper lambasting Sibley. "It is enough for [Sibley] to know that there was to be a quantity of whisky used in the enterprise to shock and horrify him," wrote Baylor. "I could not have been guilty of a greater crime in the estimation of this 'hero' than to waste whisky in killing Indians. . . . General Sibley, no doubt, would never resort to such means of ridding the country of these pests, but if the Indians could by any process be dissolved and converted into whisky, I have no doubt that he would drink the whole Apache nation in one week."[22] Certainly this response by Baylor, indicative of his fiery temper, did little to calm the feud.

Ultimately, the contents of the order reached the Confederate government in Richmond, forcing Baylor to vouch for his statements. President Jefferson Davis, along with Confederate Secretary of State George W. Randolph, asked Maj. Gen. John B. Magruder, commanding the Confederate department in which Arizona was located, to order Baylor to submit a full report of the incident. Baylor responded to Magruder on December 29, 1862, after he had already been replaced by General Sibley as commander of the Confederate troops at Mesilla. The colonel's reply came across as unapologetic: "While I sincerely regret that it has been viewed in such an unfavorable light by His Excellency the President [Jefferson Davis], as to induce him to deprive me of the command of the brave men . . . whom I was prepared to lead to battle . . . yet I cannot alter the convictions and feelings of a life time."[23] Baylor, attempting to prove himself justified in issuing the extermination order, explained, "Outrages were committed frequently; the mails were robbed; in one or two instances the messengers were found hanging up by the heels, their heads within a few inches of a slow fire, and they thus horribly roasted to death. Others were found tied to the wheels of the coach, which had been burned." In addition to these cruel acts, Baylor also attested to the fact that the Confederates themselves had continuously fallen victim to Apache raiding, noting that "upon the arrival of Sibley's brigade these Indians stole from his troops 100 head of horses and mules."[24] Owing to such atrocities, Baylor felt himself wholly justified in ordering his subordinate officers to carry out acts of extermination against the Apaches.

Baylor's explanation failed to appease his superiors. The Confederacy had previously advocated a treaty-making policy with Indian tribes, something Baylor's orders to Captain Helm completely contradicted. Additionally, there appears to have been some fear among Confederate government officials that international publication of Baylor's order could shine a negative light on their cause and might undermine their hope for foreign recognition. Thus President Davis acted promptly in the matter. Ultimately, Baylor would be stripped of his command by the Confederate leaders, due in large part to his ruthless, unforgiving Indian policy as manifested in both his letters and his actions.[25] In an ironic twist of fate, Baylor was subsequently elected to the Confederate House of Representatives and took his seat on May 25, 1864; shortly thereafter he was appointed to serve as a member of the committee on Indian affairs.[26]

The Apaches continued to pose difficulties for the Confederates during their gradual advance northward in 1862. They continually found themselves plagued by Apache raiding, much to the chagrin of not only Baylor but his successors as well. As the Confederates began their slow march northward from the Mesilla Valley in small detachments, their frustration with Indian attacks and thefts must have been profound. By the time all was said and done, many of the troops and officers alike did not deviate far from Baylor in their opinion of the Indians.

Despite the imminent threat of Apache attacks, Baylor could not afford to turn his sights away from the more important threat to the north, that of the Union garrison at Fort Craig. With several thousand enemy troops stationed there, just 130 miles to the north, the invading Confederate forces had to be careful not to become distracted by the Indians. On September 28, he wrote to the assistant adjutant general in San Antonio, Texas, informing him, "I have concentrated all the force I could muster about 9 miles above these Headquarters [Mesilla], fearing an attack from Fort Craig, and I am daily expecting a strong force from that point to move against me. . . . If I am expected to hold fifteen hundred regular troops and four regiments of New Mexican volunteers in check, with less than five hundred men, [I ask that] some other force be sent to operate against the Indians."[27] A month later, on November 10, Baylor moved these troops back to Mesilla because he had "a great deal of business to attend to as Governor of the Territory and it is essential that I should have troops here [at Mesilla] to enforce my authority and maintain order."[28] With less than a thousand troops at his disposal to oppose an estimated Union force of three thousand, and a vast territory stretching from the Rio Grande to California to govern, Baylor faced dire circumstances.

Writing to General Sibley on October 25, Baylor requested that reinforcements be sent to Mesilla as soon as practicable, noting that the Mexican contingent of the local population had begun to shift in sentiment toward the North. Perhaps the continued presence of the Rebels, and their consumption of local subsistence stores, had begun to take its toll on the attitude of the residents. "The Mexican Population are decidedly Northern in sentiment," Baylor complained, "and avail themselves of the first opportunity to rob us or join the enemy. Nothing but a strong force will keep them quiet."[29] Only a few months prior, the local population had been deemed to be decidedly pro-South, suggesting either that assumption had been gravely mistaken or else the Confederate soldiers, once having occupied Mesilla, treated the citizens poorly.

The fact that Baylor's continued presence caused turmoil among the local citizens became evident in December when Robert P. Kelley,[30] the editor of the *Mesilla Times* and an avid proponent of the Southern cause, wrote negatively about Baylor in the newspaper. Kelley disagreed with some of Baylor's actions, particularly that he had forced many of the people to abandon their property in and around Mesilla for the benefit of the troops, many of whom were quartered in buildings on the plaza. Matters came to a climax

on December 12 when, in the main plaza of Mesilla, a fight broke out between the two men. Reports stated that Baylor hit Kelley over the head with
a musket, then threw him to the ground and jumped on him. Kelley then
drew a knife, but his attempts to stab Baylor were in vain. The Confederate
officer rose, drew his pistol, and shot Kelley in the head.[31] The *Times* editor,
succumbing to the gunshot wound, had written his last slanderous word
about the governor of Arizona. In the subsequent hearing, which took place
in a Confederate court in Mesilla, a grand jury exonerated Baylor of the
murder charge. Four men took the stand to testify as witnesses on Baylor's
behalf; all four were Confederate troops under his direct command.[32]

By this time Baylor's brief tenure as military and government leader in
Arizona neared its end. The departure of General Sibley from San Antonio,
Texas, on November 18, 1861, with a force of some three thousand Confederates signified Lieutenant Colonel Baylor's eventual comeuppance. Sibley
arrived at Fort Bliss, Texas, in early December, about the same time that
the affray involving Baylor and Kelley took place on the Mesilla plaza. On
December 14, a mere two days after the killing of Robert P. Kelley and before
the grand jury had acquitted Baylor, Sibley arrived at Mesilla and assumed
the role of "Commander of the Army of New Mexico" in place of Baylor.[33]
Sibley thereafter commanded "all the forces of the Confederate States on
the Rio Grande at and above Ft. Quitman [Texas] and all in the Territory of
New Mexico and Arizona."[34]

On December 20, with Baylor still in Mesilla but now serving under
Sibley as his superior officer, the new commander issued a proclamation to
the people of Arizona, saying:

> An army under my command enters New Mexico to take posses-
> sion of it in the name and for the benefit of the Confederate States. By
> geographical position, by similarity of institutions, by commercial
> interests, and by future destinies New Mexico pertains to the Con-
> federacy. . . . Upon the peaceful people of New Mexico the Confeder-
> ate States wage no war. To them we come as friends, to re-establish a
> governmental connection agreeable and advantageous both to them
> and to us; to liberate them from the yoke of a military despotism
> erected by usurpers upon the ruins of the former free institutions of
> the United States.[35]

The Confederate general called for all Union officers and troops in New Mexico to throw down their arms immediately and espouse the Confederate cause, "the officers upon their commissions, the men upon their enlistments."[36] Obviously, such a demand was never destined for compliance, and Sibley's troops were forced to remain in occupation of Mesilla, eventually marching up the Rio Grande toward the Union strongholds in the northern part of the territory.

During the first months of 1862, General Sibley carried out his plans for the full-scale invasion of the Territory of New Mexico. After a disputable victory on February 21 at the Battle of Valverde, north of Fort Craig, the Confederates were finally defeated at Glorieta Pass a month later. With this, the grand Confederate scheme dissipated, and Sibley retreated from New Mexico by the route from which he came, through the Rio Grande valley.

As Sibley passed through the Mesilla Valley on his way to Texas, he found conditions there had changed drastically since he had departed in January. The Mexican residents in and around Mesilla, once considered staunch supporters of the Confederate cause, no longer appeared so amiable. News of the Union victory at Glorieta had reached those living in Mesilla; now, realizing the potential disaster that might befall them if they continued to support the defeated secessionists, the people turned their sentiments toward the Federals.

As the Confederates trekked back through the Mesilla Valley they found a citizenry no longer willing to provide them with food and other provisions (and, to be sure, they had been very reluctant to do so in the first place). "The Southern soldiers here are retiring," an elderly Mexican citizen of Mesilla wrote to his son, Placido Romero, "and the reason is that they have consumed and destroyed everything, even to the growing crops. The people here are with their eyes open toward the North, in the hope of being relieved from the devastation of these locusts. More than 1,000 men are waiting with open arms to receive the liberal Government of the North."[37] This change in sentiment caused a great deal of inconvenience to the already downtrodden gray-coats, who camped in and around Las Cruces for a brief period before finally returning to El Paso. Men quickly became ill from malnutrition, adding further insult to injury for Sibley's troops.

Now in a state of desperation, a group of thirteen Confederates volunteered to accompany one Captain Cleaver on a raid of Mesilla on July 1, 1862, for the purpose of stealing cattle to be butchered for food. Near the village they "found a small herd of cattle in the charge of a Mexican herder. The captain called a halt and asked for a volunteer . . . [to] take charge of the cattle." The small raiding party then split up, and a short distance south of Mesilla some of the Rebels were confronted by armed Mexicans who approached from three sides, leaving the Rio Grande as their only means for escape. In a desperate attempt to cross the river and return safely to their camp at Las Cruces, all but one of the Confederates were killed, including their commander, Captain Cleaver of the 7th Texas Infantry.[38]

Ultimately, seven Confederates were killed in this confrontation, and the losses of the Mexicans were estimated at forty, a number probably exaggerated by the Confederate officers reporting the incident. "It was a desperate fight," wrote J. A. Kirgan in his report to headquarters of July 8, "a Lieutenant of Col. Baylor's killed 3 Mexicans with his bowie-knife."[39] Among the others killed by the Mesilla citizens were Privates Thomas D. Cole, W. P. Allen, Randolph Daniels, and J. W. Herron of Company D, 7th Infantry; and Private William Bertrand of Company E, 7th Infantry.[40]

Less than a week after this unfortunate affair on the Rio Grande, the commander of Confederate forces in the Mesilla Valley, Col. William Steele, abandoned his camp and retreated to more friendly territory at Fort Bliss, Texas. This action was taken not so much to avoid further altercations with the local citizens, but rather because at that time the advance party of Union troops belonging to the California Column had arrived at Doña Ana, only a few miles to the north of the Rebel camp. Knowing this, Colonel Steele reasoned that the remainder of Major Carleton's Californians would not be far behind, and for the Confederates to remain in the Mesilla Valley would mean the certain defeat and unnecessary demise of scores of Sibley's men. Less than a week after Steele left Las Cruces, the entire Confederate contingent departed from Fort Bliss for San Antonio, and the Southern threat to take possession of New Mexico had finally ended.

CHAPTER 10

Martial Law in the Mesilla Valley

While Baylor, Sibley, and others busied themselves with the plotted Southern takeover of New Mexico, Union troops did not remain dormant in other quarters within the territory. As the Confederate invasion gradually unfolded, the Union army made preparations to resist the enemies not only in New Mexico but in California as well. A large body of volunteer troops known as the California Column was mustered into service and placed under the command of Maj. James Henry Carleton. Their orders were to march from southern California to the Mesilla Valley to serve as reinforcements for the Union troops already in New Mexico and to thwart the Confederate scheme in any way possible.

The Californians got off to a slow start, and by the time their march to New Mexico commenced the Confederates had already been defeated at Glorieta and were retreating back toward Texas. Nevertheless, Carleton's troops would still be needed in order to ensure that the federal government regained control of the Confederate Territory of Arizona, where many secessionists still resided and exercised their influence.

The march would be a slow and tedious one for Carleton's troops, causing much dissatisfaction among the men. Writing an anti-Carleton address at Mesilla in 1865 after mustering out of the service, four of Carleton's former soldiers complained bitterly of their commander and his tactics, particularly during their long march to the Mesilla Valley. "Nothing of importance characterized that march until our arrival at Fort Yuma, on the Colorado River"; they explained, "at this point commenced the series of gross derelictions of duty, frauds, unwarranted delays, marches and countermarches without any progress, which facts, when they receive the awful sentence of history, will forever shroud the name of James H. Carleton, in the darkest obloquy and disgrace." The four soldiers openly accused Carleton of stalling in order to avoid any direct confrontation with the Confederate troops who still remained in Las Cruces until the summer of 1862. They further explained that Carleton, "while at Tucson . . . knowing that the rebels were on the Rio Grande, plundering and robbing the citizens of that valley, for no good cause whatsoever, persistently delayed and refused to follow and punish them when fully within his power to do so . . . and it is an undisputable fact that he never moved from that point towards the Rio Grande until he was positively informed the enemy had retired."[1]

An advance troop of the California Column, under Lt. Col. Joseph Rodman West, reached Tucson on May 20, 1862, and took possession without opposition; the rebel troops there fled to the Rio Grande.[2] Carleton followed close behind, reaching Tucson in June and immediately declaring Arizona a federal territory and nullifying all prior Confederate laws. Carleton's first action after pronouncing Arizona a part of the United States was to make himself head of state. In doing this he differed but little from Lt. Col. John R. Baylor. Both of these men entered "Arizona" with a command of troops, both proclaimed that it belonged to their own government and made proclamations outlining this, and both elevated themselves to the position of governor. Once governor, Carleton would act surprisingly similar to the way Baylor had; that is, Union troops would be quartered in and around the Mesilla Valley settlements, and the citizens would be drawn upon for all of the necessary food stores to maintain the army and their animals. It was a trying time indeed for the people living in the area.

On August 14, Major Carleton issued his proclamation, ironically informing the people of Arizona that they "may now rest assured that the era of anarchy and misrule—when there was no protection to life or property; when the wealthy were plundered; when the poor were robbed and oppressed . . . has passed away; that now, under the sacred banner of our country, all may claim and shall receive their just rights."[3] While the era of Confederate rule had in fact passed away forever in the Mesilla Valley, it remains highly debatable as to whether or not the era of anarchy passed along with it. Carleton immediately declared martial law and promptly arrested any Southern sympathizers who crossed his path, in the process claiming their property for the federal government. All other residents were forced to take an oath of allegiance to the United States of America as evidence of their denunciation of the Confederacy.[4]

Martial law, by its very nature, has always been a controversial aspect of wartime conditions, and the incidents taking place in the Mesilla Valley during the period 1862–65 proved no exception. Usually unwritten, martial law "is invoked as an extreme measure which pressing necessity alone can justify . . . [and] is established when civil authority in the community is made subordinate to military, either in repelling invasion or when the ordinary administration of the laws fail to secure the proper objects of government."[5] It is typically justified by the notion that military action "should be prompt, meeting the danger and overcoming it on the instant. It cannot, therefore, afford to await on the deliberations of a legislative assembly." The downside to this is that it allows the military commander instituting martial law "a larger charter than the end in view requires or is consistent with freedom. Armed with the sanction of positive law, [the military commander] need no longer consider whether his acts are justified by necessity. He may abuse the undefined power entrusted to his hands, and destroy life, liberty, and property without the shadow of an excuse."[6] Major Carleton came to embody these detrimental impacts of prolonged implementation of martial law.

One man who received the brunt of Carleton's authoritarian actions was Sylvester Mowry, a prominent man who supported the South prior to Carleton's arrival. Mowry lived in the vicinity of the Sonoita River and Patagonia Mines, some forty miles south of Tucson, and upon arriving at that city Carleton dispatched Lt. Col. E. E. Eyre to arrest him at his home for treasonous activities. "It is possible I shall be obliged to hold Mr. Mowry as prisoner," Carleton wrote on June 10, 1862. "That he has been guilty of overt as well as covert acts of treason there is hardly a doubt. I consider his presence in this territory as dangerous to its peace and prosperity."[7] On June 16, by Carleton's orders, a board consisting of three Union officers convened to investigate the charges against Mowry; their findings did not bode well for him. "The board having examined the foregoing personal testimony and documentary evidence," the final report declared, "are of the opinion that said Sylvester Mowry is an enemy to the government of the United States, and that he has been in treasonable correspondence and collusion with well known secessionists, and has afforded them aid and comfort when they were known publicly to be enemies . . . to the government of the United States . . . and that there are sufficient grounds to restrain the said Sylvester Mowry of his liberty and bring him to trial before a military commission."[8] Mowry would subsequently be imprisoned at Fort Yuma, Arizona, where he was held in confinement until November 4, 1862.[9]

This action would prove to be a sign of things to come on the part of Major Carleton inasmuch as Confederate sympathizers in southern New Mexico were concerned. Historian Dan Thrapp has aptly described Mowry's involvement with the Civil War–era controversies in southern New Mexico: "He was of northern birth . . . but in Arizona he was amidst predominantly Southern partisans and sentiment; he was much more interested in Mowry and his promotions than in political embroilments back east, and being a thoroughgoing opportunist he cottoned up to the Confederates as he would have to any other conquering element."[10] Mowry had perceived the inevitable Confederate invasion at the beginning of the Civil War and acted according to his own best interests. In order to ensure their own well-being and promote themselves financially, many citizens like Mowry openly professed an advocacy for the Southern cause. Not surprisingly, once the Rebels were driven out of the territory in the summer of 1862, these same individuals reverted back to patriotism and pro-Federal sentiment quickly and nonchalantly, as if nothing had ever transpired.[11] Many individuals throughout southern New Mexico underwent the same treatment as Mowry as a result of their prior allegiances.

Major Carleton's California Column, after crossing the Butterfield Trail in the heat of the summer, reached the Rio Grande valley on August 7, 1862, and established their headquarters at Las Cruces three days later. For the soldiers, this was the first sign of substantial inhabitation since leaving California. Sgt. George Hand, in his journal, noted, "[We] arrived at Mesilla in the afternoon. Found some civilization here . . . [there is] one tenpin alley, two billiards tables, one church and plenty of houses. Fandangoes every night."[12] At that time Mesilla boasted a population of some 2,400 people, making it the largest town between San Antonio and Los Angeles. Las Cruces, meanwhile, had a population of 720, only about one-quarter that of Mesilla. In both Mesilla and Las Cruces, the soldiers comprising Major Carleton's command would have little difficulty finding entertainment and nightlife; one officer described the area as one where "whisky, gambling and women were plentiful."[13] O. M. Bryan, a military surgeon at Mesilla, found himself unimpressed with the negative effects that all of this had upon the soldiers. The sale of intoxicants went virtually uninterrupted and the local women made a career of "the retail of venereal disease in its various forms."[14]

At the time of its inspection by Maj. Henry Wallen in January 1863, the

Figure 10.1. Maj. James Henry Carleton, commanding officer of the military department of New Mexico during the Civil War years. (Courtesy National Archives)

military post at Mesilla consisted of five companies of infantry and one company of cavalry from the California Volunteers. Wallen went on to state, "the companies are as comfortably quartered as the nature of the buildings in the town of Mesilla will admit. They are wholly deficient in bunks and bed sacks. . . . There are no mess rooms to any of the company quarters,

lumber being so difficult to obtain and at such high rates, that mess tables
and benches cannot readily be obtained. At present, each man gets his meal
at the company kitchen, and leaves to eat it where he pleases."[15]

Despite the numerous distractions in the area, the Union troops could
not let their guard down. No sooner had they settled in than rumors began circulating of a plotted reinvasion attempt by Baylor. Lt. Col. Joseph R.
West, commanding in the Mesilla Valley, ordered Maj. William McMullen
to march to Franklin, Texas, on November 27, 1862, informing him that "an
attack is threatened upon that post by a force of the enemy now said to be at
the Presidio del Norte."[16] West continued: "You are sent to foil and defeat the
enemy if you can; to retire before him if he is so strong as to render a contest
hopeless, and in that event to leave no particle of property in his track. . . . Beginning at San Elizario, Ysleta, Socorro, Fort Bliss, Franklin, and Hart's Mill
all must be devastated."[17] The Union commanders were taking no chances.
With the Confederate troops having only been gone for a few months, anxiety prevailed among military and civil officials throughout the territory,
especially in the Mesilla Valley, from which point the reinvasion attempt
would undoubtedly come if indeed Baylor followed through with it.

Union commanders planned to enlist local citizens as volunteers to
fight the Confederates if they returned. Lieutenant Colonel West expressed
his concern that the Rebels proposed "to recover possession of the Mesilla
Valley." He went on to stress the importance of the citizens' involvement:
"When the time comes for active resistance the undersigned [West] will
call upon the people of the Mesilla Valley to rally for the defense of their
homes and their property, and he will place means at their disposal to do
so effectually."[18]

When Baylor arrived at San Antonio, Texas on August 1, 1862, he wasted
no time in moving forward with his plan to raise an army of some six thousand men, twice the size of Sibley's Army of New Mexico that had been
defeated in March of that year. Baylor had authorization from his superiors
at the Confederate capital in Richmond to "retake and hold New Mexico at
all hazards."[19] The Union officers in the Mesilla Valley thus had ample cause
for alarm and were justified in their concerns of a reinvasion.

In preparation for Baylor's contemplated move, Major Carleton anx-
iously wrote a letter on November 18, 1862, to Lieutenant Colonel West, then
commanding the post at Mesilla.[20] In his letter Carleton ordered West to

strip the Mesilla Valley of all excess food provisions in order to discourage Baylor's plan to retake the territory. Carleton's suggested method of accomplishing this was to "secure all the corn and grain you can possibly buy from the people at San Elizario, Socorro, Ysleta, Franklin, La Mesa, La Mesilla, Las Cruces, and Doña Ana . . . and have it all carefully guarded and stored at Mesilla. If the people will not sell it to you it must be seized and receipt given for it."[21] Pursuant to Carleton's demands, West issued General Order No. 24 on December 2, 1862, outlining the process by which citizens of the Mesilla Valley must turn over their surplus property to the federal authorities.

It was imperative that excess goods, especially food stores and supplies, not fall back into the hands of the Rebels if they did attempt a reinvasion. West wrote: "Any person found with over two months' subsistence for his family, or necessary grain for his animals, within fifteen days after the publication of this order, will be considered as an enemy to the Government of the United States and will be treated accordingly." Depots would be established at Mesilla, Franklin, and San Elizario, at which locations the people were to turn over their surplus property, and the commanding officers at each station would "give receipts in due form . . . the depot quartermaster at Mesilla will settle with the proper owners upon the presentation of these receipts."[22] The fact that the Union army promised monetary compensation for the goods offered little consolation to the local residents, who once again found themselves subjected to harsh military rule.

In several instances Union troops raided the properties of local citizens suspected of hiding surplus grain and other food stores. One such individual was Joshua Sledd, who harbored a surplus of goods in a storage facility near his home for issuance to hungry locals. On November 15, 1862, Union troops broke down Sledd's doors and confiscated all of the grain sacks in his possession. An appeal to Lieutenant Colonel West fell on deaf ears. Another defiant local citizen, José María Aguirre, likewise met with an unsympathetic West; when Aguirre refused to accept payment for his grain, the army officer promptly fined him an exorbitant $90 for defying the military during a time of martial law.[23]

To be fair, Carleton was not the first official to enact such a policy in the Mesilla Valley. Under Confederate rule in 1861–62, Lieutenant Colonel Baylor had carried out similar policies in the region. The only difference lay in the fact that Baylor's actions were aimed primarily toward those boasting sentiment for the Union; Carleton's were aimed at all citizens of the Mesilla Valley, not just Southern sympathizers. The Santa Fe mercantile firm of Elsbery & Amsberg was among several northern New Mexico companies that bore the brunt of pecuniary losses stemming from Baylor's Confederate administration. Writing to Brigadier General West[24] in 1863, after the Union reconquest of the Mesilla Valley, the merchants claimed to have lost $16,316.33 worth of merchandise to the Confederates. The goods, they claimed, had been seized from the copper mines at Santa Rita del Cobre and sold at public auction in Mesilla. A report provided by Samuel Bean affirmed this assertion; however, the firm's pleas for compensation were in vain.[25] If the citizens of southern New Mexico hoped for a change in policy under the new Union administration of Major Carleton, their hopes would soon be dashed. Much of the unwarranted seizure of personal property and subsistence stores that defined Baylor's administration would continue, and even be exacerbated, under Carleton's direction.

However unpopular the confiscations may have been, they were upheld by U.S. law. A statute of July 17, 1862, allowed for the confiscation of property belonging to civilians supporting the enemy. Section 6 of this Act specifically maintained that "all persons within a state or territory being engaged in armed rebellion against the government thereof, or aiding or abetting such a rebellion, and not ceasing so to do and returning to his allegiance within sixty days after proclamation duly made by the President, should in like manner forfeit his property."[26] This Act was subsequently upheld as being constitutional in the Supreme Court case *Miller v. U.S.*[27] Thus, legally, Major Carleton was not overstepping his bounds in ordering the confiscation of these properties in the Mesilla Valley. Still, with the Confederates having exited the territory and no longer posing an imminent threat, one must question the necessity of such excessive confiscation of private property.

Following his order that all excess provisions be seized, Carleton next ordered that all suspected Southern sympathizers in the vicinity be detained, marched north to Fort Craig, and their property destroyed. "The houses and stores owned by secessionists who ran off to Texas, the enemy will expect to repossess when they come back," he wrote to West. "These, including . . . all of those belonging to this class of men in Mesilla and Las Cruces, will be laid to ashes. . . . You will also destroy Bull's Mill,[28] at Mesilla, and Grandjean's Mill, at Las Cruces, in case you are compelled to fall back. . . . The Mexican population who prefer to remain behind can grind their corn on *metates* as of old; so that the destruction of these mills will be no serious blow to them."[29] Carleton was determined to thwart an attempted reinvasion at any cost, even if it meant potential starvation and unspeakable hardships for the civilians in the Mesilla Valley. In so doing he created a rift between himself and the inhabitants of New Mexico, especially the Hispanic population, for whom he seemed to express little sympathy.

Finally, in an attempt to prevent any local uprisings in favor of the Confederates, Carleton suggested that West "remind the Mexicans of how they were robbed before [by Baylor's troops], and animate them, as you can do, with a settled determination to attack the enemy from every cover . . . to hover by night around his camps; to set fire to the grass which his animals might otherwise get; to shoot down his men by night; and then before day scatter singly in all directions."[30] Carleton hoped that the local Mexicans, as civilians, would undertake some of the guerrilla tactics frequently employed by the surrounding Indian tribes, which could not be enacted by Carleton's regular troops without straying from the course of "civilized warfare." It is a matter of no little irony that Carleton expected such wholehearted assistance in the Mesilla Valley from the civilian population, even after he himself issued the orders depriving them of food and property.

As events progressed it gradually became clear that a reinvasion by the Texans would not take place. Baylor, had he been able to muster his intended force of six thousand fighting men, certainly would have had the manpower to accomplish the task. Ultimately, two reasons led to the scheme's demise. First, Baylor could not procure adequate and timely transportation for such a large body of troops from San Antonio to El Paso, a distance of nearly six hundred miles. Second, and perhaps more importantly, by the end of 1862 the Mesilla Valley was being protected by a much larger and more determined fighting force under Carleton than it had been in 1861 under Maj. Isaac Lynde. When Baylor first invaded New Mexico in July 1861, he did so with little opposition due to the prevalent Southern sentiment among both the citizens and the Union officers at Fort Fillmore. But now, Major Carleton and his troops, all ardent Northerners willing to go to any length to preserve the Union, presented a seemingly insurmountable obstacle for Baylor. While six thousand men might have been enough to defeat Carleton's command in the Mesilla Valley, doing so would require a major combative action and would have severely depleted Baylor's forces. "From all the information that I can gather," wrote West in December 1862, "I have arrived at the conclusion that there are no reasons at present to apprehend that we shall be troubled by the enemy's advance towards us."[31]

The Confederate reinvasion scare in the autumn of 1862 never came to fruition, and matters continued in the Mesilla Valley as they had been. Carleton remained in overall command of the troops and government alike, and the people remained subject to martial law until further notice. In order to ensure that Baylor remained idle in Texas, and that the Territory of New Mexico receive ample protection in its southern extremity, the troops of the California Column would remain stationed at the various towns in the Mesilla Valley.

It comes as little surprise, then, that discipline problems among the troops ensued. The guardhouse at Mesilla rarely sat vacant, oftentimes being occupied by several of Carleton's men.[32] Disciplinary actions reached a climax on November 26, 1862, when, pursuant to orders handed down by Brigadier General West, a firing squad executed one of the troops. The unfortunate man was Cpl. Charles Smith of Company K, 1st California Infantry, accused of assisting others to escape from jail. The firing squad assigned to carry out the execution was composed of men from Company D, 1st California Infantry (it was assumed that none of the individuals from Smith's own company could be counted upon to fire when the time came). As it were, those of Company D likewise proved reluctant to take the life of their comrade. The order was given to fire, which the men did, but when the smoke cleared, Smith remained standing uninjured on the Mesilla plaza. Every man had purposely aimed high. While this had the effect of temporarily sparing the soldier's life, it also caused several of the citizens to be injured by the stray bullets. Undaunted by his troops' lack of cooperation, West ordered that a second volley be fired at Smith. This time the bullets hit their mark.[33]

Smith's bunkmate, Pvt. William Walker, had difficulty coping with the loss of his friend. Seven weeks later, he was found dead in the Rio Grande near Mesilla, having committed suicide. According to Sgt. George Hand, Walker had been missing since shortly after Smith's execution, and when they finally found his body he had already been lying dead on the banks of the river for several weeks. Two hundred dollars, a knife, and a pistol were on his person.[34] Sergeant Hand himself later visited the location where the execution was carried out: "Here is where Corp. [Smith] . . . was shot by order of [Brigadier] General West. The houses, trees, walls round the church, all show the marks of bullets not intended to hit the man. . . . One [man] of Co. "A," 5th [Pvt. Edward Frobitz], a woman & a Mexican boy were killed [by the stray bullets]."[35] What had begun as the killing of one evolved into the hapless murder of four. The entire spectacle poses many questions, especially in light of the fact that Smith was never actually court-martialed. "When one takes into consideration all of the events leading to the execution and also the lack of evidence of a Court-Martial," wrote one historian, "one must conclude that Cpl. Smith was murdered by . . . West just as surely as if he had put his pistol to Smith's head and pulled the trigger, all for the sake of emphasizing the fact that his word was law."[36]

Despite knowledge that Baylor would not attempt to retake the Mesilla Valley by force, the widespread paranoia that had defined the previous several months continued to prevail among Union officers. In December 1862, Maj. William McMullen of the 1st Regiment of California Volunteers arrived with his troops at Franklin (El Paso) and took charge of the recently reestablished Union garrison there. He reported that Texans sympathizing with the Confederacy remained dominant among the citizenry and were well organized for another possible attack on New Mexico. West ordered McMullen to "occupy your men with throwing up some temporary defenses, loop holing houses, getting ready to lay waste so that if the enemy should come upon you suddenly, you will be quite ready to act."[37]

Owing to the strong Union force now occupying the region, many of these Southern sympathizers crossed the Rio Grande to Paso del Norte (present-day Juárez, Mexico) for safety and to avoid Major Carleton's policies of imprisoning and seizing the property of such individuals. Major McMullen, displaying the anxiety common among his contemporaries at that time, seemed convinced that these people were conniving another attack from their safe haven in Mexico. Consequently, McMullen stationed pickets of Union soldiers on the Mexican side of the Rio Grande to watch for any possible uprisings that might spread into the United States. McMullen blatantly violated international law and treaty stipulations by placing these American troops on Mexican soil, and a controversy inevitably resulted.

Figure 10.2. Brig. Gen. Joseph Rodman West, commanding officer at Mesilla during the Union occupation of southern New Mexico in 1862–63. This photograph shows him many years after the Civil War, probably in the 1870s. (Courtesy National Archives)

José María Uranga, a top Mexican leader in Paso del Norte, wrote to McMullen on December 24, 1862, saying in part that "this office has been informed . . . that a picket of soldiers of your command has been camped . . . on the right banks of the Rio Grande. . . . If this act, Major, has actually been done, there is no doubt that, without your knowledge, international rights have been violated and treaties existing between the two nations have been broken." McMullen made no attempt to deny the fact that he had ordered his troops to station themselves on the Mexican side of the river. The picket, consisting of eight Union soldiers, had been placed in Mexico "with my knowledge and by my order . . . my sense of duty to my government will not permit Mexican soil to shield our enemies." In a letter to Brigadier General West at Mesilla, McMullen explained that his actions were necessary in order to thwart an attack by Southern sympathizers residing in Mexico. West curtly agreed with him: "You did perfectly right and your straightforward letter to the prefect [Uranga] will be too much for Mexican Diplomacy, I think."[38] Nothing became of this intrusion on Mexican sovereignty by the Union forces along the border, although it exemplifies the levels to which they were willing to digress in order to protect New Mexico from Confederate control.

In January 1863, as tensions gradually eased in the Mesilla Valley, Carleton and West turned their attentions partially toward the Apaches, whose plundering habits had continued virtually without hindrance. West departed Mesilla with the intention of establishing a new fort near the headwaters of the Gila River, one destined to bear his own name. Two companies of cavalry and two of infantry left Mesilla on January 12, with West as their commander, and marched first to Piños Altos and thence to the Gila River. Here these four companies were permanently stationed and charged with the duty of constructing the new post, located atop a prominent bluff overlooking the Gila River valley and named Fort West.[39]

Writing in January 1863, West acknowledged the efforts being undertaken in view of discouraging Apache raiding. "By direction of General James H. Carleton . . . a vigorous warfare is being prosecuted by the U.S. troops against the various tribes of Apache Indians who infest the country lying east and west of the Rio Grande," he wrote.[40] By the end of February so much attention had been turned toward thwarting Apache raiding in the vicinity that Sergeant Hand reported that only twenty-two men were available for duty in Mesilla. Many of the troops were dispatched to other regions in southern New Mexico, where they built not only Fort West but also Fort McRae (near the Jornada del Muerto) for the purpose of inducing the Apaches to cease their plundering of the Rio Grande settlements.[41]

The efforts of the California troops ultimately had little effect on Apache depredations. Reports of skirmishes and attacks continued to trickle in from the field. In June 1863, Apaches attacked a party of New Mexico volunteers on the Jornada del Muerto, killing Lieutenant Bargie, "mutilating his body, and carrying his head off as a trophy. At the same time a mail rider from Fort Craig was killed and the mail destroyed," lamented Brigadier General West. The Apache culprits had been identified as belonging to the Mimbres band residing west of the Rio Grande. He subsequently ordered Maj. William McCleave to "scour every foot of ground and beat up all their haunts . . . this band of Miembres [sic] River Indians must be exterminated to a man."[42] West and Carleton both frequently issued orders such as this throughout 1862 and 1863, but in most instances troop movements against the Apaches proved to be in vain.

Many of the troops who were not out fighting Apaches during this time found themselves marching back and forth between Las Cruces and Mesilla. Sergeant Hand's company was transferred from Mesilla to Las Cruces on March 27, where they "found very good quarters but lots of work to put them into order." According to Sergeant Hand, Las Cruces bore the appearance of a "dirty, miserable, dusty looking place."[43] Hand remained there until April 20, when his company transferred again, this time to El Paso.

In August 1863, an incident occurred at Mesilla that served as a vivid reminder of cultural tensions between the Anglo soldiers and the local Mexicans. A Union trooper from Sergeant Hand's company, referred to in his journal only by his last name, "Grimes," had left Las Cruces and gone to Mesilla to "see a senorita with whom he had been intimate, and some Spaniard, thinking that he had money . . . set upon him with a small hatchet . . . the greaser was taken and confined in the guardhouse at Las Cruces." Owing either to the poor jail facilities or the public sentiment being in his favor, the Mexican escaped that night. In doing so, however, he was reportedly shot through the thigh by the guard. The following day, the same Mexican appeared in Mesilla and was recognized by another soldier from the same company as Grimes. Hand explained that the soldier, "seeing the fellow[,] got in conversation with him . . . the Mexican [then] assaulted him with a hatchet on the back of the head. Spencer drew his revolver and shot him. He fought very desperately and Spencer put 6 revolver balls in him, then went out, got a double-barrel shotgun and gave him the contents." The commanding officer, West, subsequently placed Private Spencer under arrest, although all who witnessed the spectacle agreed that the killing had been perpetrated in self-defense.[44]

Martial law had first been declared in New Mexico in September 1862, about the same time that Carleton had assumed command of the military department in place of Col. Edward R. S. Canby. Those living in the Mesilla Valley, both because of their distance from the capital in Santa Fe and because of the widespread knowledge that they had openly supported Baylor and Sibley's invasion in 1861–62, became the most burdened of all the territory's citizens by martial law. The fact that the Mesilla Valley would be the point from which any reinvasion attempt was launched, if indeed it were, caused Carleton to exercise greater diligence in the enforcement of martial law in that vicinity.

In its basic principles, martial law has always been frowned upon in American society and has historically been reverted to as a last resort in desperate times. In the opinion of Carleton, and perhaps rightfully so, times were desperate enough in New Mexico in 1862 to justify the implementation of military rule. Doña Ana County probate judge Frank Higgins, in a correspondence with Major Carleton, explained the circumstances under which martial law could be acceptably implemented:

> You will certainly admit that martial law is a measure only to be resorted to in most urgent emergencies, and those are such as endanger the existence and security of a nation. Rebellion against national authorities, imminently impending war, or formidable attempts to subvert national or local law . . . require this extreme remedy. Does such a condition of affairs exist in the Mesilla Valley, as calls for this resort? As for treason, it may exist in a few men's breasts, but finds no sympathy to call forth its utterance—Never before has there existed in this valley a more universal respect for government and desire for its success and triumph.[45]

In a blunt letter to Carleton, Higgins stated, "If you will visit this community, General, you will find that a necessity for martial law, so far as the dignity, honor and security of our nation, does not exist."[46] His denunciation of martial law and assertion that it be discontinued in the Mesilla Valley came as his own personal response to five separate petitions submitted by local Mexicans favoring martial law.[47] Some of the locals viewed the military presence in the Mesilla Valley as a benevolent thing, providing protection from the dangers of raiding Apaches. However, this point of view starkly contrasted with that of local merchants and businessmen whose interests were blatantly undermined by martial law. Indeed, with public stores and merchants' property being seized by the army, it proved almost impossible to run a successful business in Mesilla during the Civil War years. One can thus see the rift developing between the two components of the local population, the Mexican farmers and laborers and the Anglo merchants.

Probate Judge Frank Higgins held an interesting opinion concerning the Mexicans' favoring of martial law. Writing to Major Carleton, he explained, "There is nothing more painful and irksome, than to live in a com-

munity where it is neither politic or safe to express your disapproval of what
you know to be manifest injustice—where you feel it dangerous to discuss
the issues of the day, if your opinions should be the opposite of those in
power."[48] In a New Mexican society in which native Mexicans were marginalized by Anglos possessing political and military power, these feelings of
oppression oftentimes went unexpressed, except in the occasional but rare
form of a petition. This widespread feeling of subjugation among the local
population manifested itself in a letter written to Carleton: "Our trouble is,
that many of our Mexican citizens think that certain parties have the influence to accomplish what they please, and that martial law was a matter of
course, and they are afraid to make themselves conspicuous in opposition
to the measures."[49]

At least one man, however, was powerful enough to challenge Carleton
directly. Judge Joseph G. Knapp, presiding over the 3rd Judicial District at
Mesilla, openly abhorred martial law and the effects it had on the people.[50]
Knapp, along with most other citizens of Las Cruces and Mesilla, believed
that a Confederate reinvasion was no longer a concern, rendering the continued implementation of martial law entirely unnecessary. A resolution
against martial law adopted by the people in 1863 noted, "The confederates
had abandoned all of their positions, and their whole power in New Mexico
had been broken by July 4, 1862, and that by Sept. 26, 1862, the date of Carleton's order extending martial law, the last remnants of the invading army
had reached San Antonio."[51]

The initial disagreement between Carleton and Knapp arose with the
requirement that all individuals apply for and obtain a military pass before traveling anywhere in the territory. Knapp absolutely refused to do
this when traveling on official business, stating that it insulted his personal
dignity and honorable position as a judge. With this mindset, Judge Knapp
departed Mesilla and rode north to Santa Fe, without a pass, where he arrived on January 2, 1863, to attend a session of the Supreme Court. Carleton,
not surprisingly, was indignant with the judge for his refusal to secure a
military pass.

On August 1, 1863, troops arrested Knapp in Las Cruces and confined
him in the guardhouse for five days "for failure to properly cooperate with
the military." If Knapp had considered the policy of requiring a travel pass
to be derogatory toward his office as judge, his imprisonment must have

pushed him over the edge. In a letter to Brigadier General West, Knapp remained steadfast in his refusal to cooperate: "In my character as a judge," he wrote, "I cannot and will not take a pass, and shall not call for one. When I desire to travel on private business I will cheerfully submit to any rule you may make, not inconsistent with the dignity of a man; but as a judge my duty not less than my rights prevent me from submitting to any rule or order which can in any manner lower the dignity of that office."[52] West's reply was equally staunch and unwavering: "You cannot go from place to place within my command without the usual pass; this pass will be furnished you upon your application at these headquarters."[53]

After failing in his appeals to West and Carleton, Knapp wrote directly to General-in-Chief of the Union Army Henry W. Halleck, explaining to him the conditions prevailing in New Mexico. Halleck agreed with Knapp, writing to Carleton and informing him that the procedure currently being implemented in New Mexico should be "immediately discontinued."[54] Knapp also enlisted the aid of Attorney General Edward Bates, who, discussing it with President Lincoln, decided not to become involved. His response to Knapp was much less favorable than that of General Halleck: "I regret exceedingly the existence of the difficulties of which you so strongly complain, and would be glad to remove them, if it were in my power. But I have no control over the military authorities in New Mexico."[55] With the Civil War raging in the east, officials in Washington had far more important things to tend to than the complaints of a judge in a far removed western territory.

The involvement of those in Washington would prove to be of no consequence to Carleton, and his martial law policies continued as before. In a special session of court in Mesilla on June 10, 1864, a grand jury (with the assistance of Knapp, no doubt), wrote a resolution declaring, among other things, that "instead of being protected in the rights secured to us, General Carleton through his subordinates, has imprisoned citizens, has fined and compelled them to submit to the performance of labor without conviction or trial; has taken away property without just compensation, and refused to restore it upon demand being made, or to pay for the same. Setting up courts of his own creation in our midst, he has compelled citizens to answer before them for offenses unknown to the law, and has prevented the courts established by law from discharging their duty."[56]

It comes as little surprise, given the close relationship between Carleton and West, that tensions between West and Knapp would arise and come to the forefront. "It is much to be regretted that a great want of accord exists between the heads of the military and civil authorities here between Gen'l. West and Judge Knapp," observed Frank Higgins. "There is a wide differ-ence between them as to where their respective jurisdiction commences and ends. The effect has been an almost complete military rule—and the paralization [sic] of the power and objects of the civil authorities."[57] Higgins went on to request that the commander, Carleton, set forth a clear definition of the jurisdictions of each man so as to alleviate further disagreements.

Whatever the relationship may have been between West and Knapp, General Carleton had had enough of the judge from Mesilla. Carleton, who very much enjoyed exercising absolute control over the territory, would not allow Knapp to continue questioning his authority and making a mockery of his policies. Writing once again to the attorney general, Carleton was blunt in his assessment of the judge. "Knapp is a compound of a knave and a fool, or else crazy," criticized Carleton.[58] In another letter to General Thomas in Washington, Carleton further explained:

> The inevitable Judge Joseph G. Knapp, who has written so many . . . scurrilous articles for the press against the officers serving in this department, claiming that New Mexico is under a military despotism . . . that I have subverted the liberties of the people, and other claptrap of the sort, came here [Santa Fe] last week to sit as an associate justice. After the court was organized and had transacted some business which he, Knapp, wanted to have done, he got up and said he would do no more business until my order with reference to passports was rescinded unconditionally; and, so, the court stopped. The judge would not take a passport for Mesilla, 300 miles off, but started without one. As he might have known before he left, he was stopped at the first military post he came to.[59]

By this time Knapp had gained a significant following in the territory, and the widespread discontent with Carleton's martial law policy became increasingly obvious. An editorial published in the *Santa Fe New Mexi-can* in 1864 maintained that "the deplorable condition of this Territory and the wants and starvation staring our people in the face, [are] owing to the ruinous policy pursued by the political General commanding this department."[60]

All of these personal and political feuds were not without their effect upon the population. There were two factions in the Mesilla Valley: one favoring martial law, consisting primarily of the Mexican population and the military, and one opposing it, consisting primarily of merchants and civil authorities. Frank Higgins assessed the situation: "Our district judge J. G. Knapp appears to us to be inclined to be jealous of the military authorities, to be desirous of raising questions of jurisdiction, and making issues decidedly impolitic and unnecessary. On the other hand there seems to have been in the local military authorities a jealousy of the civil authorities, and there exists, much to my regret, a want of friendly intercourse between the military and civilian officers."[61]

Furthermore, Knapp had brought with him to the Mesilla Valley George R. Withers, who was generally looked down upon by many in the region. Probate Judge Higgins described Withers as being "given to what lawyers call 'sharp practice' and is inclined to be quite unscrupulous as to the means with which he accomplishes his end." Higgins went on to write, with apparent sarcasm, that Withers served as clerk of the U.S. District Court, clerk of the County Court, U.S. commissioner, and "is or wants to be agent of the United States district attorney and it is alleged has entire control of the district judge."[62]

Mesilla and Las Cruces, perhaps because of Knapp's presence, tended to be a gathering place for the anti-Carleton contingent in New Mexico. Knowing this, Carleton ventured to the Mesilla Valley on December 16, 1864, where he gave a speech in response to recent accusations by New Mexico newspapers and citizens alike. The speech was printed as a pamphlet and distributed all over the territory. The oration, interestingly enough, pertained almost entirely to Carleton's Indian policies, specifically the internment of the Navajos at Bosque Redondo, and effectively dodged the matter of martial law, the primary concern of those to whom he spoke in Las Cruces.

Another policy of Major Carleton that had a decided impact on southern New Mexico was his strong support of mining interests. Carleton frequently encouraged his subordinate officers to prospect for gold and other minerals while on expeditions in New Mexico. In southern Arizona, several ore discoveries led to a mining boom in the region, and those living in the Mesilla Valley, perhaps because of their proximity to southern Arizona and the easy access provided by the Butterfield Trail, quickly packed up their belongings and headed to the mines. Carleton received complaints from civil officials in Mesilla concerning the detrimental effects this had on the local population. "Seventy-five men left here for the mines in Arizona on the 19th inst., one hundred fifty on the 23rd ult., and some twenty-five will leave tomorrow," wrote one official. "Continued reports from these mines will have the effect of almost depopulating this valley . . . from all I can learn from the new mines they are a decided success, and extend over a large extent of country, and will have the best possible results towards the development of the Territory of Arizona."[63]

By the close of the Civil War, Carleton's days were coming to an end as the supreme commander of New Mexico. In January 1866, the territorial legislature issued a memorial to President Andrew Johnson and the War Department, condemning Carleton for his failed Indian policies and the implementation of martial law, among other things. On September 19, 1866, Secretary of War Edwin M. Stanton ordered that Carleton be relieved of his command in New Mexico. The *Santa Fe New Mexican,* not at all distraught with this decision, proclaimed, "it thus appears that our territory will be relieved from the presence of this man . . . who has so long lorded it amongst us. For five years or more he has been in supreme command in New Mexico, and during that whole time, has accomplished nothing for which he is entitled to the thanks or gratitude of our people. . . . He has, however, succeeded in gaining for himself the detestation and contempt of almost the entire population of our territory."[64]

With this, General Carleton's martial law would no longer be a burden upon the people of New Mexico. Throughout the duration of the Civil War, the citizens had been subjected to rule by the military, had lost their property and freedom, and generally had been subjugated and taken advantage of by military leaders. It had been a process of mutual reciprocation; historian Jerry Thompson appropriately assessed the situation in the Mesilla Valley when writing, "Perhaps nowhere in New Mexico was the military as oppressive and as big a burden on the local population as in the Mesilla Valley. Conversely, nowhere was the local population as sullen and uncooperative."[65]

The Civil War years had been exceedingly difficult on those living in the vicinity of Mesilla. They had seceded from New Mexico, welcomed with open arms an invading Confederate army, and had been admitted into the Confederacy as the Territory of Arizona, only to be once again reverted back to an entity of the North, all in a period of just three years. Owing to all of this, their suffering upon the arrival of Carleton and his troops cannot be understated. In the eyes of Carleton, the people deserved it. In the eyes of the people, they were merely trying to choose the course that would best promote their own livelihood.

Conclusion

Located in the southernmost portion of New Mexico and only a short distance from the Mexican border, the Mesilla Valley has always been defined by cultural aspects. This was evident in the earliest settlements, where disputes over land and cultural misunderstandings became the norm. What began in 1843 as a fertile valley with only one village, Doña Ana, became the location of numerous Mexican towns within only a few years due primarily to the arrival of the Americans and the resultant cultural disparities. Following the culmination of the Mexican War in 1848, three separate entities claimed the Mesilla Valley as their own: Mexico, New Mexico, and Texas (not to mention the Apaches, who had called the region home for centuries). It took many years and countless millions of dollars to sort out these issues satisfactorily and with minimal bloodshed.

The arrival of the Americans in 1846 brought about an entirely new era in New Mexico history. Two vastly different cultures would attempt to live in harmony among each other, and in many cases this was not just improbable, but impossible. The people already living in New Mexico were firmly set in their traditions, and it would take more than a few thousand newcomers from the United States to enact any profound change. These cultural differences remain, in some cases, partially unchanged and are a distinctive characteristic of New Mexico to this day.

One thing that did not change when the Americans arrived was the raiding habits of the Indians. The Apaches had been a constant burden upon the citizens of New Mexico, Chihuahua, and Sonora since the arrival of the first Spaniards, and this held true long after the United States extended its jurisdiction over New Mexico. Those in the Mesilla Valley enjoyed a considerable amount of military protection in the form of U.S. troops stationed in the immediate vicinity: first at Doña Ana beginning in 1848, then at Fort Fillmore in 1851. The last Apaches surrendered to the U.S. Army in September 1886. However, raiding of the Mesilla Valley settlements had nearly ceased by the 1870s, owing to the continually increasing population of the area. Mesilla and Las Cruces continued to grow, and the influx of Americans from the east overwhelmed the Apaches to the point that it simply became too risky for them to raid near these towns.

More than anything else, the Civil War years had been a trying time for the residents. The banner of the Confederacy waved high above the Mesilla plaza in 1861, openly embraced by many of the residents. Mesilla became the capital of a new Confederate territory—Arizona—only to once again revert to its original status as a traditional Mexican farming village and commercial center less than a year later. The Union army, arriving at the same time the Confederates retreated, proved to be unforgiving to the people. Martial law forced a heavy burden upon all classes and ethnicities, with the military commanders confiscating food stores and supplies from the citizens; many former Confederate sympathizers abandoned everything and fled for their lives lest Major Carleton get a hold of them.

The Rio Grande would continue to be an unpredictable, sometimes dangerous river for decades to come. Since the time of its founding in 1850, the town of Mesilla had been situated on the west bank of the river. However, two major floods of the Rio Grande in 1862 and 1865 forever changed the course of the river. The town then became, and remains to this day, situated on the eastern bank.

Mesilla had been a place of importance throughout this era, being the largest town between San Antonio, Texas, and Los Angeles, California, for many years. This all began to change shortly after the Civil War. Nearby Las Cruces, which previously consisted of only a few dozen scattered adobe homes, began to grow. In 1880 the railroad arrived in the valley but bypassed Mesilla entirely, instead laying its rails directly through Las Cruces. This simple act spelled tragedy for Mesilla's prosperity. The county seat was moved away from Mesilla soon thereafter. To this day the population of the village remains almost the same as it was in 1860: about three thousand. By contrast, Las Cruces, a town that in 1860 claimed a mere seven hundred inhabitants, now approaches one hundred thousand.

Much transpired during the brief time span from 1846 to 1865, and those events laid the groundwork for the continuous development of the valley. This account ends with the Civil War for a number of reasons. The pre–Civil War and post–Civil War years in southern New Mexico are two distinctly different time periods. Many things changed in a matter of just a few years. Las Cruces boomed and Mesilla stagnated. The coming of the railroad was a monumental occurrence, completely changing the way people lived their lives. Transportation became easier and nearby mining towns boomed; no longer did it take days or weeks to travel from one part of New Mexico to another. The local economy prospered, and politics took on an increased importance. Many of the men who had been involved in local politics during the Civil War years continued in that role; additionally, a number of the soldiers who had arrived with Carleton's California Column made the area their home and began a life in the public arena. The Apache troubles gradually dissipated, but a new burden in the form of thieves and cattle rustlers quickly replaced them. The region became a part of the Wild West, with outlaw gangs springing up and violence being the inevitable result.

Thus there are two very distinct eras in the territorial history of the Mesilla Valley, and to attempt to cover both in one volume would be difficult, if not impractical. It has been my purpose in this work to recount some perhaps previously unfamiliar items of local interest. When one considers it as a whole, it is truly a unique and captivating history of which the Mesilla Valley can proudly boast.

Notes

INTRODUCTION

1. Quoted by Twitchell, *Leading Facts,* vol. 2, 20. In an address given at the Santa Fe Plaza, Kearny proclaimed: "New Mexicans: we have come amongst you to take possession of New Mexico, which we do in the name of the government of the United States. We have come with peaceable intentions and kind feelings toward you all. We come as friends, to better your condition and make you a part of the republic of the United States . . . you are now American citizens, subject only to the laws of the United States." Quoted in Keleher, *Turmoil in New Mexico,* 15–16.

2. Historian Robert W. Frazer writes: "Regardless of his reason for going to New Mexico, the average visitor displayed very little tolerance for, or understanding of, the culture of the New Mexican people . . . the average American who bothered to set down his views was critical of the New Mexican male's lack of intelligence, his cowardice, his slothfulness, and his habits generally." Frazer, *New Mexico in 1850,* 55.

3. Averell, *Ten Years in the Saddle,* 107.

4. Davis, *El Gringo,* 273.

5. Frazer, *New Mexico in 1850,* 14. John Slidell, of Louisiana, was sent by President Polk to Mexico in 1845 to negotiate a purchase of New Mexico and California, but his attempt was in vain, and the Mexican War broke out not long afterward. President Polk had provided Slidell with the map of New Mexico, the only one then in the possession of the U.S. government, to assist him in his venture. Evidently, the map was never returned to Washington and remained in Mexico where it was of no use to anybody from the United States.

6. Army inspector George A. McCall estimated the American population of New Mexico to be 1,200 in the year 1850. Territorial Governor James Calhoun, in 1851, gave the probable number as just 300. Frazer, *Mansfield on the Condition of Western Forts,* 5n2.

7. Davis, *El Gringo,* 252–53. The reference to the "irresponsible individual" is undoubtedly aimed toward Manuel Armijo, the last Mexican governor of New Mexico before Kearny's arrival in 1846.

8. Bartlett, *Personal Narrative,* vol. 2, 391. During his stay at El Paso, Bartlett

commented on the variety of character traits in the Mexicans, depending on their background and family origins. "There are a few respectable old families," he wrote. "A vast gulf intervenes these Castilians and the masses, who are a mixed breed, possessing none of the virtues of their European Ancestors, but all their vices, with those of the aborigines superadded. The Indian physiognomy is indelibly stamped upon them; and it requires little sagacity to discriminate between the pure and the mixed race." Quoted by Paredes, "The Mexican Image in American Travel Literature," 22.

9. Averell, *Ten Years in the Saddle,* 114n1.

10. Reid, *Reid's Tramp,* 145. Reid went on to state: "The national characteristics of the people of the United States and Mexico are antipodal. You know those of our country, and if curious to know those of Mexico, place the two opposite. If you know that as a nation the former are brave, honest and enlightened, my word for it, the latter are the reverse in the particular. Individually or collectively, whether high or low, perfidy is next of kin to their nature; and their transactions reek with it. Faithlessness characterizes their compliance with national stipulations with all governments and all persons." Ibid., 225.

11. Davis, *El Gringo,* 50. For a detailed description of the interiors of these early adobe homes in New Mexico, see ibid., 50–52.

12. Bloom, "New Mexico Viewed by Americans," 177.

13. Davis, *El Gringo,* 85.

14. Ibid., 54–55.

15. Susan Shelby Magoffin, in her diary from the years 1846–47, describes a fandango in Santa Fe, which was attended by all of the military officers and Mexicans alike. Magoffin, *Down the Santa Fe Trail and into Mexico,* 118–24.

16. Averell, *Ten Years in the Saddle,* 114–15. Another observer wrote: "The music is applauded by the smiles of all, and by the clapping of the hands of the male dancers. At the end of each set your partner takes your arm and deliberately conducts you to a corner of the room, where the proprietor of the fandango 'tends bar,' and where you are expected to treat her to a glass of wine, or something stronger if desired; or, should she prefer it, she joins you in a smoke." Reid, *Reid's Tramp,* 147.

17. Davis, *El Gringo,* 165.

18. Ibid., 60–61.

19. Ibid., 49.

20. Carmony, *The Civil War in Apacheland,* 107.

21. Davis, *El Gringo,* 64.

22. *Mesilla Times,* October 25, 1860.

23. When the American troops entered Santa Fe in 1846, "There were probably not more than 500 or 700 rich Mexicans in the territory. They were able to read and write; some were educated in the east; their hair was short, their dress and appearance that of the Spanish gentleman. The lower class, and in fact all, more or less were intermixed with Indian blood." Ayers, "A Soldier's Experience in New Mexico," 260–61.

24. Frazer, *New Mexico in 1850,* 57. In the early 1850s, Bishop John Lamy established one of the first successful schools at Santa Fe. During the 1855–56 session of the territorial legislature, an act was passed that established a school system in New Mexico, calling for at least one school in each territorial precinct, and enacting a tax to fund the act. "The law is defective in many particulars, but it exhibits a desire, on the people's representatives, to do something to enlighten the minds of the rising generation." Davis, *El Gringo,* 251–52.

25. Davis, *El Gringo,* 88–89. As a reason for the loose marital bonds and irreverence for the sanctity of that institution, Davis mentions the fact that formal marriages were extremely expensive in New Mexico; only the richest and most influential could afford the exorbitant fee charged by the Catholic priests.

26. Ibid., 97.

27. Bloom, "New Mexico Viewed by Americans," 174.

CHAPTER 1

1. Edwards, *A Campaign in New Mexico,* xxiv.

2. General Kearny credited Doniphan, an attorney by profession, with assisting in the writing of these laws. On September 22, 1846, Kearny wrote: "I am entirely indebted for these laws to Colonel A. W. Doniphan, of the first regiment of Missouri Volunteers, who received much assistance from Private Willard P. Hall, of his regiment. These laws are taken, part from the laws of Mexico—retained as in the original—a part with such modifications as our laws and constitution made necessary, a part are from the laws of the Missouri territory; a part from the laws of Texas; and also of Texas and Coahuila; a part from the statutes of Missouri and the remainder from the Livingston Code." Quoted by Keleher, *Turmoil in New Mexico, 1846–1868,* 118n25.

3. Before leaving Santa Fe for Paso del Norte, Doniphan embarked on a campaign against the Navajos in November 1846, the first American military campaign against that tribe. See McNitt, *Navajo Wars,* 95–123.

Later in his life, during the Civil War, he opposed secession and remained loyal to the Union but took no active military role in the conflict. Doniphan lived the remainder of his life pursuing civil affairs in his home state of Missouri. He died in Richmond, Missouri, on August 8, 1887, still widely revered for his heroic actions in the Mexican War. Launius, *Alexander William Doniphan,* 219–83.

4. Tucker, "The Missourians and The Battle of Brazito," 161.

5. Edwards, *A Campaign in New Mexico,* 48.

6. The Jornada del Muerto, or Journey of Death, was described in the 1850s as being "a barren stretch of country, which extends nearly a hundred miles . . . without water except the little found in holes after a rain, and is bounded on each side by a range of mountains. . . . [This] desert has ever been the dread of travelers, and many a one has entered upon it and never been heard of afterward." Davis, *El Gringo,* 209.

7. *New Orleans Daily Picayune,* January 9, 1847.

8. Ibid.

9. Ruhlen, "Brazito," 7.

10. Bieber, *Marching with the Army of the West,* 223.

11. Tucker, "The Missourians and The Battle of Brazito," 163.

12. Hafen, Porter, and Porter, *Ruxton of the Rockies,* 168.

13. Edwards, *A Campaign in New Mexico,* 51. It should be noted that Paso del Norte references modern-day Ciudad Juárez, Mexico, on the west bank of the Rio Grande. The current city of El Paso, Texas, on the east side of the Rio Grande, was not yet a location of significance. Mexico had maintained a permanent garrison of soldiers at Paso del Norte for many years, and it was from this post that the Mexican troops departed to confront Doniphan.

14. Estimates on the size of the Mexican force varied. Several accounts place the number at or near 1,200. Lieutenant Kribben estimated 1,100, Gibson said between 800 and 1,000, and Doniphan estimated 1,300. It is important to note that this included both Mexican regulars and volunteers. The regulars were estimated at around 500. Dawson, *Doniphan's Epic March,* 262n19.

15. Mangum, "The Battle of Brazito," 218.

16. Bieber, *Marching with the Army of the West,* 224–25.

17. Mangum, "The Battle of Brazito," 220.

18. Gallaher, "Official Report of the Battle of Temascalitos (Brazito)," 386–89.

19. Ibid.

20. Doniphan estimated the Mexican force to be 1,220, with 537 of them being

cavalry. Doniphan to Brig. Gen. Roger Jones, March 4, 1847, Senate Exec. Doc. No. 1, 30th Cong., 1st Sess., 498.

21. Before leaving Doña Ana, Doniphan left behind a cannon for the citizens to use as a defensive measure against hostile Apaches. Although few primary sources mention this, it is recorded in Susan Magoffin's diary entry of February 10, 1847. She wrote: "Colonel Doniphan has left them a cannon, and by the way we came near getting ourselves into a fine scrape last night by the wild impudence of some of the waggoners. They went into the village, 'got on a spree' and ran off with the cannon, brought it to the camp and persisted in taking it as being *unfit for Mexicans.* As 'twas done without provocation, and with seeming hostile intentions, the Alcalde told us this morning, that if *mi alma* [Samuel Magoffin] had not sent him an apology then—by Gabriel that the men were drunk and he would have it returned in the morning, he intended raising a fource [*sic*] . . . the men on finding they were not allowed to retain their trophy, spiked the touch-hole so that it will not fire, and if the Indians were to come they would be without protection." Magoffin, *Down the Santa Fe Trail and into Mexico,* 201.

22. Tucker, "The Missourians and The Battle of Brazito," 163.

23. Edwards, *A Campaign in New Mexico,* 120.

24. Quoted by Mangum, "The Battle of Brazito," 220.

25. Dawson, *Doniphan's Epic March,* 111.

26. Edwards, *A Campaign in New Mexico,* 53.

27. Mangum, "The Battle of Brazito," 222.

28. Edwards, *A Campaign in New Mexico*, 54.

29. Bieber, *Marching with the Army of the West,* 231.

30. Quoted by Tucker, "The Missourians and The Battle of Brazito," 161.

31. Dawson, *Doniphan's Epic March,* 112–13. This flag was later picked up on the Sacramento battlefield by Maj. Meriwether Lewis Clark and is described as "a small black flag, on one side of which, in white, are painted two skulls, with cross-bones below each. On the other side is the following inscription: *Libertad o Muerto.*" Twitchell, *Leading Facts,* vol. 2, 220n158. The flag is now on display at the Missouri Historical Society Museum in St. Louis.

32. Doniphan to Brig. Gen. Roger Jones, March 4, 1847, Senate Exec. Doc. No. 1, 30th Cong., 1st Sess., 497.

33. Edwards, *A Campaign in New Mexico,* 121.

34. Doniphan to Brig. Gen. Roger Jones, March 4, 1847, Senate Exec. Doc. No. 1, 30th Cong., 1st Sess., 497.

35. Susan Magoffin recorded on December 29, 1846, that Lt. James Lea of Doniphan's regiment "passed us post-haste this morning, for the artillery, as they must have it before el Passo [*sic*] can be taken." At the time the battle was fought, Magoffin was traveling south down the Camino Real toward El Paso. Magoffin, *Down the Santa Fe Trail and into Mexico,* 180.

36. Edwards, *A Campaign in New Mexico,* 119.

37. Connelly, *Doniphan's Expedition,* 374–75. Emphasis in original.

38. Lieutenant Kribben reported: "After their fire had been spent, their front column being at about 100 steps from the front of our flank, our line poured a volley into them, which being a few times repeated, created havoc in their columns." Edwards, *A Campaign in New Mexico,* 120–21.

39. Connelly, *Doniphan's Expedition,* 374–75.

40. Gallaher, "Official Report of the Battle of Temascalitos (Brazito)," 386–89.

41. Altamirano and Villa, *Chihuahua: Textos de su historia,* vol. 1, 489. The Mexican National Guard present at Brazito consisted of 180 troops; the Veracruz Dragoons, 46. Ibid.

42. Bieber, *Marching with the Army of the West,* 235.

43. Edwards, *A Campaign in New Mexico,* 55.

44. Connelly, *Doniphan's Expedition,* 374–75. Doniphan noted that "we had succeeded in mounting twenty men under the intrepid Captain Reid, and at this point he was ordered to charge the Vera Cruz dragoons." Doniphan to Brig. Gen. Roger Jones, March 4, 1847, Senate Exec. Doc. No. 1, 30th Cong., 1st Sess., 498.

45. Edwards, *A Campaign in New Mexico,* 57.

46. Mangum, "The Battle of Brazito," 222.

47. Edwards, *A Campaign in New Mexico,* 55.

48. Ibid., 121.

49. Ibid., 55.

50. Doniphan to Brig. Gen. Roger Jones, March 4, 1847, Senate Exec. Doc. No. 1, 30th Cong., 1st Sess., 498.

51. Mangum, "The Battle of Brazito," 224; Baldwin, "A Short History of the Mesilla Valley," 317.

52. Antonio Ponce de León to Lt. Col. Luis Vidal, Jan. 17, 1847. Quoted in Gallaher, "Official Report of the Battle of Temascalitos (Brazito)," 386–89.

53. Edwards, *A Campaign in New Mexico,* 57.

54. Susan Magoffin summarized the events of the battle in her diary entry of December 29, 1846. Traveling from Santa Fe to El Paso, her party was overtaken

by Lieutenant Lea, who informed her of the battle, which "lasted about 20 or 30 minutes, and is calculated to inspire our troops with more confidence than we had expected. Just as they had gotten into camp & staked out their horses, not expecting the enemy to be any ways near, for scouts had been out in all directions, a dust was seen rising and in a few moments a fource [*sic*] of some five or seven hundred dragoons, and nearly as many volunteers and pressed soldiers stood before them. Of course all was in confusion; order was soon restored though, and as will long be remembered of him, Doniphan's first order in battle to his men was 'prepare to squat,' rather a ludicrous command—but a wise one as the sequel will show, as they squatted the enemy fired, and of course all the bullets *passed over their heads,* killing none and wounding only five and they not seriously. It was now our turn for a round—the *first* that, perhaps, every one in our little army of six or seven hundred ever fired. Thirty of the Mexicans were shot dead, five were taken prisoners of war, the wounded we have not heard of and the remaining portion *fled,* leaving one field piece. I believe the only one they had, a good deal of ammunition, and some muskets, which of course our Col. has taken as trophies of victory,—on the whole 'twas quite a nice little skirmish." Magoffin, *Down the Santa Fe Trail and into Mexico,* 180–81.

55. Edwards, *A Campaign in New Mexico,* 55.

56. Ibid., 57.

57. Ibid.

58. Vasquez, "Brazito Remembered," 62.

59. Ponce de León to Lt. Col. Luis Vidal, January 17, 1847. Quoted by Gallaher, "Official Report," 386–89.

60. Ibid.

61. Bieber, *Marching with the Army of the West,* 235n167.

62. Smith, "The 'King of New Mexico' and the Doniphan Expedition." Kirker, who spoke Spanish fluently, was a widely acclaimed Apache scalp hunter both before and after the arrival of the Americans. He died in 1853. Edwards says: "The Mexicans look upon [Kirker] as almost superhuman; but I have heard, from credible authority, that his bravery is rather lukewarm, and that his victories have always been achieved through cunning. . . . He joined us the morning after the fight at Brazito, having given up hunting the Indians, in consequence of the government having forgotten to pay him. He was very useful to us, serving as guide and interpreter, during all the time we remained in the country." Edwards, *A Campaign in New Mexico,* 63.

63. Ibid., 58.

64. Bieber, *Marching with the Army of the West,* 238.

65. Quoted by Dawson, *Doniphan's Epic March,* 120.

66. Edwards, *A Campaign in New Mexico,* 58.

67. Davis, *El Gringo,* 216.

68. Bieber, *Marching with the Army of the West,* 238.

69. Ramón Ortíz was born in Santa Fe in 1814 and was a descendant of one of the original Spanish colonizing families. He became a *cura* in 1838 at Paso del Norte. Ortíz's jurisdiction as *cura* extended from Paso del Norte northward as far as Doña Ana. In 1841 he was instrumental in relieving and caring for the captured Texans comprising the ill-fated Texan–Santa Fe Expedition from the torturous Damasio Salazar. "This was the first of many public and defiant acts on the part of the young priest in defense of those without hope," writes one historian. Almada, *Diccionario de historia, geografía y biografía chihuahuenses,* 385; Taylor, *A Place as Wild as the West Ever Was,* 15–18.

70. Puckett, "Ramón Ortíz," 280–82.

71. Gilbert, "The U.S. Military Occupation of El Paso del Norte, 1846–47," 116.

72. Dawson, *Doniphan's Epic March,* 117.

73. Magoffin, *Down the Santa Fe Trail and into Mexico,* 202.

74. Davis, *El Gringo,* 212.

CHAPTER 2

1. The treaty was signed at Guadalupe Hidalgo, the location of a revered religious shrine near Mexico City. The Mexican government ratified the treaty on May 30, 1848, and Congress quickly followed suit, doing so on July 4. Keleher, *Turmoil in New Mexico,* 36.

2. Twitchell, *Leading Facts,* vol. 2, 194–278.

3. The treaty was submitted to the Senate on February 23. President Polk recommended its approval, except for Article IX. It was ratified on March 10. Drexler, *Guilty of Making Peace,* 127–28.

4. Garber, *The Gadsden Treaty,* 5.

5. Miller, *Treaties and Other International Acts,* vol. 5, 213–16.

6. In 1841 a force of several hundred Texans led by Gen. Hugh McLeod left Austin and marched for Santa Fe. The purpose of the expedition had been debated; some said it was for trading, others said it was to forcibly take possession of New

Mexico. The entire contingent was captured and led on a forced march into Mexico. Many of the Texans died along the way, and Mexican officers were notoriously brutal in their treatment of the prisoners. This did nothing to ease preexisting tensions between Texas and the Republic of Mexico. Numerous firsthand accounts exist, the most noteworthy and colorful of which is George Wilkins Kendall's *Narrative of the Texan Santa Fé Expedition.*

7. Quoted by Keleher, *Turmoil in New Mexico,* 125n45.

8. General Winfield Scott to Colonel John Munroe, August 6, 1850. Quoted in Abel, *Official Correspondence of James S. Calhoun,* 164–65.

9. An editorial published in the Santa Fe *Republican* on August 31, 1848, proclaimed: "We would inform our Texian friends that it is not necessary to send us a Judge or a District Attorney to settle out affairs or to 'put things to rights,' for there is not a citizen, either American or Mexican, that will ever acknowledge themselves as citizens of Texas, until it comes from higher authorities. . . . Oh Texas, do show some little sense and drop this question, and not have it publicly announced that Texas' smartest men were tarred and feathered by attempting to fill the office assigned them." Quoted by Edrington, "Military Influence on the Texas–New Mexico Boundary Settlement," 378.

10. A census taken on April 16, 1843, lists fourteen settlers at Doña Ana, probably all the heads of family living there at the time: Pablo Melendres (the first alcalde), José María Costales (to whom the land grant had been issued), Juan José Benavidez, Francisco Rodríguez, Jesús Olivares, José María Bernál, Francisco Lucero, Geronimo Lujan, José Inéz García, Saturnino Albillar, Gabriel Dábalos, Ramón de la Serna, and one unknown. Frietze, *History of La Mesilla,* 19.

11. Ibid., 11n2.

12. Ibid., 19.

13. Price, *Pioneers of the Mesilla Valley,* 67.

14. When Sackett arrived to survey Las Cruces, there were already 120 families living there, mostly in *jacales.* After the survey had been completed, the people held a gathering during which individuals drew names out of a hat to determine which plot of land would belong to them. Sackett's original survey split the town into thirty-seven blocks. Owen, "The Mesilla Valley's Pioneer Settlements," 10. Several years later, another observer of the town said, "[Las Cruces] is a modern-built Mexican village, and, in Yankee style, stretches mostly along one broad street with a population of about a thousand souls." Davis, *El Gringo,* 217. Dr. S. W. Woodhouse, who passed through the Mesilla Valley in 1851, wrote: "When within six miles of

Don Anna [*sic*], we passed through a Mexican town of about 500 inhabitants [Las Cruces]. It was a miserable looking place. The houses are adobe and very low. The natives look poor and the corn, backwards." Woodhouse, *From Texas to San Diego in 1851,* 59–60.

15. Bartlett, *Personal Narrative,* vol. 2, 212–14.

16. Stegmaier, *Texas, New Mexico, and the Compromise of 1850,* 70.

17. Colonel John Munroe to AAG Roger Jones, May 20, 1850. Quoted by Stegmaier, "The Guadalupe Hidalgo Treaty as a Factor in the New Mexico–Texas Boundary Dispute," 48.

18. Bartlett, *Personal Narrative,* vol. 2, 212–14.

19. Taylor, *A Place as Wild as the West Ever Was,* 20–27.

20. Rafael Ruelas was quite young at the time he led his fellow citizens across the Rio Grande to found Mesilla. The 1860 U.S. census notes his birth date as "about 1820," which would have made him about thirty years old in 1850. In the 1860 census he is noted as being married to Blusa Ruelas and as having five children between the ages of six and fourteen. 1860 U.S. Census: Doña Ana County, New Mexico Territory.

21. Bartlett to A. H. H. Stuart, August 8, 1851, Senate Exec. Doc. No. 119, 32nd Cong, 1st Sess., 148.

22. In order to assuage the Texans, Congress included a provision in the act of September 9, 1850, allowing $10 million to be paid to Texas in exchange for the relinquishment of their claim to the Rio Grande as a western boundary. Keleher, *Turmoil in New Mexico,* 39–42.

23. At this time, the Rio Grande did not follow its present course, but rather flowed to the east of Mesilla. By all accounts, the Rio Grande was a wild, unpredictable river up until the construction of the Elephant Butte Dam in the early twentieth century. Josiah Gregg, passing through in the 1830s, commented: "We reached the usual ford of the Rio del Norte six miles above El Paso; but the river being somewhat flushed we found it impossible to cross over with our wagons. . . . This river, even when fordable, often occasions a great deal of trouble, being, like the Arkansas, embarrassed with many quicksand mires. In some places, if a wagon is permitted to stop in the river but for a moment it sinks to the very body. Instances have occurred where it became necessary not only to drag out the mules by the ears and to carry out the loading package by package, but to haul out the wagon piece by piece—wheel by wheel." Gregg, *Commerce of the Prairies,* 241–42.

24. Miller, *Treaties and Other International Acts,* vol. 5, 216.

25. Bender, "Military Transportation in the Southwest," 142.

26. Miller, *Treaties and Other International Acts,* vol. 5, 219–22.

27. Quoted by Garber, *The Gadsden Treaty,* 27.

28. Calhoun to Orlando Brown, February 12, 1850. Quoted in Abel, *Official Correspondence of James S. Calhoun,* 150.

29. Garber, *The Gadsden Treaty,* 3.

30. Ibid., 30.

31. Juan N. Almonte to William L. Marcy, October 22, 1853, RG59, M54, Roll 4.

32. Garber, *The Gadsden Treaty,* 32–33.

33. Coffey, "Some General Aspects of the Gadsden Treaty," 151–52.

CHAPTER 3

1. Fillmore to Congress, August 6, 1850, House of Representatives Exec. Doc. No. 82, 31st Cong., 1st Sess., 5.

2. The Mexican government chose the Disturnell map because it showed El Paso del Norte being located within the recognized boundaries of the State of Chihuahua. A Mexican law of 1824 describing the boundaries of Chihuahua did so in a manner open to interpretation, and use of the Disturnell map resulted in a favorable outcome for Mexico, which considered it imperative that this town be retained and not ceded to the United States along with the rest of New Mexico. Werne, *The Imaginary Line,* 12.

3. According to Bartlett, "two gross errors in the [Disturnell] map . . . [were] that the Rio Grande was laid down on this map, more than two degrees too far to the eastward—the river, where it is intersected by the southern boundary of New Mexico, being really in 106° 40′ west longitude, instead of 104° 40′." Bartlett, *Personal Narrative,* vol. 1, 210.

4. Hine, *Bartlett's West,* 32.

5. Baldwin, "A Historical Note on the Boundaries of New Mexico," 126.

6. Emory, "Running the Line," 224.

7. Born on October 21, 1817, Amiel Weeks Whipple was a member of the 1841 graduating class at West Point. He was assigned to the Army Corps of Topographical Engineers and later worked on the Mexican Boundary Survey. During the Civil War, Whipple became Chief Topographical Engineer for the Army of the Potomac, attaining the rank of major general for meritorious service at the Battle of

Chancellorsville where he was mortally wounded on May 7, 1863. Heitman, *Historical Register and Dictionary of the United States Army,* 1025.

8. Pedro García Conde was born in Arizpe, Sonora, Mexico, on February 8, 1806, and like many young Mexican boys, began his military career early. By age twelve he was a cadet at a military academy in Durango and by 1828 had attained the rank of captain in the Mexican Corps of Engineers. After engaging in cartographic work in Chihuahua during the 1830s, he became director of the Colegio Militar and by 1837 was a brigadier general. He played an active role in the Mexican War and took part in the Battle of Sacramento in 1847, where he fought against Doniphan's Missouri Volunteers. He died in December 1851. Almada, *Diccionario de historia, geografía y biografía chihuahuenses,* 218.

9. José Salazar Ylarregui was born in Sonora and first came to Chihuahua in 1850 to serve on the boundary commission. Beginning in 1855 he served as the Mexican commissioner and surveyed the Gadsden Purchase boundary line. He served as a representative in the Mexican Congress starting in 1857; Salazar Ylarregui died in 1892 at the age of sixty-nine. Almada, *Diccionario de historia, geografía y biografía chihuahuenses,* 476.

10. Prieto, *Memorias de mis tiempos,* 167.

11. Salazar Ylarregui, *Datos de los trabajos,* 8–9.

12. In addition to García Conde and Salazar Ylarregui, principal officials comprising the Mexican commission included Francisco Jímenez and Francisco Martinez de Chavero (Ingenieros de Primera Clase), Agustín García Conde and Ricardo Ramirez (Ingenieros de Segundo Clase), and Felipe de Iturbide (Interpreter). Salazar Ylarregui, *Datos de los trabajos,* 8.

13. Goetzmann, *Army Exploration in the American West,* 163. Although the order relieving Weller from command and replacing him with Frémont had been issued on June 20, 1849, Weller continued working on the boundary survey until early 1850.

14. Hine, *Bartlett's West,* 5.

15. Ibid.

16. John Russell Bartlett was born on October 23, 1805, in Providence, Rhode Island, and lived in Ontario, Canada, until the age of eighteen. He developed a profound interest in the study of American Indians and ethnology, and was a cofounder of the American Ethnological Society in 1842. After working as boundary commissioner, he returned to Rhode Island, where he served as secretary of state from 1855 until 1872. He published numerous important books during his lifetime,

among them his famed *Personal Narrative* of the boundary surveys. The books, published in two volumes, were an instant classic, and were used as a reference for travelers across southern New Mexico and Arizona for many years. He died on May 26, 1886, at the age of eighty. Bartlett, edited by Mueller, *Autobiography of John Russell Bartlett.*

17. In receiving the appointment as boundary commissioner, Bartlett enjoyed the endorsements of such prominent politicians as Albert Gallatin, Jefferson Davis, Stephen A. Douglas, Thomas Hart Benton, and John C. Calhoun. Grassham, "The United States–Mexico Boundary Commission," 18.

18. Bartlett, edited by Mueller, *Autobiography of John Russell Bartlett,* 23–24.

19. Ibid., 37.

20. Quoted by Hine, *Bartlett's West,* 10.

21. Bartlett, edited by Mueller, *Autobiography of John Russell Bartlett,* 24.

22. Werne, *The Imaginary Line,* 51.

23. Bartlett, edited by Mueller, *Autobiography of John Russell Bartlett,* 38. "On assuming the duties of my new office," Bartlett wrote, "I found hundreds of applications for places in the Boundary Commission which I proceeded to fill, nearly all upon the recommendations of Senators and Members of Congress." Ibid.

24. Wallace, *The Great Reconnaissance,* 8–12.

25. McClellan to A. H. H. Stuart, January 13, 1850, Senate Exec. Doc. No. 60, 32nd Congress, 1st Sess., 2–3.

26. Bartlett to McClellan, December 4, 1851, Senate Exec. Doc. No. 60, 32nd Cong., 1st Sess., 10; Bartlett, *Personal Narrative,* vol. 2, 28.

27. Bartlett to McClellan, December 16, 1851, Senate Exec. Doc. No. 60, 32nd Cong., 1st Sess., 12.

28. Ibid., 10–11. The detachment of Mexican troops consisted of only about fifteen men (whereas the American commission boasted a military escort exceeding eighty troops). The unwillingness of the Mexican government to provide an adequate military escort would be a severe shortcoming for the commission. Werne, *The Imaginary Line,* 54.

29. Bartlett to Ewing, December 23, 1850. Quoted by Werne, *The Imaginary Line,* 57.

30. Baldwin, "A Historical Note on the Boundaries of New Mexico," 127.

31. Hine, *Bartlett's West,* 31.

32. García Conde to Mexican Minister of Relations, December 24, 1850. Quoted by Werne, *The Imaginary Line,* 56–57.

33. Faulk, *Too Far North, Too Far South,* 65.

34. Bartlett to Stuart, December 28, 1850, Senate Exec. Doc. No. 119, 32nd Cong., 1st Sess., 392.

35. The exact language of the Treaty of Guadalupe Hidalgo stated that the boundary was to follow the Rio Grande northward until "the point where it strikes the southern boundary of New Mexico; thence westward along the whole southern boundary of New Mexico (which runs north of the town called Paso) to its western termination; thence northward along the western line of New Mexico until it intersects the first branch of the river Gila (or if it should not intersect any branch of that river, then to the point on the said line nearest such branch, and thence in a direct line to the same); thence down the middle of said branch and said river until it empties into the Rio Colorado." Miller, *Treaties and Other International Acts,* vol. 5, 213.

A Mexican law passed July 24, 1824, stipulated that the northern boundary of Chihuahua, where it struck the Rio Grande, was just north of the "town called Paso del Norte," and gave a detailed description of where that point was. Thus previously existing Mexican law had established the boundary at the same point Bartlett had fought for but failed to obtain. García Conde seems to have conveniently neglected to inform Bartlett of this law. Werne, *The Imaginary Line,* 165.

36. Bartlett to Stuart, December 28, 1850, Senate Exec. Doc. No. 119, 32nd Cong., 1st Sess., 391.

37. Citizens of Mesilla to James S. Calhoun, August 25, 1851. Quoted in Abel, *Official Correspondence,* 404–405. The petition contains some errors on the part of those writing it. There is no evidence to suggest that Mesilla was founded as an American village; contrarily, all evidence states that the town was founded by people wishing to avoid becoming American, and even more specifically, Texas, citizens.

38. Quoted by Devine, *Slavery, Scandal, and Steel Rails,* 42.

39. William L. Marcy to James Gadsden, July 15, 1853. Quoted in Abel, *Official Correspondence,* 46–47.

40. Devine, *Slavery, Scandal, and Steel Rails,* 70.

41. Ibid., 72.

42. Garber, *The Gadsden Treaty,* 15.

43. "American civilian and military personnel selected to carry out significant assignments on the survey continually quarreled over who was in charge," writes one historian. "Mexico, on the other hand, appointed their commissioner and

survey party promptly and with little difficulty." Grassham, "The United States–Mexico Boundary Commission," 15.

44. Bartlett to Stuart, August 8, 1851, Senate Exec. Doc. No. 119, 32nd Cong., 1st Sess., 147–48.

45. This would have been allowed under the Treaty of Guadalupe Hidalgo, which maintained that any New Mexican wishing to remain a citizen of Mexico could do so. Individuals were to make their choice of citizenship known within one year following ratification of the treaty. In this way more than one thousand New Mexicans moved back to Mexico to retain their Mexican citizenship. Miller, *Treaties and Other International Acts,* vol. 5, 217–18.

W. W. H. Davis described the resultant situation: "In the eighth article of [the Treaty of Guadalupe Hidalgo] there is a clause which provides that all Mexicans living in the territory ceded to the United States might, if they desired it, retain the rights of Mexican citizens by making their election to that effect within one year after the ratification of said treaty. . . . In accordance with said provisions, Colonel [John M.] Washington, in the Spring of 1849, while acting as civil and military governor of the Territory, issued a proclamation calling upon all those who desired to make their election to do so in the manner therein pointed out." Davis, *El Gringo,* 177–78.

46. William Helmsley Emory was born on September 7, 1811, in Maryland. As a child, Emory grew up with the likes of Henry Clay Jr. and Jefferson Davis, both of whom came from families who were close friends of the Emorys. He became a first lieutenant in the Topographical Engineers on July 7, 1838. After the boundary surveys, he was a part of the Pacific Railway surveys in the mid-1850s, afterward returning to service as a major in his 2nd Cavalry regiment. He participated in the Mormon War of 1858 and when the Civil War broke out in 1861 refused a commission as major general in the Confederate Army, opting instead to remain loyal to the North. Fighting for the Union, he achieved the rank of brevet major general of volunteers by the end of the war. Emory retired on July 1, 1876, with the rank of brigadier general, having served forty-three years in the U.S. Army. Heitman, *Historical Register and Dictionary of the United States Army,* 405–406.

47. Goetzmann, *Army Exploration in the American West,* 182.

48. Writing of his experience, Emory said that when he arrived in New Mexico, "the commissioner [Bartlett] was absent on an expedition into Sonora, the commission was in debt, and not one cent was at my disposal to prosecute the survey. Beyond running an erroneous line a degree and a half west of the Del Norte [Rio

Grande], and starting a party with limited means under Lieut. Whipple to survey the Gila, and another to survey the Rio del Norte, nothing had been accomplished." Quoted by Bancroft, *History of Arizona and New Mexico,* 469n46.

49. William H. Emory to A. D. Bache, January 21, 1852. Quoted by Hine, *Bartlett's West,* 71.

50. George Clinton Gardner to his Father, April 9, 1852, in Weber and Elder, *Fiasco,* 188.

51. Wallace, *The Great Reconnaissance,* 95.

52. Hine, *Bartlett's West,* 12.

53. Goetzmann, *Army Exploration in the American West,* 183.

54. Kajencki, "Charles Radziminski and the United States–Mexican Boundary Survey," 223–24.

55. Bartlett, *Personal Narrative,* vol. 1, 197.

56. George Clinton Gardner to his Father, February 16, 1852, in Weber and Elder, *Fiasco,* 180.

57. Bartlett, edited by Mueller, *Autobiography of John Russell Bartlett,* 35–41.

58. Quoted by Baldwin, "A Historical Note on the Boundaries of New Mexico," 127.

59. Emory, "Running the Line," 234.

60. George Clinton Gardner to his Father, March 1852, in Weber and Elder, *Fiasco,* 183.

CHAPTER 4

1. Devine, *Slavery, Scandal, and Steel Rails,* 9.

2. Garber, *The Gadsden Treaty,* 18–19.

3. Coffey, "Some General Aspects of the Gadsden Treaty," 154.

4. "There is but one thing that can possibly open a new era in the prosperity of New Mexico, which is the building of a railroad through the Territory to the Pacific. It would give a new impetus to all her interests, and do more to develop her resources than all other causes combined." Davis, *El Gringo,* 251.

5. Lane to his Wife, February 15, 1853. Quoted in Bieber, "Letters of William Carr Lane," 192.

6. Proclamation of William Carr Lane, March 13, 1853, RG59, M54, Roll 1.

7. Quoted in Carson, "William Carr Lane Diary," 300.

8. *El Siglo Diez y Nueve* (Mexico City), "Agresión Americana en Chihuahua," April 10, 1853.

9. Ibid., "La Cuestión de La Mesilla," June 6, 1853. See also articles in *El Siglo Diez y Nueve,* one of May 13, 1853, titled "Noticias Nacionales: La Cuestión de Mesilla en Chihuahua," and another of April 27, 1853, titled "Ministerio de Relaciones."

10. Trías to Lane, March 28, 1853, in *Alcance al Centinela* (Chihuahua City), March 29, 1853.

11. Werne, *The Imaginary Line,* 163.

12. D. R. Diffendorfer to William L. Marcy, March 23, 1853, RG59, M54, Roll 1.

13. Carson, "William Carr Lane Diary," 218–23.

14. Miles to Sumner, April 1853, RG393, M1102, LR, DNM, Roll 7.

15. Frazer, *Mansfield on the Condition of the Western Forts,* 57.

16. Ibid., 77

17. Lane to his Wife, April 5, 1853. Quoted in Bieber, "Letters of William Carr Lane," 193.

18. William Carr Lane, Statement written in Washington, D.C., January 23, 1854, House of Representatives Exec. Doc. No. 81, 33rd Cong., 1st Sess., 2.

19. J. Miguel Arroyo to Alfred B. Conkling, April 8, 1853, RG59, M97, Roll 17.

20. Conkling to Marcy, June 14, 1853, ibid., Roll 18.

21. Conkling to Lane, April 8, 1853, ibid.

22. Lane to Conkling, May 13, 1853, ibid.

23. Lane to his Wife, June 8, 1852. Quoted in Bieber, "Letters of William Carr Lane," 196.

24. David Meriwether was born in Virginia on October 30, 1800. He served thirteen nonconsecutive terms in the Kentucky General Assembly between the years 1832 and 1883. In 1852 he was named as Henry Clay's successor to the U.S. Senate, a position he held for only a brief period. He gave up his seat in the Senate to replace Governor Lane. Meriwether acted as the governor of New Mexico Territory until October 31, 1857, being the first to serve a full term in that position. Horn, *New Mexico's Troubled Years,* 53.

25. A native Virginian, John Garland saw his first military action during the War of 1812. He took an active part in the Mexican War, fighting at the Battles of Palo Alto, Monterrey, and Veracruz before being severely wounded at Mexico City. He was the father-in-law of the famed Confederate general, James Longstreet, although he himself did not fight for the Confederacy during the Civil War.

26. Davis, *El Gringo,* 108–109.

27. Mullin, "David Meriwether, Territorial Governor of New Mexico," 87.

28. Ibid.

29. Marcy to James Gadsden, July 15, 1853. Quoted in Miller, *Treaties and Other International Acts,* vol. 6, 345.

30. Ibid., 347.

31. Born in 1788, Gadsden graduated from Yale University in 1806. He enlisted in the Army Corps of Engineers during the War of 1812 and eventually reached the rank of colonel. When his friend, Andrew Jackson, built a military post in Florida, he named it Fort Gadsden in his honor. Gadsden owed much of his career to the spoils system, as it was his friendships with Andrew Jackson and Jefferson Davis that allowed him to advance to such noteworthy positions. Devine, *Slavery, Scandal, and Steel Rails,* 7.

32. Coffey, "Some General Aspects of the Gadsden Treaty," 152–53.

33. Garber, *The Gadsden Treaty,* 74–82.

34. Ibid., 85–87.

35. The location that stood to gain the most from the construction of a railroad was El Paso. The proposed route would have passed through this town, and thence westward, effectively bypassing Mesilla and Las Cruces. One witness, writing in the mid-1850s, noted that "if the proposed Atlantic and Pacific railroad should be constructed through Texas, El Paso will be an important point on the route, and it will be the means of settling this whole valley with an enterprising population. The place of crossing [the Rio Grande] is just below the mill of Judge Hart, which is said to be the most eligible point for the purpose upon the river." Davis, *El Gringo,* 214.

36. Faulk, *Too Far North, Too Far South,* 129–30.

37. Garber, *The Gadsden Treaty,* 88–89. Gadsden detailed Santa Anna's money problems in an undated letter to President Franklin Pierce in 1853. Miller, *Treaties and Other International Acts,* vol. 6, 349–53.

38. James Gadsden to William L. Marcy, October 18, 1853. Quoted by Schmidt, "Manifest Opportunity and the Gadsden Purchase," 253.

39. William L. Marcy to Christopher L. Ward, October 22, 1853. Quoted in Miller, *Treaties and Other International Acts,* vol. 6, 361–64.

40. Devine, *Slavery, Scandal, and Steel Rails,* 48.

41. "The Mexican Treaty," *New York Daily Times,* January 18, 1854.

42. Coffey, "Some General Aspects of the Gadsden Treaty," 155–56; Garber, *The Gadsden Treaty,* 91–93.

43. "Later from Mexico," *New Orleans Daily Picayune,* January 13, 1854.

44. Hackler, *The Butterfield Trail in New Mexico,* 58.

45. Quoted by Garber, *The Gadsden Treaty,* 107.

46. "The Important Treaty," *Richmond Enquirer,* January 18, 1854.

47. Garber, *The Gadsden Treaty,* 114.

48. Coffey, "Some General Aspects of the Gadsden Treaty," 159–63.

49. Garber, *The Gadsden Treaty,* 140.

50. Ibid., 155.

51. Miller, *Treaties and Other International Acts,* vol. 6, 295–97.

52. Schmidt, "Manifest Opportunity and the Gadsden Purchase," 264n54.

53. Goetzmann, *Army Exploration in the American West,* 196.

54. Faulk, *Too Far North, Too Far South,* 143.

55. Kajencki, "Charles Radziminski and the United States–Mexican Boundary Survey," 233.

56. Ibid., 236. According to John Reid in 1857: "The line between the territories of the United States and Mexico . . . is told by blocks of gray marble placed at conspicuous points along the line. Durable objects stand, within short distances of each other, the entire length of the line. . . . On each public road which crosses this line monuments (obelisks) have been built, whereon is engraved the name of the boundary commissioner, Maj. Emory, etc., purpose of the monuments, and time when the line was run." Reid, *Reid's Tramp,* 165.

57. Maj. William H. Emory first suggested that the Mexican troops at Tucson be relieved by a force of American regulars in a letter to General Garland on August 11, 1855. As of September 1, 1855, some six months prior to their ultimate removal from Tucson, the Mexican garrison there consisted of fifty-two troops under the command of Capt. Hilarion García. Benjamin H. Sacks Manuscript Collection, MSS110, Box 7, Folder 3, Arizona Historical Foundation, Tempe, Arizona.

58. Faulk, *Too Far North, Too Far South,* 150.

59. Mullin, "David Meriwether," 88.

60. Ibid., 91.

61. Bennett, *Forts and Forays,* 74.

62. Quoted by Mullin, "David Meriwether," 91.

63. General Orders 27, November 1855. Constance Wynn Altshuler Collection, MSS113, Box 12, Folder 10, Arizona Historical Foundation, Tempe, Arizona.

64. Garber, *The Gadsden Treaty,* 156–57.

65. Reid, *Reid's Tramp,* 156.

CHAPTER 5

1. The 9th Military Department was organized in 1848. At that time the United States was divided into two military divisions, the Eastern and Western, of which there were eleven different departments. The 9th Department included all of modern-day New Mexico and Arizona as well as portions of southern Utah and Colorado. This area would prove far too vast for a small body of troops to control; between the years 1848 and 1853 the government spent over $12 million on defensive measures in the territory. By 1850, two years after the creation of the department, twenty-one companies of infantry and dragoons (a total of 1,188 officers and privates) were stationed in New Mexico. Frazer, *Forts and Supplies,* 33–59.

2. Bartlett, *Personal Narrative,* vol. 2, 384–85.

3. "The bottomlands of the Mesilla Valley directly opposite Fort Fillmore, and about forty-five miles above El Paso on the Rio Grande del Norte, comprising about thirty square miles, have latterly been occupied by the Mexicans, although the village was laid out by Major E. Steen of the U.S. Dragoons, and a flourishing population of about three thousand souls produces as good crops as are to be found in New Mexico." Frazer, *Mansfield on the Condition of the Western Forts,* 13.

4. Company B, 3rd Infantry, arrived for duty at Doña Ana on December 6, 1849, and was commanded by 1st Lt. John Trevitt, who also served in the roles of acting assistant quartermaster and assistant commissary of subsistence. Frazer, *New Mexico in 1850,* 167.

5. Ibid., 168.

6. Woodhouse, *From Texas to San Diego in 1851,* 60.

7. Born in Harrodsburg, Kentucky, on February 22, 1800, Enoch Steen joined the 1st Regiment of U.S. Dragoons in 1833 and served thirty-four years as an officer with that regiment. He fought in the Mexican War and was brevetted major on February 23, 1847, for meritorious conduct at the Battle of Buena Vista. On August 16, 1849, while in command at Doña Ana, he was wounded in a skirmish with the Mimbres Apaches near Santa Rita del Cobre. In 1856 he was sent to establish a new post at Tucson; arriving there, he decided differently and instead established Fort Buchanan forty miles away. He left Arizona in April 1858 and by 1860 had been reassigned to the Oregon Territory. He retired as a lieutenant colonel of the 2nd Cavalry on September 23, 1863. He was described as being "a man of splendid physique, of the most temperate habits, and he had the endurance of old Daniel Boone himself." He lived the remainder of his civilian life in Missouri until his death on

January 22, 1880. Heitman, *Historical Register and Dictionary of the United States Army,* 919.

8. Frazer, *New Mexico in 1850,* 166–67.

9. The theft of animals and property in southern New Mexico was not limited to Apache pillaging, but was a mutual practice in which both the Indians and Mexicans participated. In 1855, agent Steck reported that the Mescaleros had stolen several head of cattle near Doña Ana, but went on to state, "the Mexicans have stolen more than double that number from the Indians." Steck to Meriwether, July 30, 1855, *Inventory of the Michael Steck Papers,* Series 2. Also in 1855, three Mexicans from El Paso were reported to have stolen six horses and a mule from the camp of a peaceful band of Mescaleros near Doña Ana. Steck to U.S. Consul at El Paso, July 28, 1855, ibid.

10. Steen to McLaws, December 9, 1849, RG393, M1102, LR, DNM, Roll 2.

11. Steen to McLaws, July 8, 1850, ibid.

12. Steen to McLaws, February 5, 1850, ibid.

13. Steen to McLaws, March 26, 1850, ibid.

14. Frazer, *New Mexico in 1850,* 168.

15. In accordance with this order troops were permanently withdrawn from Socorro, Doña Ana, El Paso, and San Elizario south of El Paso. In their place, Fort Conrad was established twenty miles south of Socorro, Fort Bliss near El Paso, Fort Webster at the Santa Rita Copper Mines, and Fort Fillmore south of Mesilla. Secretary of War Charles M. Conrad supported this plan, saying: "The Department is induced to believe, that both economy and efficiency of the service would be promoted by removing the troops out of the towns where they are now stationed, and stationing them more towards the frontier and nearer to the Indians." Quoted by Frazer, *Forts and Supplies,* 61.

16. Frazer, *New Mexico in 1850,* 182.

17. The land on which Fort Fillmore was constructed belonged to local entrepreneur Hugh Stephenson, who had owned silver mines in the vicinity during the Mexican colonial period. The military leased this land from him at the rate of ten cents per year for twenty years. Stephenson, recognizing the benefits of having military protection in the vicinity of his landholdings, made this offer to Colonel Sumner in order to ensure that this location would be chosen for the fort, rather than Brazito or Cottonwoods farther south.

18. Miles to Buell, September 26, 1851, RG393, M1102, LR, DNM, Roll 3. Fort Fillmore would be garrisoned at various times by Company B, 1st Dragoons, from

1854 to 1855; Company H, 1st Dragoons, from 1851 to 1852; Company D, 1st Dragoons, from 1852 to 1854 and 1859 to 1860; and Company K, 2nd Dragoons, in 1852, along with numerous companies of the 3rd Infantry and Regiment of Mounted Rifles. Agnew, *Garrisons of the Regular U.S. Army*, 19–21.

19. Davis, *El Gringo*, 375.

20. Ibid., 374.

21. Lane, *I Married a Soldier*, 99–100.

22. Buford to AAG, December 20, 1851, RG393, M1102, LR, DNM, Roll 4.

23. Quoted by Frazer, *New Mexico in 1850*, 188.

24. Buford to McFerran, December 19, 1851, RG393, M1102, LR, DNM, Roll 4. The post was named for Daniel Webster, who was serving as secretary of state at the time it was established. The fort remained at the copper mines for less than a year, being abandoned in November 1852, and then moved a short distance away to a bluff overlooking the Mimbres River. The second Fort Webster was abandoned on December 20, 1853. The sentiment of the Apaches toward this post was obvious when, after abandoning Fort Webster, the troops looked back and saw that the Indians had already set fire to the buildings.

25. Governor Lane eventually challenged Sumner to a duel, which the military commander declined. The disagreement stemmed from the moment of Lane's arrival at Santa Fe when Sumner moved his headquarters from Santa Fe to Albuquerque and took with him the U.S. flag that had been flying over the plaza. When Lane asked Sumner to return it, he responded, "I am not authorized by the govt. to furnish you with govt. stores." A dispute between Lane and Sumner ensued, one that would last until both men left the territory, which ironically occurred almost simultaneously. Wadsworth, *Forgotten Fortress*, 79.

26. Tittman, "By Order of Richard Campbell," 398.

27. The majority of Mescalero Apache depredations were carried out by a small contingent of the tribe. Frequently, the vast majority of the tribe was innocent of any wrongdoing and was entirely unaware of any raids that their kinsmen had perpetrated. Because of this it was not uncommon for some of these Indians to be living peaceably near the settlements (usually Doña Ana) while others were raiding in the same area. The result of this was many misunderstandings by both parties, at times resulting in the unnecessary death of individuals on both sides.

28. McFerran to Sturges, August 1853, RG393, M1102, LR, DNM, Roll 7.

29. McFerran to Sturges, August 1853, ibid.

30. Frazer, *Mansfield on the Condition of the Western Forts*, 54–57. Fort Fillmore

was formally inspected for the last time on September 9, 1859, by Lt. Col. Joseph E. Johnston. The garrison's strength at that time was 163 enlisted men, excluding officers. Thompson, *Texas and New Mexico on the Eve of the Civil War,* 58.

31. Ibid. In addition to a lack of horses and ammunition, Fort Fillmore suffered from other shortcomings as well. In August 1855, Miles complained to headquarters that he lacked enough men to perform various duties at the post, to the extent that he could spare only one man at a time to serve as sentinel. He wrote: "There is of necessity, as at all posts, certain labor required ... this can be avoided and permit me to mount additional guard, if the quartermaster is permitted to hire but a few Mexicans, not over 5 or 6, who can be obtained at 5 or 6 bits per day ... this is decidedly cheaper to the government that the employment of soldiers." Miles to Nichols, August 11, 1855, RG393, M1120, LR, DNM, Roll 4.

32. Sweeney, *Mangas Coloradas,* 289.

33. Miles to Nichols, October 1854, RG393, M1120, LR, DNM, Roll 3.

34. When the troops returned to Fort Fillmore a grim scene unfolded: "Mrs. Stanton, the Captain's wife, stood in the door awaiting her husband. If a person had one drop of pity, here he could use it. Poor woman! She asks for her husband, the answer is evaded. An hour passes. Her smiles are fled. Her merry laugh is turned to sighs, and tears stain her cheek. Him she loved, she never more shall behold." Bennett, *Forts and Forays,* 63.

35. Miles to Steck, April 3, 1855, Steck Papers, Series 2.

36. Fort Thorn was named for Capt. Herman Thorn who drowned in 1849. The drowning was described by George Clinton Gardner, an assistant surveyor with the boundary commission. Captain Thorn, in command of a company of dragoons, "got drowned by being capsized in crossing the Gila [River] with two Mexicans and one dragoon; it seems that Capt. Thorn was quite a good swimmer but the two Mexicans who were drowning also got hold of him—one by the leg the other by his arm and carried him under." George Clinton Gardner to his Father, October 28, 1849, in Weber and Elder, *Fiasco,* 65–66. Gardner erred in stating that Thorn drowned in the Gila River; the incident actually occurred in the Colorado River, near Fort Yuma.

Fort Thorn was the successor to Fort Webster, and was established on the western banks of the Rio Grande in December 1853. The post sat on a small mesa overlooking the river, about five miles north of the present town of Hatch, New Mexico. Nothing remains of the post today, several large floods having washed away the entire bluff upon which the fort sat. The location of Fort Thorn was a poor one, with malaria prevalent due to the nearby marshy bottomlands of the river valley. For this reason the fort was abandoned in 1859. Kraemer, "Sickliest Post in the Territory of New Mexico."

37. Steck wrote General Garland on January 7, 1856: "I left word for Col. J. H. Eaton comdg. Ft. Thorn that I knew the thieves & murderers & requested him to take no steps until I returned [from leave of absence], but from certain information that he received from other sources . . . [he] fitted up an expedition . . . the unexpected movement of the troops into the Indian country without their knowing the particular objective alarmed the whole tribe, who left the vicinity of the agency to watch the movement of the troops." Steck to Garland, January 7, 1856, Steck Papers, Series 2.

38. Manypenny to Meriwether, May 9, 1854, RG75, T21, LR, NMS.

39. President Fillmore appointed Steck as an Indian agent in New Mexico for the term of four years, beginning on September 1, 1852, at an annual salary of $1,550. Steck accepted the appointment on September 7, 1852. Lea to Steck, September 4, 1852, Steck Papers, Series 1.

Steck was born on October 6, 1818; he graduated from Jefferson Medical College in Philadelphia in 1843. He came to New Mexico in 1849 as a surgeon with the army. Steck became superintendent of Indian affairs in New Mexico during the Civil War, a position that caused him much anguish owing to continuous disputes with military commander Maj. James H. Carleton. Afterward, Steck returned to Pennsylvania, where he made an unsuccessful attempt to become lieutenant governor. He died on October 6, 1883. Thrapp, *Encyclopedia of Frontier Biography,* vol. 3, 1361–62.

40. Miles to Nichols, October 28, 1855, RG393, M1120, LR, DNM, Roll 4. Mescalero chief Palanquito visited Miles at Fort Fillmore on October 28 to proclaim the innocence of his band in stealing Fletcher's stock, offering to follow the trail of the stolen animals and recover them if possible. Miles was openly skeptical of Fletcher. Writing to Steck, he said, "I have so little confidence in Fletcher, that I must have the evidence of someone besides himself to believe he ever lost any mules at all—this is my private opinion, which I would thank you to keep to yourself." The colonel further noted, "The people of Cruzces [*sic*] and Mesilla have treated these Indians [Palanquito's band] most shamefully & I doubt not Fletcher was [involved in] any outrages committed against them." Miles to Steck, October 29, 1855, Steck Papers, Series 2.

41. Gibbs to Whipple, March 11, 1857, RG393, M1120, LR, DNM, Roll 5.

42. Miles to Nichols, August 16, 1857, RG393, M1120, LR, DNM, Roll 7.

43. Barrick and Taylor, *The Mesilla Guard,* 29–30.

44. Sweeney, *Mangas Coloradas,* 272.

45. Ruelas to Steck, August, 1857, quoted by Taylor, *A Place as Wild as the West Ever Was,* 58.

46. Miles to Nichols, February 18, 1858, RG393, M1120, LR, DNM, Roll 7.

47. Miles to Nichols, March 4, 1858, ibid.

48. Miles to County Prefect, February 9, 1858, ibid.

49. Mesilla Citizens to Garland, March 24, 1858, ibid. Three years later the same citizens once again petitioned the military department: "The number of troops within this portion of the territory notwithstanding their desire to stay the hands of our ruthless enemies, is insufficient to protect us. We therefore respectfully request that not only will the troops now at [Fort Fillmore] be permitted to remain, but that others may be ordered there; that we may be protected against the incursions of those numerous bands of savages that are devastating our otherwise flourishing and rapidly increasing communities." Doña Ana County Citizens to Colonel Fauntleroy, February 13, 1861, in Altshuler Collection, MSS113, Box 13, Folder 1, Arizona Historical Foundation, Tempe, Arizona.

50. Garland to Mesilla Citizens, April 1858, RG393, M1120, LR, DNM, Roll 7.

51. Miles to Nichols, March 4, 1858, ibid.

52. Alley to Hildt, February 8, 1858, ibid.

53. Miles to Nichols, March 1858, ibid.

54. Thrapp, *Victorio and the Mimbres Apaches,* 59–60.

55. Quoted in ibid., 60.

56. Averell, *Ten Years in the Saddle,* 139.

57. Wood to Nichols, April 17, 1858, RG393, M1120, LR, DNM, Roll 8.

58. Ibid.

59. Taylor, *A Place as Wild as the West Ever Was,* 60.

60. Barrick and Taylor, *Mesilla Guard,* 33.

61. Quoted by Sweeney, *Mangas Coloradas,* 365.

62. Averell, *Ten Years in the Saddle,* 142.

63. Steck wrote: "Their poverty and rapid decline, which they themselves feel and their leaders see . . . makes it more easy to control them and convince them of the necessity of a change in their mode of life. . . . Human nature exhibits itself as well in the Indian as in the Anglo-Saxon: supply the wants of either, and the disposition to revolt is suppressed or materially weakened. This was clearly shown by the

Mescalero and Gila Apaches, from 1854–1860. Liberally supplied with food during that period by their agents, they remained quiet and planted large breadths of corn. But for the discovery of the gold mines . . . which attracted a population not exactly adapted to the best interests of the Indians, and the Texan invasion, they would at this time be at peace." Steck to Manypenny, August 27, 1856, Steck Papers, Series 2.

64. Sweeney, *Mangas Coloradas,* 388.

65. *San Francisco Herald,* June 16, 1861.

66. This was the same Pablo Melendres who had served as alcalde of Doña Ana in 1843.

67. In 1863, during the occupation of the Mesilla Valley by Union troops, volunteer regiments were again called upon to fight Apaches and protect the isolated mining towns of southern New Mexico and Arizona. Probate Judge Frank Higgins wrote in 1863: "The [mines] will also effect the raising of volunteers for the two additional regiments of New Mexico. In this valley I do not think more than one company could be raised, and these chiefly from peons who enlist to escape servitude." Higgins to Carleton, September 25, 1863, RG393, M1120, LR, DNM, Roll 19.

68. *Mesilla Times,* July 20, 1861.

69. Ibid.

70. Special Order 97, June 30, 1861. Altshuler Collection, MSS113, Box 12, Folder 10, Arizona Historical Foundation, Tempe, Arizona. Fort Buchanan was the first military post established in the Gadsden Purchase lands of modern southern Arizona, being built in the Sonoita Valley south of Tucson in 1857 by troops of the 1st Dragoons under Maj. Enoch Steen. It was abandoned on July 23, 1861, just two days before the Confederates reached Mesilla. Wilson, "Retreat to the Rio Grande," 4–8.

71. Steck to Dole, September 19, 1863. *Annual Report of the Commissioner of Indian Affairs,* 107.

72. *Mesilla Times,* October 3, 1861.

73. Ibid.

74. *Santa Fe Gazette,* October 19, 1861.

75. Quoted by Thrapp, *Victorio and the Mimbres Apaches,* 88–89.

CHAPTER 6

1. Frietze, *History of La Mesilla,* 9.

2. Prior to the creation of Doña Ana County in 1851, Mesilla and Doña Ana

were both located in El Paso County. Created in 1849, El Paso County "included all of the area between the Rio Grande and the Pecos River, south of a line running due east from a point on the Rio Grande twenty miles north of San Diego." San Diego was a river crossing about fifteen miles north of Doña Ana. Hence, El Paso County, as originally established, included a portion of present-day New Mexico. Frazer, *Mansfield on the Condition of the Western Forts,* 4n1.

3. A personal friend of Abraham Lincoln, Benedict's political opponents attempted in vain to have him removed from office. Charges against Benedict, including a proclivity for intoxication while occupying the bench, were submitted to Lincoln, who responded, "Well, gentlemen, I know Benedict. We have been friends for thirty years. He may imbibe to excess, but Benedict drunk knows more law than all the others on the bench in New Mexico sober. I shall not disturb him." Twitchell, *Old Santa Fe,* 351.

4. Price, *Pioneers of the Mesilla Valley,* 18.

5. Quoted by Tittman, "By Order of Richard Campbell," 392.

6. Price, *Pioneers of the Mesilla Valley,* 21.

7. Davis, *El Gringo,* 217–18.

8. Ibid., 373.

9. Quoted by Keleher, *Turmoil in New Mexico,* 272n67.

10. James A. Lucas arrived in New Mexico in 1846 with General Kearny, serving as a private in Company A, 1st Regiment of Missouri Volunteers. He took part in the Battle of Brazito on Christmas Day in 1846, and after mustering out of the service returned to the Mesilla Valley where he became a merchant and justice of the peace in 1852. He was an ardent Southern sympathizer, supporting Colonel Baylor and his invading Confederate army in 1861. Price, *Pioneers of the Mesilla Valley,* 83.

11. Ibid., 15, 84.

12. Years later, in recalling this event, Poston remarked: "in 1856, I met at El Paso, William Claude Jones, the then [U.S. Attorney] of New Mexico, and on a journey up the Rio Grande we discussed the propriety of making a petition to Congress for the organization of a territorial government between the Rio Grande and Colorado [River]. At La Mesilla, Jones . . . wrote a petition, and when it came to giving the proposed Territory a name he wrote in ARIZONA. The petition was signed by everybody in Mesilla who could write and some who could not." Quoted by Sacks, *Be It Enacted,* 10.

13. Donnell, "The Confederate Territory of Arizona," 149.

14. Granville H. Oury was born on March 25, 1825. Oury practiced law in California before moving to Tucson in 1856. He espoused the Arizona territorial movement, raising a regiment of volunteer militia and serving with the Arizona Mounted Volunteers. He remained in Arizona his entire life, holding several political positions until his death in Tucson on January 11, 1891. Thrapp, *Encyclopedia of Frontier Biography,* vol. 2, 1094–95.

15. On December 17, 1857, following recommendations by President Buchanan for the construction of a territorial government for Arizona, Senator Gwin introduced a bill to organize such a government. The New Mexico legislature passed a resolution favoring this measure in 1858; however, Congress did not pass the bill. Bancroft, *History of Arizona and New Mexico,* 504–505.

16. Donnell, "The Confederate Territory of Arizona," 149.

17. Walker, "Causes of the Confederate Invasion of New Mexico," 93.

18. Quoted by Lamar, *The Far Southwest, 1846–1912,* 78.

19. Walker, "Causes of the Confederate Invasion of New Mexico," 93.

20. *Santa Fe Weekly Gazette,* October 9, 1858.

21. Walker, "Causes of the Confederate Invasion of New Mexico," 95.

22. Judge Kirby Benedict denied that the court had neglected the Mesilla Valley and southern New Mexico. "I have now to state," the judge wrote, "that during the whole time, from the fall of 1853, up to the time of leaving that District for this . . . in 1858, I never failed going twice a year to the County of Doña Ana, to Las Cruces, or Mesilla to hold the terms of court as fixed by Law." Benedict to J. S. Black, August 18, 1859. Quoted by Sacks, *Be It Enacted,* 33.

23. Frietze, *History of La Mesilla,* 50.

24. *The Weekly Arizonian,* July 14, 1859.

25. Ibid., June 30, 1859.

26. Sylvester Mowry was born in Providence, Rhode Island, in 1833. After being arrested by the Union army in 1862 as a Southern supporter he was not allowed to remain in Arizona. He died in London on October 13, 1871. For a detailed account of the life of Mowry, consult Sacks, "Artilleryman, Libertine, Entrepreneur," Sacks Manuscript Collection, MSS110, Box 6, Folder 16, Arizona Historical Foundation, Tempe, Arizona.

27. *Mesilla Times,* October 25, 1860.

28. *San Francisco Herald,* November 22, 1860.

CHAPTER 7

1. *San Francisco Herald,* November 20, 1860.

2. *Mesilla Times,* November 8, 1860.

3. McKee, *Narrative of the Surrender,* 7.

4. *San Francisco Herald,* December 4, 1860.

5. *Mesilla Times,* March 9, 1861.

6. Price, *Pioneers of the Mesilla Valley,* 87.

7. *Mesilla Times,* March 16, 1861.

8. Keleher, *Turmoil in New Mexico,* 390.

9. Lamar, *The Far Southwest, 1846–1912,* 100.

10. Capt. Richard S. Ewell, commanding at nearby Fort Buchanan, and for whom one of the newly established Arizona counties was named, occupied a seat at the convention by special invitation. Bancroft, *History of Arizona and New Mexico,* 507n26.

11. Like many early New Mexico pioneers, Samuel G. Bean first came to the territory in 1846 with General Kearny's Army of the West; serving with the Missouri Volunteers under Col. Alexander Doniphan, he took part in the Battle of Brazito in December 1846. After the Mexican War, Bean returned to the Mesilla Valley, where he served three consecutive terms as sheriff between the years 1855 and 1860. When the Confederate army arrived at Mesilla in June 1861, Col. John R. Baylor appointed him justice of the peace for Mesilla. Bean, though not as avid a supporter of the Confederacy as many of his Mesilla counterparts, traded openly with the Southern troops during their stay at the town. When Gen. James H. Carleton and his California Column arrived in 1862 to help thwart the Confederate invasion, Bean fled to Texas realizing that he would be exiled as a secessionist if he remained in Mesilla. His home and property were confiscated, although he returned several years later. Price, *Pioneers of the Mesilla Valley,* 100.

12. Ibid., 16.

13. Donnell, "The Confederate Territory of Arizona," 150.

14. Lamar, *The Far Southwest, 1846–1912,* 369.

15. Bancroft, *History of Arizona and New Mexico,* 506–507.

16. Lucas to Labadie, June 14, 1861, *The War of the Rebellion: A Compilation of the Official Records,* Series 1, vol. 4, 39.

17. *Mesilla Times,* March 30, 1861.

18. Ibid., March 9, 1861.

19. *San Francisco Herald,* June 26, 1861.

20. The *Mesilla Times* was aimed more toward Texas citizens than the Mexican population residing in the Mesilla Valley, as the *Times* hoped to garner outside support for the Arizona cause. The majority of the newspaper's circulation was outside of the Mesilla Valley, with authorized agents in forty-eight different locations to sell subscriptions and advertising space; twenty-four of those locations were in Texas and only three were in "Arizona." The last known issue of the *Times* was printed on March 1, 1862. "The Mesilla Times," Small Manuscript Collection, MSM175, Box 16, Folder 13, Arizona Historical Foundation, Tempe, Arizona.

21. Wilson, *When the Texans Came,* 27.

22. *San Francisco Herald,* March 26, 1861.

23. Quoted by Keleher, *Turmoil in New Mexico,* 390–91.

CHAPTER 8

1. Bender, "Military Transportation in the Southwest," 137n69.

2. Baylor to Van Dorn, September 24, 1861, *The War of the Rebellion: A Compilation of the Official Records,* Series I, vol. 4, 109.

3. Quoted by Walker, "Causes of the Confederate Invasion," 85.

4. Hackler, *The Butterfield Trail in New Mexico,* 7–8.

5. Need to Cameron, September 27, 1861, *The War of the Rebellion: A Compilation of the Official Records,* Series I, vol. 50, pt. 2, 635.

6. Quoted by Twitchell, *Old Santa Fe,* 368–69.

7. Quoted by Walker, "Causes of the Confederate Invasion," 81.

8. Ibid., 83.

9. Mills to Watts, June 23, 1861, *The War of the Rebellion: A Compilation of the Official Records,* Series I, vol. 4, 56.

10. *Mesilla Times,* May 11, 1861.

11. Mills to Watts, June 23, 1861, *The War of the Rebellion: A Compilation of the Official Records,* Series I, vol. 4, 56.

12. Born on May 25, 1816, in Louisiana, Henry Hopkins Sibley graduated from West Point in 1838 and fought against the Seminoles in Florida from 1838 to 1839. He was active as an officer in the Mexican War and participated in the Mormon War of 1857–59 before joining Col. Edward R. S. Canby on a Navajo Campaign in 1860. Having resigned from the U.S. Army in April 1861, Sibley left the territory

for Richmond and received a commission in the Confederate Army as brigadier general. After the Civil War, Sibley served as general of artillery in the Egyptian Army from 1869 to 1873. He died on August 23, 1886. Heitman, *Historical Register and Dictionary of the United States Army,* 886.

13. Taylor, *A Place as Wild as the West Ever Was,* 11.

14. Texas had been swept from the control of the Union in February 1861, when the commander of that military department, Gen. David E. Twiggs, surrendered all federal equipment stores and funds to the Confederacy. Crimmins, "Fort Fillmore," 330.

15. Cooper to Sibley, July 8, 1861, *The War of the Rebellion: A Compilation of the Official Records,* Series I, vol. 4, 93. Cooper wrote: "In view of your recent service in New Mexico and knowledge of that important country and the people, the President has entrusted you with the important duty of driving the Federal troops from that department. . . . You will proceed without delay to Texas, and . . . organize, in the speediest manner possible, from the Texas troops . . . forces as you may deem necessary."

16. Col. John Robert Baylor was born on July 22, 1822, in Kentucky. He spent most of his youth in Texas, where he fought Indians throughout the 1840s and 1850s. By the time he commanded the invasion of New Mexico in 1861, he was already well known for his Indian-fighting exploits during the preceding two decades. Baylor was relieved of his command in the Mesilla Valley by Brig. Gen. Henry Hopkins Sibley on December 14, 1861. The Confederate Congress never reinstated Baylor to his position as an officer, due mainly to his harsh Indian policies. Thompson, *John Robert Baylor,* 1–22.

17. Alberts, *Rebels on the Rio Grande,* 31.

18. Mills fled to Mexico to avoid being captured by the Confederates. However, he was eventually taken prisoner at Mesilla by Colonel Baylor and was incarcerated at Fort Bliss for about a month before making his escape to Fort Craig. Mills, *Forty Years at El Paso,* 51–55.

19. Anderson to Lynde, June 23, 1861, *The War of the Rebellion: A Compilation of the Official Records,* Series I, vol. 4, 45.

20. Lynde to AAAG, July 21, 1861, ibid. Lynde wrote: "In compliance with instructions received yesterday from department headquarters the enlistment of volunteers is suspended. About 50 names were on the list up to that time." Ibid.

21. Lane, *I Married a Soldier,* 106.

22. McKee, *Narrative of the Surrender,* 8–9.

23. Ibid., 7.

24. Quoted in Wilson, *When the Texans Came,* 47.

25. McMaster, "Canby's Captains of the Southwest, 1860–62," 89.

26. Mills, *Forty Years at El Paso,* 44.

27. Canby wrote to Lynde: "I had occasion on the 24th inst. to put you on your guard against the alleged complicity of Colonel Loring in the treasonable designs of the Texas authorities at Ft. Bliss and El Paso. . . . Sibley's letter shows the Texas authorities . . . count upon Colonel Loring's aid in furthering their plans [of invading New Mexico by way of the Mesilla Valley] . . . any failure to act at once, or any hesitancy in acting, may be in the highest degree disastrous." Canby to Lynde, June 30, 1861, *The War of the Rebellion: A Compilation of the Official Records,* Series I, vol. 4, 57.

28. *Mesilla Times,* July 6, 1861.

29. Quoted in Wilson, *When The Texans Came,* 46.

30. On July 20, 1861, Lynde received instructions from headquarters: "The garrison of Fort Fillmore will be retained at that post long enough to cover the movements of the troops withdrawn from the interior of Arizona . . . these troops, unless you should need them at Fort Fillmore, will take the direct route to Fort Craig. . . . The removal of the supplies from Fort Fillmore should be completed, if possible, by the time the troops from Arizona have passed up, in order that the abandonment of the post may succeed that event as soon as possible." Wilson, *When The Texans Came,* 38.

31. Peyton S. Graves, a Confederate soldier, wrote on July 24: "We rode up to within 600 yards of the fort [Fillmore], stopped and were ordered to look to our guns and be ready. Our intention being to charge in to the fort just at daylight, rush to the doors of the barracks and shoot anyone who appeared until they surrendered. . . . About 3 o'clock in the morning of the 25th we were awakened by the beating of the alarm roll within the fort. Our guard was called in and we found out that one of it, a member of Teel's Co, had deserted our ranks and gone in the Fort and told on us." Quoted by Wadsworth, "The Battle of Mesilla: A Rebel View," 9.

32. McKee, *Narrative of the Surrender,* 14.

33. Baylor to Washington, September 21, 1861, *The War of the Rebellion: A Compilation of the Official Records,* Series I, vol. 4, 16.

34. The *Mesilla Times* of July 29, 1861, reported: "On the night of the 24th a position had been taken by the Confederate troops, within six hundred yards of Fort Fillmore, and pickets were placed out and every precaution taken to storm the fort by surprise the next morning at daybreak. The plan would have been a complete

success, but for the desertion of a picket who went into the fort and gave the alarm. The fort was alive in a few minutes, and it was evident the surprise was a failure."

35. *Mesilla Times,* July 29, 1861.

36. Thompson, *Colonel John Robert Baylor,* 30.

37. Ibid.

38. The troops accompanying Baylor were: Captain Stafford's cavalry company (eighty-five men); Captain Hardeman's cavalry company (ninety men); Lieutenant Bennett's artillery company (eighty-eight men); and Captain Coopwood's spy company (forty men). Maj. Trevanion Teel remained behind at Fort Bliss, Texas, with the artillery and was not ordered to advance to Mesilla until June 27. Ibid., 31, 37.

39. Quoted by Hall, "The Skirmish at Mesilla," 346. The *Santa Fe Gazette* reported that the Confederates "were received with every manifestation of joy by the citizens . . . preparations were made to receive an attack from the U.S. troops and the citizens offered all the forage and supplies that they had at their command." Quoted by Frietze, *History of La Mesilla,* 59.

40. McKee, *Narrative of the Surrender,* 17.

41. *Mesilla Times,* July 27, 1861.

42. Ibid. It was also noted that "several of the citizens had positioned themselves on top of a sand hill at the edge of town to watch the battle. They had commenced cheering when McNally's men were seen to be in retreat." Quoted by Thompson, *Colonel John Robert Baylor,* 33. Upon learning of this, Major Lynde became angered and ordered his artillery commander to fire upon the spectators. Surgeon J. Cooper McKee would later write, "I heard Lynde order Crilly to fire a shell at a group of women, children and unarmed men on one of the sand hills to our left front." McKee, *Narrative of the Surrender,* 19.

43. Peyton Graves, in his letter of August 8, 1861, recalled, "A flag of truce came marching up to our line borne by Lieut. McNally commanding their cavalry, who approaching Col. Baylor said 'I am authorized to demand an unconditional surrender of the town and yourself and forces.' Their force amounted 535 men. Col Baylor replied, 'If you want the town! Come and take it! And as for myself and forces, we will fight a little on that!' The officer returned and in a few minutes the deafening roar of the cannon sounded on our ears! The first bomb struck the corner of the house upon the top of which Teel's Co. were stationed in full view and run them off in a hurry. The next one struck and busted at the tree just over Stafford's Co., They also being on the top of a house and rousted them from their place. They were then ordered to another part of the town and we saw no more of either Co. until after

the fight. Our position was behind an adobe wall 2 feet high with a cornfield on our left." Wadsworth, "The Battle of Mesilla," 8–9. Graves's reference to the flag of truce being borne by Lieutenant McNally is erroneous, as the flag was in fact carried by Lieutenant Brooks and Surgeon McKee.

44. Hall, "The Skirmish at Mesilla," 347. In his report, Baylor wrote: "A flag was sent in to demand the 'unconditional surrender of the Texas forces,' to which I answered that, 'we would fight them first, and surrender afterward.' The answer was followed by the enemy opening on us with their howitzers." Baylor to Washington, September 21, 1861, *The War of the Rebellion: A Compilation of the Official Records,* Series I, vol. 4, 17.

45. *Mesilla Times,* July 27, 1861.

46. Ibid.

47. One Union officer filed the following report of the Battle of Mesilla: "This was 9 A.M. on the 25th [of July]. At the same time positive word was brought back that the Texans were in the town of Mesilla. After that we laid quietly in garrison [at Fort Fillmore] until 4 P.M. when he [Lynde] moved the whole forward, putting McNally, with 22 men, in front, with the order to go on and feel his way. He had four twelve-pounder mountain howitzers. He first fired two shells at long range. Ordered McNally to form and go ahead. McNally kept ahead until he got within 60 or 70 yards of the Texans. Halted, and reported in person that they were there in the jacals and cornfields. First McNally knew they fired one shot that cut away his saber; the second struck him. Then fired a volley of about 80 shots. They had no artillery. McNally dismounted and fired at random. They fired another volley. Remounted, not being supported by infantry or artillery, ordered his men to retreat. In this fire one sergeant and one corporal were wounded and one man killed. In retreating, the Seventh Infantry fired into us. I retreated behind the battery, and found the infantry still in the rear. There McNally fainted from loss of blood and was carried from the field. The last he heard was an order from Major Lynde to retreat." Quoted by Twitchell, *Leading Facts,* vol. 2, 362n287.

48. McKee, *Narrative of the Surrender,* 19.

49. Wadsworth, "The Battle of Mesilla," 9.

50. *Mesilla Times,* July 27, 1861.

51. Colonel Canby believed this incident was perpetrated purposefully by Confederate sympathizers within the Union ranks. This is the only accusation of this that I have encountered; all other sources state that the incident was an accident, the Union troops having mistook their comrades for Confederate troops. Canby,

in 1866, wrote: "The effect upon [Lynde's] mind [made by the Southern sympathizers in the Mesilla Valley] was still furthered by the fact, as he represented it, that in the skirmish at Mesilla his own men fired upon him instead of firing upon the enemy. From that moment he appears to have lost all confidence in his officers and men . . . [and] to have experienced a mental paralysis that rendered him incapable of acting with judgment or energy." Canby to AAG, March 16, 1866, RG94, L736, Isaac Lynde Records.

52. Quoted by Wilson, *When the Texans Came,* 50.

53. McKee, *Narrative of the Surrender,* 20.

54. Ibid.

55. Ibid., 21.

56. The wounded were: Lt. Edward J. Brooks, 7th Infantry; Lt. Christopher H. McNally, Regiment of Mounted Rifles; Sgt. James Callaghan (mortally); and Privates Meyers, Farber, Gross, all of the 7th Infantry. Wilson, *When the Texans Came,* 40. In his report Baylor erroneously placed Union casualties at four killed and seven wounded. Baylor to Washington, September 21, 1861, *The War of the Rebellion: A Compilation of the Official Records,* Series I, vol. 4, 18.

57. Quoted in Wilson, *When the Texans Came,* 48.

58. *Mesilla Times,* October 17, 1861.

59. Quoted in Wilson, *When the Texans Came,* 43.

60. Quoted by Thompson, *From Desert to Bayou,* 11n70.

61. Ibid., 25.

62. Thompson, *John Robert Baylor,* 39. The *Mesilla Times* wrote: "The soldiers destroyed much of their company property, muskets, clothing, a blacksmith shop, bakery, and one of the quartermaster's storerooms had been completely burned down. The majority of the buildings were uninjured, and can be immediately occupied by the Confederate forces. The hospital stores, medicines, and furniture were most completely broken up, and nearly all the arms and a large quantity of ammunition were destroyed. A great deal of valuable commissary stores and other property was unharmed, to the amount of several thousand dollars. The Mexicans, as eager as ever for plunder, entered the Fort soon after it was evacuated, and commenced a general pillage, carrying off property on their backs, on animals, and by cartloads. They must have pillaged property to the amount of several thousand dollars." *Mesilla Times,* July 27, 1861.

63. Quoted in Wilson, *When the Texans Came,* 48.

64. Wrote Lt. William Lane's wife: "The officers and families lost everything

they owned, as they could not take their property with them, beyond a change of clothes. The Mexicans in the neighborhood reaped a harvest after the soldiers left the post that night." Lane, *I Married a Soldier,* 114.

65. Quoted in Wilson, *When the Texans Came,* 43.

66. Wilson, "Whiskey at Fort Fillmore," 117.

67. Mills to Watts, June 23, 1861, *The War of the Rebellion: A Compilation of the Official Records,* Series I, vol. 4, 56. A report received by Canby in January, 1862, sent from El Paso, mentioned this treachery: "S. Hart has done more to aid and assist [the Confederates] than the balance of the capitalists have, and has gone so far as to give a list of the principal capitalists in New Mexico, to confiscate their property, and that is their aim." Canby to AAG, January 25, 1862, ibid., 89.

Lydia Spencer Lane, wife of Lt. William B. Lane who commanded Fort Fillmore for a brief period prior to the Confederate invasion, also spoke of treachery at the post. "Fighting had begun between North and South, and we were most unpleas-antly situated. There were at Fillmore several officers and their families with de-cided Southern sentiments. One of the officers quietly retired to Texas, leaving his family to follow as best they could, showing how implicitly he relied on the chivalry of his old companions-in-arms to take care of his wife and children until they were able to join him. We knew not friend from foe." Lane, *I Married a Soldier,* 105.

68. *Daily Conservative* (Leavenworth, Kansas), October 19, 1861. Quoted by Wilson, *When The Texans Came,* 50–51. Baylor's report also referenced the pos-sible drunkenness of the Union soldiers: "The road for 5 miles was lined with the fainting, famished soldiers, who threw down their arms as we passed and begged for water." Baylor to Washington, September 21, 1861, *The War of the Rebellion: A Compilation of the Official Records,* Series I, vol. 4, 18.

69. Ibid.

70. McKee, *Narrative of the Surrender,* 26–27.

71. *Mesilla Times,* July 27, 1861.

72. Wilson, *When the Texans Came,* 45.

73. Capt. J. H. Potter, Report, July 27, 1861, *The War of the Rebellion: A Compila-tion of the Official Records,* Series I, vol. 4, 15.

74. Lynde to AAG, August 7, 1861, RG393, M1120, LR, DNM, Roll 13.

75. *Mesilla Times,* July 27, 1861.

76. Quoted by Wilson, *When the Texans Came,* 41.

77. "Particulars of the Surrender of the Federal Troops in the Mesilla Valley," *Daily Alta California,* September 3, 1861.

78. Captain Alfred Gibbs to AAG, November 7, 1861, *The War of the Rebellion: A Compilation of the Official Records,* Series I, vol. 4, 10–11. Surgeon McKee commented: "I am unable to express . . . the deep grief, mortification, and pain I, with the other officers, have endured from this cowardly surrender of a brave, true command to an inferior force of the enemy, without having one word to say or firing a single shot. I, among the other officers, entered my solemn protest against the surrender, but we were peremptorily told by Major Lynde that he was the commanding officer. To see old soldiers and strong men weep like children, men who had faced the battle's storm in the Mexican War, is a sight that I hope I may never again be present at. A braver or truer command could not be found than that which has in this case been made a victim of cowardice and imbecility." McKee to Surgeon General, August 16, 1861, ibid., 11.

79. Baylor to Capt. T. A. Washington, September 21, 1861, ibid., 19.

80. Baylor acknowledged that he did not have the ability, "with less than 300 men, [to] guard over 600 and meet another force of 240 of the enemy that is looked for daily." Report of Lt. Col. Baylor, August 3, 1861, ibid., 16–17.

81. *Mesilla Times,* August 10, 1861. Captain Potter of the 7th Infantry reported the number of prisoners as sixteen (one sergeant and fifteen privates). He noted that twenty-six Union troops deserted prior to the arrival of Baylor, presumably to join the Confederacy. Capt. J.H. Potter, Report, July 27, 1861, ibid., 15.

82. McKee, *Narrative of the Surrender,* 30.

83. Lynde to AAG, August 7, 1861. Quoted by Thompson, *John Robert Baylor,* 43.

84. Wadsworth, *Forgotten Fortress,* 330. The *New York Tribune* also compared Lynde to Benedict Arnold, writing that his actions were "the most shameful thing ever done by an officer of the United States Army." Quoted by Thompson, *John Robert Baylor,* 44.

85. Major Isaac Lynde Records, Judge Advocate General to Secretary of War, January 4, 1866; General Orders 94, November 27, 1866. RG94, File L736, CB1866.

CHAPTER 9

1. *Mesilla Times,* July 27, 1861.

2. Baylor Proclamation, August 1, 1861, *The War of the Rebellion: A Compilation of the Official Records,* Series I, vol. 4, 20–21.

3. *Mesilla Times,* August 3, 1861.

4. Probate Judge Frank Higgins issued the following decree on August 8, 1861:

"Ordered, that the tax upon Public Balls or Fandangoes be & is hereby fixed at Three Dollars for each ball. The same to be collected by the Sheriff of the County." Higgins also announced that "a License Tax of Three Dollars be & is hereby assessed upon a Theatrical Exhibition and Circuses for each representation or exhibition." Walker, "Confederate Government in Doña Ana County," 258–62.

5. Ibid., 299–300.

6. Ibid., 283.

7. Ibid., 256.

8. Donnell, "The Confederate Territory of Arizona," 159.

9. Thompson, *John Robert Baylor,* 44–45.

10. *Mesilla Times,* August 10, 1861.

11. In his report Baylor stated: "by express from Fort Stanton I learn that upon receipt of the news that Major Lynde had surrendered, Colonel Roberts, in command of that post, fled in haste, leaving the post on fire, which was extinguished by a storm of rain. Most of the commissary and quartermaster's supplies were saved." Baylor to Van Dorn, August 14, 1861, *The War of the Rebellion: A Compilation of the Official Records,* Series I, vol. 4, 23.

12. Baylor to Washington, September 21, 1861, ibid., 19.

13. Ibid.

14. Quoted in Wilson, *When the Texans Came,* 148.

15. Baylor tendered his resignation "as Colonel and Governor of this Territory" on March 17, 1862, following the arrival of Gen. H. H. Sibley as his replacement. Wrote Baylor: "I should be wanting in self respect were I to serve or hold a Commission under an Officer who has shown so palpable a want of confidence in my courage or ability." Baylor to Jackson, March 17, 1862, ibid.

16. Donnell, "The Confederate Territory of Arizona," 153.

17. Quoted by Sweeney, *Mangas Coloradas,* 420.

18. The Arizona Guards took no part in the actual invasion of New Mexico. The Guards were used solely for fending off Apache raiding parties. When Sibley pushed northward from Mesilla in 1862, they served only as a rear guard for the Confederate troops. Hall, "Thomas J. Mastin's 'Arizona Guards,'" 143–45.

19. *Mesilla Times,* October 3, 1861.

20. Baylor to Helm, March 20, 1862, *The War of the Rebellion: A Compilation of the Official Records,* Series I, vol. 50, pt. 1, 942.

21. Baylor's letter was first published in the Marshall *Texas Republican* in September 1862, and later in the Houston *Tri-Weekly Telegraph,* both of which openly

denounced Baylor. Hall, "Planter vs. Frontiersman," 58–60. Baylor later explained: "I have no hesitation in stating that the order referred to was not intended for publication, nor did I suppose that it would be paraded before the country as it has been by the malice of those who entertain no good feeling toward me. Such an order excites no surprise in Arizona or Texas, while it may not be read well in Richmond. Still I do not deem it consistent with my opinions and feelings on the subject of Indians and Indian policy to retract or disavow a word of the order referred to." Baylor to Magruder, December 29, 1862, *The War of the Rebellion: A Compilation of the Official Records,* Series I, vol. 15, 918.

22. *Houston Tri-Weekly,* October 17, 1862.

23. Baylor to Magruder, December 29, 1862, *The War of the Rebellion: A Compilation of the Official Records,* Series I, vol. 15, 918.

24. Baylor abhorred any treaty-making policy, writing, "If the Confederate Government adopts the policy of making treaties and endeavors to purchase peace and affords no more adequate protection from Indians than the Government of the United States has afforded on the frontier in this State of Arizona, the result will be that the citizens there will be reduced to the condition of stock raisers and herders for the benefit of the Indian tribes alone." Ibid., 916–17.

25. Hall, "Planter vs. Frontiersman," 63–64. Confederate Secretary of War George W. Randolph wrote: "In consequence of [Baylor's] order with regard to the Indians, the authority to raise troops granted him by the Department is revoked." Quoted by Thompson, *John Robert Baylor,* 78.

26. Hall, "Planter vs. Frontiersman," 71.

27. Baylor to Stith, September 28, 1861. Quoted in Wilson, *When the Texans Came,* 149–150.

28. Ibid., 152.

29. Baylor to Sibley, October 25, 1861, *The War of the Rebellion: A Compilation of the Official Records,* Series I, vol. 4, 132–33.

30. Robert Kelley, a native of Kentucky, was thirty-six years old when he began printing the newspaper in 1860 and served as its principal editor until his death at the hands of Baylor. "The Mesilla Times," Small Manuscript Collection, MSM175, Box 16, Folder 13, Arizona Historical Foundation, Tempe, Arizona.

31. Hall, "The Baylor-Kelley Fight," 87–88.

32. Although Baylor was acquitted, the case was reopened after Union forces occupied the valley, whereupon a grand jury convened in Mesilla on June 1, 1863, and reversed the acquittal as a symbolic gesture. Thompson, *John Robert Baylor,* 60–61.

33. General Orders No. 10, December 14, 1861, *The War of the Rebellion: A Compilation of the Official Records,* Series I, vol. 4, 157–58.

34. Quoted by Taylor, *Bloody Valverde,* 16.

35. Quoted by Donnell, "The Confederate Territory of Arizona," 155–56.

36. Ibid.

37. Connelly to Canby, June 15, 1862, *The War of the Rebellion: A Compilation of the Official Records,* Series I, vol. 50, pt. 1, 1141.

38. Jenkins, "Foraging in the Mesilla Valley," 162.

39. Quoted in Wilson, *When the Texans Came,* 311.

40. Jenkins, "Foraging in the Mesilla Valley," 172n16.

CHAPTER 10

1. Quoted by Keleher, *Turmoil in New Mexico,* 453. Carleton was an extremely controversial figure; people either adamantly supported him or openly despised him. Many of his soldiers, after being discharged, expressed extreme discontent with their commanding officer. On September 15, 1864, some of these troops met at Mesilla and wrote an indictment against their former commander, which they submitted for publication in newspapers all across the west. In what they titled "An Address to Our Late Commander, James H. Carleton," the ex-soldiers charged him with tyranny and cowardice: "As an officer, he is incompetent—he is wanting in all those qualities which endear and adorn the citizen and characterize the true soldier." These indictments were published in the January 6, 1865, issue of the *Santa Fe New Mexican.* Miller, *The California Column in New Mexico,* 33.

2. Wright to Thomas, June 10, 1862, *The War of the Rebellion: A Compilation of the Official Records,* Series I, vol. 50, pt. 1, 1128.

3. General Orders No. 15, August 14, 1862, *The War of the Rebellion: A Compilation of the Official Records,* Series I, vol. 50, pt. 2, 65.

4. Lamar, *The Far Southwest, 1846–1912,* 371.

5. Birkhimer, *Military Government and Martial Law,* 32, 371.

6. Hare, *American Constitutional Law,* vol. 2, 968.

7. Carleton to Drum, June 10, 1862, *The War of the Rebellion: A Compilation of the Official Records,* Series I, vol. 50, pt. 1, 1129.

8. "Proceedings of a Board of Officers," in Small Manuscript Collection MSM455, Folder 12, Arizona Historical Foundation, Tempe, Arizona.

9. Mowry Files, Altshuler Collection, MSS113, Box 9, Folder 1, Arizona Histori-

cal Foundation, Tempe, Arizona. Mowry ultimately sued Carleton and West for $1,129,000.00 in damages. Ibid., Folder 2.

10. Thrapp, *Encyclopedia of Frontier Biography,* vol. 2, 1029–30.

11. The U.S. Congress passed an act on July 17, 1862, just prior to Carleton's arrival in the Mesilla Valley, allowing for the confiscation of property belonging to Southern sympathizers, including those in the territories. In addition to Mowry, Union commanders confiscated items from Rafael Armijo (brother of former New Mexico Governor Manuel Armijo), valued at almost $59,000. Other victims included James Magoffin, Simeon Hart, James A. Lucas, Samuel and Roy Bean, Hugh Stephenson, and at least twenty others. Tittman, "The Exploitation of Treason," 138–42.

12. Carmony, *The Civil War in Apacheland,* 95.

13. Quoted by Miller, *The California Column in New Mexico,* 29. Several of the California soldiers would end up marrying Hispanic women whom they met while stationed in Mesilla and Las Cruces. By 1864 at least four Union soldiers had been married to local women at San Albino Catholic Church in Mesilla and St. Genevieve's in Las Cruces. These were: Mariana Bernal and James Malone of Company D, 1st Infantry; Anamaría Lueras and Frederick Burkner, a scout for the Union army; Perfeta Sanches and Patrick Helms; and Juana María Chávez and John Ryan of the 1st Infantry. Taylor, *A Place as Wild as the West Ever Was,* 90.

14. Bryan to West, February 26, 1863. Quoted by Thompson, *New Mexico Territory during the Civil War,* 83–84.

15. Ibid., 85–88.

16. The rumors of Confederates organizing in Chihuahua continued for many months. In the summer of 1863, Carleton received numerous reports apprising him of a force being drawn up by a Confederate named Skillman. This never materialized, but the reports threw Carleton into a frenzy of anxiety. Creel to West, May 3, 1863, *The War of the Rebellion: A Compilation of the Official Records,* Series I, vol. 50, pt. 2, 425–26.

17. West to McMullen, November 27, 1862, ibid., 232.

18. General Orders No. 24, December 2, 1862, ibid., 239.

19. Thompson, *John Robert Baylor,* 81–86.

20. West received the appointment as commanding officer in the Mesilla Valley on August 13, 1862, pursuant to General Orders No. 14 issued by Major Carleton. West would serve as "military commander of the towns of La Mesilla, La Mesa, El Picacho, and of such other places on the western bank of the Rio Grande as lie

between the Chihuahua line and Fort Thorn." General Orders No. 14, August 13, 1862, *The War of the Rebellion: A Compilation of the Official Records,* Series I, vol. 50, pt. 2, 62.

21. Carleton to West, November 18, 1862, *The War of the Rebellion: A Compilation of the Official Records,* Series I, vol. 15, 509–601. The price West was authorized to pay for grain, $3 per *fanega,* was well below market value. Miller, "Hispanos and the Civil War in New Mexico," 116.

22. General Orders No. 24, December 2, 1862, *The War of the Rebellion: A Compilation of the Official Records,* Series I, vol. 50, pt. 2, 239–40.

23. Taylor, *A Place as Wild as the West Ever Was,* 91.

24. Joseph Rodman West was commissioned a lieutenant colonel on August 5, 1861. On November 28, 1862, Carleton wrote West informing him that he had promoted him to brigadier general, noting, "You have worked hard and earnestly and well deserve this reward." He attained the rank of brevet major general of volunteers on January 4, 1866, the same day he mustered out. West died on October 31, 1898. RG94, Microcopy A2, California Column Muster Rolls, August, 1861; Carleton to West, November 28, 1862, *The War of the Rebellion: A Compilation of the Official Records,* Series I, vol. 50, pt. 2, 234.

25. Giershouse to West, January 9, 1863, RG393, M1120, LR, DNM.

26. United States Statutes at Large XII, Section 6, Chapter 195, 590–91; Birkhimer, *Military Government and Martial Law,* 38.

27. Randall, "Some Legal Aspects of the Confiscation Acts of the Civil War" 87–88.

28. Thomas J. Bull professed neutrality during the Civil War but held contracts with the federal government to supply Fort Fillmore with various provisions, making some think he favored the Northern cause. This was of little consequence to Carleton, whose order clearly stipulated that Bull's mill at Mesilla be destroyed in the event Baylor did reinvade. Price, *Pioneers of the Mesilla Valley,* 21.

29. Carleton to West, November 18, 1862, *The War of the Rebellion: A Compilation of the Official Records,* Series I, vol. 15, 509–601. On December 2, West ordered all people in the Mesilla Valley to surrender any surplus grain to the army. This made the people indignant, and many of them consequently fled to Mexico. On March 10, 1863, the Union army held an auction at Mesilla of goods that had been confiscated. Carmony, *The Civil War in Apacheland,* 105.

30. Carleton to West, November 18, 1862, *The War of the Rebellion: A Compilation of the Official Records,* Series I, vol. 15, 509–601.

31. West to Cutler, December 28, 1862, *The War of the Rebellion: A Compilation of the Official Records,* Series I, vol. 50, pt. 2, 266. In this same communication West outlined Baylor's difficulties in staging the reinvasion: "Governor Baylor returned from Richmond . . . endeavoring to raise a force of 6,000 men for a movement in this direction. Great difficulties were experienced; transportation and supplies were not to be had and the people at large were averse to the enterprise. They cited the failure of Sibley's expedition; claimed that the country was not worth possessing." Ibid.

32. In September 1862, after Union troops occupied the Mesilla Valley, post returns showed seven men in arrest/confinement. By November that number had risen to twenty-three. RG94, M617, Roll 1518, Mesilla Post Returns. By February 1863, West began suggesting that the garrison be removed from Mesilla entirely and transferred to a more southerly location, citing disciplinary problems as one reason. "The adjacent town of Franklin [Texas] has less than 100 inhabitants," West wrote. "The selling of liquor to soldiers can be entirely prohibited." West to Cutler, February 27, 1863, *The War of the Rebellion: A Compilation of the Official Records,* Series I, vol. 50, pt. 2, 329–30.

33. Carmony, *The Civil War in Apacheland,* 95–96.

34. Ibid., 99.

35. Ibid., 95. The boy killed in the incident is identified by one historian as the son of Dr. William Black. The other casualties are not identified. Taylor, *A Place as Wild as the West Ever Was,* 93.

36. Frietze, *History of La Mesilla,* 66.

37. Sonnichsen, "Major McMullen's Invasion of Mexico," 39.

38. Ibid., 40–43.

39. West to Cutler, January 28, 1863, *The War of the Rebellion: A Compilation of the Official Records,* Series 1, vol. 50, pt. 2, 296–97.

40. West to Uranga, January 30, 1863, ibid., 299.

41. Carmony, *The Civil War in Apacheland,* 104.

42. West to McCleave, June 21, 1863, *The War of the Rebellion: A Compilation of the Official Records,* Series I, vol. 50, pt. 2, 490.

43. Carmony, *The Civil War in Apacheland,* 124.

44. Ibid., 133–34.

45. Higgins to Carleton, August 1, 1863, RG393, M1120, LR, DNM, Roll 19.

46. Higgins to Carleton, August 20, 1863, ibid.

47. These five petitions, sent to Carleton in August 1863, are written in Spanish

and bear the signatures of hundreds of local Mexican residents. In response, probate judge Frank Higgins wrote: "Does the petition set forth measures which suggest to you an obligation as citizen and officer, that its prayers should be granted? I would suggest that this is a matter peculiarly pertaining to the consideration of Congress, and involves a number of Constitutional questions. . . . I believe that I have the welfare of this community in which I live at heart, and I do not wish to see it distracted by political and personal feuds, and this I deem would be the effect of granting the prayer of this petition." Higgins to Carleton, August 1, 1863, ibid.

48. Ibid.

49. Higgins to Carleton, August 20, 1863, ibid.

50. Joseph Gilette Knapp was born in New York in 1805 and died in Florida on July 2, 1888. His studies of law began in Wisconsin in the 1850s; he was admitted to the bar and shortly thereafter appointed to serve on the Third Judicial District in the Territory of New Mexico, where he would find himself continually at odds with Carleton. Keleher, *Turmoil in New Mexico,* 505n125.

51. Ibid., 400.

52. *Rio Abajo Weekly Press,* April 5, 1864.

53. Keleher, *Turmoil in New Mexico,* 401.

54. Halleck to Carleton, February 4, 1864, *The War of the Rebellion: A Compilation of the Official Records,* Series I, vol. 34, pt. 2, 671.

55. *National Intelligencer,* February 26, 1864.

56. *Santa Fe New Mexican,* July 1, 1864.

57. Higgins to Carleton, September 25, 1863, RG393, M1120, LR, DNM, Roll 19.

58. Quoted by Keleher, *Turmoil in New Mexico,* 405.

59. Ibid., 406.

60. *Santa Fe New Mexican,* October 31, 1864.

61. Higgins to Carleton, August 20, 1863, RG393, M1120, LR, DNM, Roll 19.

62. Ibid.

63. Higgins to Carleton, September 25, 1863, Ibid.

64. *Santa Fe New Mexican,* October 27, 1866.

65. Thompson, *New Mexico Territory during the Civil War,* 84.

Bibliography

MANUSCRIPTS, UNPUBLISHED DOCUMENTS, ARCHIVAL COLLECTIONS

Arizona Historical Foundation, Tempe. Constance Wynn Altshuler Collection, MSS 113, Box 9, Folders 1–2, Sylvester Mowry Files; "Proceedings against Sylvester Mowry," Small Manuscript Collection, MSM 455, Box 48, Folder 12; "Sylvester Mowry: Artilleryman, Libertine, Entrepreneur," Benjamin H. Sacks Manuscript Collection, MSS 110, Box 6, Folder 16; unknown author, "The Mesilla Times," Unpublished Manuscript, Small Manuscript Collection, MSM 175, Box 16, Folder 13.

Center for Southwest Research, University of New Mexico. *Inventory of the Michael Steck Papers, Series 1, 1839–1853,* Microfilm E93, Reels 1–3; *Series 2, 1854–1862,* Microfilm E93, Reels 1–4.

Eighth Census, 1860. Dona Ana County, New Mexico Territory, National Archives, Washington, D.C.

United States, National Archives and Records Center, Washington, D.C. Record Group 59 (RG59), State Department Records, Microcopy 54, Roll 1, Despatches from United States Consuls in Ciudad Juárez, 1850–1906; Microcopy 54, Roll 4, Notes from the Mexican Legation in the United States to the Department of State, 1821–1906; Microcopy 97, Roll 17, Despatches from U.S. Ministers to Mexico, 1821–1906.

———. Record Group 75 (RG75), Records of the Bureau of Indian Affairs, Letters Received 1824–80, New Mexico Superintendency, 1849–80, Microcopy 234; Microcopy T21.

———. Record Group 94 (RG94), Records of the Adjutant General's Office (AGO), 1780s–1917, Letters Received, Main Series, Microcopy 617, Roll 1518 (Mesilla Post Returns); Mircocopy 619, Roll A2 (California Column Muster Rolls); Selected Records from File L736, CB1866, Major Isaac Lynde.

———. Record Group 393 (RG393), Records of the United States Army Continental Commands, 1821–1920, Microcopy 1102, Registers of Letters Received by Headquarters, Department of New Mexico, 1849–53; Microcopy 1120, Registers of Letters Received by Headquarters, Department of New Mexico, 1854–1865.

UNITED STATES GOVERNMENT PUBLICATIONS

30th Congress, 1st Session

Senate Executive Document No. 1, Report of Colonel Alexander W. Doniphan on the Battle of Brazito, March 4, 1847.

31st Congress, 1st Session

House of Representatives Executive Document No. 82, Message of President Millard Fillmore to Congress, August 6, 1850.

32nd Congress, 1st Session

Senate Executive Document No. 60, Correspondence Relative to McClellan's Removal from the International Boundary Commission.

Senate Executive Document No. 119, Correspondence Relative to the International Boundary Commission.

33rd Congress, 1st Session

House of Representatives Executive Document No. 81, Statement of William Carr Lane, January 24, 1854.

Abel, Annie Heloise, ed. *The Official Correspondence of James S. Calhoun While Indian Agent at Santa Fe and Superintendent of Indian Affairs in New Mexico, 1849–1852.* Washington, D.C.: Government Printing Office, 1915.

Heitman, Francis B. *Historical Register and Dictionary of the United States Army, From Its Organization, September 29, 1789, to March 2, 1903,* 2 vols. Washington, D.C.: Government Printing Office, 1903.

Miller, Hunter, ed. *Treaties and Other International Acts of the United States of America,* 8 vols. Washington, D.C.: Government Printing Office, 1931–48.

Report of the Commissioner of Indian Affairs for the Year 1863. Washington, D.C.: Government Printing Office, 1864.

United States Statutes at Large XII, Section 6, Chapter 195.

The War of the Rebellion: A Compilation of the Official Records of the Union and Confederate Armies. Series I, 53 vols. Washington, D.C.: Government Printing Office, 1880–1901.

NEWSPAPERS

Alcance al Centinela, Chihuahua City

Daily Alta California, San Francisco

El Siglo Diez y Nueve, Mexico City

Houston Tri-Weekly

Mesilla Times

National Intelligencer

New Orleans Daily Picayune

New York Daily Times

Richmond Enquirer

Rio Abajo Weekly Press

San Francisco Herald

Santa Fe New Mexican

Santa Fe Weekly Gazette

Weekly Arizonian, Tubac

BOOKS: PRIMARY SOURCES

Alberts, Don. E. *Rebels on the Rio Grande: The Civil War Journal of A. B. Peticolas.* Albuquerque: Merit Press, 1993.

Averell, William Woods. *Ten Years in the Saddle: The Memoir of William Woods Averell, 1851–1862.* Edited by Edward K. Eckert and Nicholas J. Amato. San Rafael, CA: Presidio Press, 1978.

Bartlett, John Russell. *Personal Narrative of Explorations and Incidents in Texas, New Mexico, California, Sonora, and Chihuahua, 1850–1853,* 2 vols. New York: D. Appleton, 1854.

———. *Autobiography of John Russell Bartlett, 1805–1886.* Edited by Jerry E. Mueller. Providence, RI: John Carter Brown Library, 2006.

Bennett, James A. *Forts and Forays.* Albuquerque: University of New Mexico Press, 1948.

Bieber, Ralph P., ed. *Marching with the Army of the West: The Journals of Abraham R. Johnston, 1846; Marcellus Ball Edwards, 1847–48; and Philip Gooch Ferguson, 1847–48.* Glendale, CA: Arthur H. Clarke, 1936.

Carmony, Neil B., ed. *The Civil War in Apacheland: Sergeant George Hand's Diary.* Silver City, NM: High-Lonesome Books, 1996.

Davis, William Watts Hardy. *El Gringo; or, New Mexico and Her People.* Santa Fe: Rydal Press, 1938.

Frazer, Robert W., ed. *Mansfield on the Condition of the Western Forts, 1853–54.* Norman: University of Oklahoma Press, 1963.

———. *New Mexico in 1850: A Military View.* Norman: University of Oklahoma Press, 1968.

Gibson, George R. *Journal of a Soldier under Kearny and Doniphan.* Edited by Ralph P. Bieber. Glendale, CA: Arthur H. Clarke, 1935.

Hafen, Leroy R., Clyde Porter, and Mae Reed Porter, eds. *Ruxton of the Rockies.* Norman: University of Oklahoma Press, 1950.

Kendall, George Wilkins. *Narrative of the Texan Santa Fé Expedition.* New York: Harper Brothers, 1844.

Lane, Lydia Spencer. *I Married a Soldier.* Albuquerque: University of New Mexico Press, 1987.

Magoffin, Susan Shelby. *Down the Santa Fe Trail and into Mexico: The Diary of Susan Shelby Magoffin, 1846–1847.* Edited by Stella M. Drumm. New Haven, CT: Yale University Press, 1926.

McKee, James Cooper. *Narrative of the Surrender of a Command of U.S. Forces at Fort Fillmore, New Mexico in July, A.D. 1861.* Houston: Stagecoach Press, 1960.

Merrick, Morgan Wolfe. *From Desert to Bayou: The Civil War Journal and Sketches of Morgan Wolfe Merrick.* Edited by Jerry Thompson. El Paso: Texas Western Press, 1991.

Prieto, Guillermo, *Memorias de mis tiempos, 1840 a 1853.* Mexico City: Librería de la Vda. de C. Bouret, 1906.

Reid, John C. *Reid's Tramp, or a Journal of the Incidents of Ten Months Travel through Texas, New Mexico, Arizona, Sonora, and California.* Austin: Steck, 1935.

Salazar Ylarregui, Jose, *Datos de los trabajos astronómicos y topográficos, dispuestos en forma de diario, practicados durante el año de 1849 y principios de 1850 por la Comisión de Límites Mexicana en la Línea que Divide esta Republica de la de los Estados Unidos.* Mexico City: Imprenta de Juan R. Navarro, 1850.

Thompson, Jerry D., ed. *New Mexico Territory during the Civil War: Wallen and Evans Inspection Reports, 1862–1863.* Albuquerque: University of New Mexico Press, 2008.

———. *Texas and New Mexico on the Eve of the Civil War: The Mansfield and Johnston Inspections, 1859–1861.* Albuquerque: University of New Mexico Press, 2001.

Weber, David J., and Jane Lenz Elder, eds. *Fiasco: George Clinton Gardner's Correspondence from the U.S.-Mexico Boundary Survey, 1849–1854.* Dallas: Southern Methodist University Press, 2010.

Wilson, John P., *When the Texans Came: Missing Records from the Civil War in the Southwest, 1861–1862.* Albuquerque: University of New Mexico Press, 2001.

Woodhouse, S. W. *From Texas to San Diego in 1851: The Overland Journal of Dr.*

S. W. Woodhouse, Surgeon-Naturalist of the Sitgreaves Expedition. Edited by Andrew Wallace and Richard H. Hevly. Lubbock: Texas Tech University Press, 2007.

BOOKS: SECONDARY SOURCES

Agnew, S. C. *Garrisons of the Regular U.S. Army, New Mexico, 1846–1899.* Santa Fe: Press of the Territorian, 1971.

Almada, Francisco R. *Diccionario de historia, geografía y biografía chihuahuenses.* Chihuahua, Mexico: Ediciónes Universidad de Chihuahua, 1968.

Altamirano, Graziella, and Guadalupe Villa, eds. *Chihuahua: Textos de su historia, 1824–1921,* 3 vols. Ciudad Juárez, Chihuahua: Universidad Autónoma de Ciudad Juárez, 1988.

Bancroft, Hubert Howe. *History of Arizona and New Mexico, 1530–1888.* San Francisco: The History Co., 1889.

Bandelier, Adolph P. *The Discovery of New Mexico by the Franciscan Monk, Friar Marcos de Niza, in 1539.* Translated by Madeleine Turrell Rodack. Tucson: University of Arizona Press, 1981.

Barrick, Norma, and Mary Taylor. *The Mesilla Guard, 1851–1861.* El Paso: Texas Western Press, 1976.

Birkhimer, William E. *Military Government and Martial Law.* Kansas City: Franklin Hudson Publishing, 1914.

Connelly, William E. *Doniphan's Expedition and the Conquest of New Mexico and California.* Topeka, KS: Published by the author, 1907.

Dawson, Joseph G., III. *Doniphan's Epic March: The 1st Missouri Volunteers in the Mexican War.* Lawrence: University Press of Kansas, 1999.

Devine, David. *Slavery, Scandal, and Steel Rails: The 1854 Gadsden Purchase and the Building of the Second Transcontinental Railroad across Arizona and New Mexico Twenty-Five Years Later.* New York: iUniverse, 2004.

Drexler, Robert W. *Guilty of Making Peace: A Biography of Nicholas P. Trist.* Lanham, MD: University Press of America, 1991.

Edwards, Frank S. *A Campaign in New Mexico with Colonel Doniphan.* Philadelphia: Carey and Hart, 1847.

Faulk, Odie B. *Too Far North, Too Far South.* Los Angeles: Westernlore Press, 1967.

Frazer, Robert W. *Forts and Supplies: The Role of the Army in the Economy of the Southwest, 1846–1861.* Albuquerque: University of New Mexico Press, 1983.

Frietze, Lionel C. *History of La Mesilla and Her Mesilleros.* Las Cruces, NM: L. C. Frietze, 1995.

Garber, P. N. *The Gadsden Treaty.* Philadelphia: University of Pennsylvania Press, 1923.

Goetzmann, William H. *Army Exploration in the American West, 1803–1863.* Lincoln: University of Nebraska Press, 1959.

Gregg, Josiah. *Commerce of the Prairies.* New York: Langley, 1844.

Hackler, George. *The Butterfield Trail in New Mexico.* Las Cruces, NM: Yucca Enterprises, 2005.

Hammond, George P., and Agapito Rey. *Don Juan de Oñate, Colonizer of New Mexico, 1595–1628.* Albuquerque: University of New Mexico Press, 1953.

Hare, J. I. Clark. *American Constitutional Law,* vol. 2. Boston: Little, Brown, 1889.

Hine, Robert V. *Bartlett's West: Drawing the Mexican Boundary.* New Haven, CT: Yale University Press, 1968.

Horn, Calvin. *New Mexico's Troubled Years: The Story of the Early Territorial Governors.* Albuquerque: Horn and Wallace, 1963.

Julyan, Robert. *The Place Names of New Mexico.* Albuquerque: University of New Mexico Press, 1996.

Keleher, William A. *Turmoil in New Mexico, 1846–1868.* Albuquerque: University of New Mexico Press, 1952.

Lamar, Howard R. *The Far Southwest, 1846–1912: A Territorial History.* New Haven, CT: Yale University Press, 1966.

Launius, Roger D. *Alexander William Doniphan: Portrait of a Missouri Moderate.* Columbia: University of Missouri Press, 1997.

McNitt, Frank. *Navajo Wars: Military Campaigns, Slave Raids, and Reprisals.* Albuquerque: University of New Mexico Press, 1972.

Miller, Darlis A. *The California Column in New Mexico.* Albuquerque: University of New Mexico Press, 1982.

Mills, W. W. *Forty Years at El Paso, 1858–1898.* Edited by Rex Strickland. El Paso: Carl Hertzog, 1962.

Moorhead, Max L. *New Mexico's Royal Road: Trade and Travel on the Chihuahua Trail.* Norman: University of Oklahoma Press, 1958.

Price, Paxton. *Pioneers of the Mesilla Valley.* Las Cruces: Yucca Tree Press, 1995.

Sacks, Benjamin. *Be It Enacted: The Creation of the Territory of Arizona.* Phoenix: Arizona Historical Foundation, 1964.

Stegmaier, Mark J. *Texas, New Mexico, and the Compromise of 1850.* Kent, OH: Kent State University Press, 1996.

Sweeney, Edwin R. *Mangas Coloradas.* Norman: University of Oklahoma Press, 1998.

Taylor, John. *Bloody Valverde: A Civil War Battle on the Rio Grande, February 21, 1862.* Albuquerque: University of New Mexico Press, 1995.

Taylor, Mary Daniels. *A Place as Wild as the West Ever Was: Mesilla, New Mexico, 1848–1872.* Las Cruces: New Mexico State University Museum, 2004.

Thompson, Jerry D. *Colonel John Robert Baylor: Texas Indian Fighter and Confederate Soldier.* Hillsboro, TX: Hill Junior College Press, 1971.

Thrapp, Dan L. *Encyclopedia of Frontier Biography,* 3 vols. Lincoln: University of Nebraska Press, 1988.

———. *Victorio and the Mimbres Apaches.* Norman: University of Oklahoma Press, 1974.

Twitchell, Ralph Emerson. *The Leading Facts of New Mexican History,* 2 vols. Cedar Rapids, IA: Torch Press, 1911.

———. *Old Santa Fe: The Story of New Mexico's Ancient Capital.* Chicago: Rio Grande Press, 1963.

Wadsworth, Richard. *Forgotten Fortress: Ft. Millard Fillmore and Antebellum New Mexico.* Las Cruces, NM: Yucca Tree Press, 2002.

Wallace, Edward S. *The Great Reconnaissance: Soldiers, Artists, and Scientists on the Frontier, 1848–1861.* Boston: Little, Brown, 1955.

Werne, Joseph Richard. *The Imaginary Line: A History of the United States and Mexican Boundary Survey, 1848–1857.* Fort Worth: Texas Christian University Press, 2007.

JOURNAL ARTICLES AND BOOK CHAPTERS

Ayers, John. "A Soldier's Experience in New Mexico." *New Mexico Historical Review* 24 (October 1949): 259–66.

Baldwin, P. M. "A Historical Note on the Boundaries of New Mexico." *New Mexico Historical Review* 5 (April 1930): 117–37.

———. "A Short History of the Mesilla Valley." *New Mexico Historical Review* 3 (July 1938): 314–24.

Bender, Averam B. "Military Transportation in the Southwest, 1848–1860." *New Mexico Historical Review* 31 (April 1957): 123–50.

Bieber, Ralph P., ed. "Letters of William Carr Lane, 1852–1854." *New Mexico Historical Review* 3 (April 1928): 179–203.

Bloom, John P. "New Mexico Viewed by Americans, 1846–1849." *New Mexico Historical Review* 34 (July 1959): 165–98.

Carson, William G. B., ed. "William Carr Lane Diary." *New Mexico Historical Review* 39 (October 1964): 274–332.

Coffey, Frederic A. "Some General Aspects of the Gadsden Treaty." *New Mexico Historical Review* 8 (July 1933): 145–64.

Crimmins, Colonel M. L. "Fort Fillmore." *New Mexico Historical Review* 6 (October 1931): 327–33.

Donnell, F. S. "The Confederate Territory of Arizona, as Compiled from Official Sources." *New Mexico Historical Review* 17 (April 1942): 148–63.

Edrington, Thomas S. "Military Influence on the Texas–New Mexico Boundary Settlement." *New Mexico Historical Review* 59 (October 1984): 371–93.

Emory, Deborah Carley. "Running the Line: Men, Maps, Science, and Art of the United States and Mexico Boundary Survey, 1849–1856." *New Mexico Historical Review* 75 (April 2000): 221–65.

Gallaher, F. M. "Official Report of the Battle of Temascalitos (Brazito)." *New Mexico Historical Review* 3 (October 1928): 385–98.

Gilbert, Thomas D. "The U.S. Military Occupation of El Paso del Norte, 1846–47." *Pass-Word* 40 (Fall 1995): 106–18.

Grassham, John. "The United States–Mexico Boundary Commission." In *The Treaty of Guadalupe Hidalgo, 1848: Papers of the Sesquicentennial Symposium, 1848–1998,* edited by John Porter Bloom. Las Cruces, NM: Doña Ana County Historical Society, 1999.

Haecker, Charles M. "Brazito Battlefield: Once Lost, Now Found." *New Mexico Historical Review* 72 (July 1997): 229–38.

Hall, Martin Hardwick. "The Baylor-Kelley Fight: A Civil War Incident in Old Mesilla." *Pass-Word* 5 (July 1960): 83–90.

———. "Planter vs. Frontiersman: Conflict in Confederate Indian Policy." In *Essays on the American Civil War.* Austin: University of Texas Press, 1968.

———. "The Skirmish at Mesilla." *Arizona and the West* 1 (Winter 1959): 343–51.

———. "Thomas J. Mastin's 'Arizona Guards.'" *New Mexico Historical Review* 49 (April 1974): 143–51.

Jenkins, Frank. "Foraging in the Mesilla Valley: The Last Confederate Fight in New Mexico." *Pass-Word* 46 (Winter 2001): 159–73.

Kajencki, Francis C. "Charles Radziminski and the United States–Mexican Boundary Survey." *New Mexico Historical Review* 63 (July 1988): 211–40.

Kraemer, Paul. "Sickliest Post in the Territory of New Mexico: Fort Thorn and Malaria, 1853–1860." *New Mexico Historical Review* 71 (July 1996): 221–36.

Loyola, Sister Mary. "The American Occupation of New Mexico, 1821–1852." *New Mexico Historical Review* 14 (January 1939): 34–75.

Mangum, Neil C. "The Battle of Brazito: Reappraising a Lost and Forgotten Episode in the Mexican-American War." *New Mexico Historical Review* 72 (July 1997): 217–28.

McMaster, Robert K. "Canby's Captains of the Southwest, 1860–62." *Pass-Word* 6 (Summer 1961): 123–40.

Miller, Darlis. "Hispanos and the Civil War in New Mexico: A Reconsideration." *New Mexico Historical Review* 54 (April 1979): 105–23.

Mullin, Robert N. "David Meriwether, Territorial Governor of New Mexico: A Sidelight on the Mexican Boundary Controversy of 1853." *Pass-Word* 8 (Fall 1963): 83–98.

Owen, Gordon R. "The Mesilla Valley's Pioneer Settlements." *Southern New Mexico Historical Review* 6 (January 1999): 10.

Paredes, Raymund A. "The Mexican Image in American Travel Literature, 1831–1869." *New Mexico Historical Review* 52 (January 1977): 5–29.

Puckett, Fidelia Miller. "Ramón Ortíz: Priest and Patriot." *New Mexico Historical Review* 25 (October 1950): 265–95.

Randall, James G. "Some Legal Aspects of the Confiscation Acts of the Civil War." *American Historical Review* 18 (October 1912): 79–96.

Ruhlen, George. "Brazito—The Only Battle in the Southwest between American and Foreign Troops." *Pass-Word* 2 (February 1957): 4–13.

Schmidt, Louis Bernard. "Manifest Opportunity and the Gadsden Purchase." *Arizona and the West* 3 (Autumn 1961): 245–64.

Smith, Ralph A. "The 'King of New Mexico' and the Doniphan Expedition." *New Mexico Historical Review* 38 (January 1963): 29–55.

Sonnichsen, C. L. "Major McMullen's Invasion of Mexico." *Pass-Word* 2 (May 1957): 38–43.

Stegmaier, Mark J. "The Guadalupe Hidalgo Treaty as a Factor in the New Mexico–Texas Boundary Dispute." In *The Treaty of Guadalupe Hidalgo, 1848: Papers of the Sesquicentennial Symposium, 1848–1998,* edited by John Porter Bloom. Las Cruces, NM: Doña Ana County Historical Society, 1999.

Tittman, Edward D. "By Order of Richard Campbell." *New Mexico Historical Review* 3 (October 1928): 390–98.

———. "The Exploitation of Treason." *New Mexico Historical Review* 4 (April 1929): 128–45.

Tucker, Phillip Thomas. "The Missourians and the Battle of Brazito." *Pass-Word* 34 (Winter 1989): 159–69.

Vasquez, Enrique Tamez. "Brazito Remembered: One Hundred Fifty Years Ago; Another Look." *Pass-Word* 43 (Summer 1998): 54–68.

Wadsworth, Richard. "The Battle of Mesilla: A Rebel View." *Southern New Mexico Historical Review* 12 (January 2005): 8–9.

Walker, Charles S. "Causes of the Confederate Invasion of New Mexico." *New Mexico Historical Review* 8 (April 1933): 76–97.

———. "Confederate Government in Doña Ana County: As Shown in the Records of the Probate Court, 1861–1862." *New Mexico Historical Review* 6 (July 1931): 253–302.

Wilson, John P. "Retreat to the Rio Grande: The Report of Captain Isaiah N. Moore." *Rio Grande History* 2 (3 & 4) (1975): 4–8.

———. "Whiskey at Fort Fillmore: A Story of the Civil War." *New Mexico Historical Review* 68 (April 1993): 109–32.

Index

West, Brig. Gen. Joseph Rodman: 190,
    255n20; and Apaches, 201–202;
    background, 256n24; as com-
    mander in Mesilla Valley, 194–201;
    condones invasion of Mexico,
    200; confiscates property, 195–97,
    256n21, 256n29; executes troops,
    198–99
Whipple, Lt. Amiel Weeks: 52, 59, 62,
    72, 82, 229n48; background, 225n7
whiskey, *see* liquor
Withers, George R., 207

women: 247n42, 250n67; Apache, 118,
    123, 130; killed by troops, 199;
    Mexican, 4, 6, 8, 9–10, 202, 215n16;
    255n13
Wood, Lt. William H., 123, 124
Wood, Samuel, 148
Wordsworth, Palatine, 145
Wright, Lt. Nicholas B., 22

Ysleta, Tex., 194, 195

Zacatecas, Mex., 74

ELMA DILL RUSSELL SPENCER SERIES
IN THE WEST AND SOUTHWEST

Hispanics in the Mormon Zion, 1912–1999, Jorge Iber

Comanche Society: Before the Reservation, Gerald Betty

True Women and Westward Expansion, Adrienne Caughfield

The Robertson, the Sutherlands, and the Making of Texas, Anne Sutherland

Life Along the Border: A Landmark Tejana Thesis, Jovita González, edited by María Eugenia Cotera

Lone Star Pasts: Memory and History in Texas, Gregg Cantrell and Elizabeth Hayes Turner

The Secret War for Texas, Stuart Reid

Colonial Natchitoche: A Creole Community on the Louisiana-Texas Frontier, Burton/Smith

Yeomen, Sharecroppers, and Socialists: Plain Folk Protest in Texas, 1870–1914, Kyle G. Wilkison

More Zeal Than Discretion: The Westward Adventures of Walter P. Lane, Jimmy L. Bryan

On the Move: A Black Family's Western Saga, S. Rudolph Martin

Texas That Might Have Been: Sam Houston's Foes Write to Albert Sidney Johnston, Margaret Swett Henson

Tejano Leadership in Mexican and Revolutionary Texas, Jesús F. De la Teja

Texas Left: The Radical Roots of Lone Star Liberalism, David O'Donald Cullen

How Did Davy Die? And Why Do We Care So Much? Commemorative Edition, Dan Kilgore/Crisp

Drumbeats from Mescalero: Conversations with Apache Elders, Warriors, and Horseholders, H. Henrietta Stockel

CPSIA information can be obtained at www.ICGtesting.com
Printed in the USA
LVOW12s2201220914

405287LV00004B/55/P